Blindsided by Grace

Entering the World of Disability

Robert F. Molsberry

Augsburg Books

MINNEAPOLIS

Table of Contents

Dedication   v

Introduction   vii

1. Blindsided by Grace   1

2. While I Was Sleeping   18

3. You Can't Go Home Again   32

4. More Than an Inspiration   51

5. A Pilgrim's Progress   62

6. A Cross-Cultural Safari   76

7. The Bible Tells Me So   86

8. Disabled by Definition   109

9. Crippled by Culture   127

10. Rights or Rehab?   141

11. Rolling Reflections   157

Bibliography   173

Dedication

When Ann agreed to marry me twenty-six years ago, she had no idea what she was in for. She was unaware of the heart-wrenching vigil she would undergo at my bedside waiting to see if I would live or die following a hit-and-run accident. She hadn't signed up as a caregiver for a paraplegic in a wheelchair. She thought she was just getting a lover and a friend, a life partner.

She did know some other things about me. She knew my obsessive/compulsive tendencies, for example. She knew that when I carry a ballpoint pen in my pocket, you don't borrow that pen and then return it with the clip mutilated or bent. That causes the pen to slip out of my pocket when I bend over, and then I lose it. A pen without a functional clip is useless. If Ann borrows my pen and returns it with the clip mangled, she might at well start packing. Damaging my ballpoint pen is tantamount to initiating divorce proceedings. Ann acknowledges my idiosyncrasies, and is very careful about using my pens.

So when I asked her who I should dedicate this book to, she responded in kind. "This is your book, Dear, and you may dedicate it to whomever you wish. Of course, if you dedicate it to someone other than me, you're sleeping on the couch the rest of your life."

A debilitating accident doesn't just happen to the victim. It affects every relationship, beginning with those closest and extending outward like ripples in a pond. Ann has borne the brunt of my experience of disability. It happened to me and I'm responsible for my recovery and return to life, but her experience may have been the more devastating. While I was in a coma, she and the rest of my family were coming to grips with the possibility of my demise. As I recovered, there was the very real likelihood that I would emerge with insurmountable mental and emotional impairments. As I continue to adjust to a life with limited mobility, she has had to make peace with my limitations.

Three months ago Ann and I went to hear a band play in the parking lot of a local bar. After we listened to a few songs she pushed me out onto the dance floor. Dancing, to a person who uses a wheelchair, is a fluid choreography of spins and turns and wheelies. It takes much skill to pull it off with a partner. Awkward at first, we became more and more confident in our movements, until the rest of the dancers parted for us and we felt as though we were alone on the floor.

Through Ann's patience, persistence, and perseverance, we have learned to dance again. It has been a Herculean act on her part, for my idiosyncrasies have only become more pronounced through injury and disability. But she's still here and we're still dancing. So this book is for her. May the adventure continue.

Robert Molsberry
December 2003

Introduction

I t was not what I would have chosen for my life. But I have, over the course of the last five years, *decided* to choose it. And that has made all the difference.

In the late spring of 1997, while I was out on a hard bicycle ride training for the summer racing season, I was struck from behind by a hit-and-run driver. I never heard him coming. The resulting injuries were almost fatal. I survived, but was robbed permanently of the use of my legs. I know it was permanent because the handicap-parking permit I received from the Department of Transportation reads, "Permanent, non-expiring." And the DOT doesn't lie. I use a wheelchair now.

My efforts to return to my former life as husband, father, parish pastor, and athlete have consumed me almost entirely for the past five years. That's why I felt the need to take a sabbatical from my duties as a parish pastor and sit down to write this book. It's high time that I reflect on where I've been. I need that reflection time as therapy, to continue the closure and healing process. It has been a journey of almost epic proportions, made all the more difficult by a lack of certainty as to the end goal. Who am I now, post injury? All my friends, colleagues, parishioners, and family members are inspired by the progress I've made in returning to my old life. I was at death's door, and now I'm just about back to "normal." But what does that mean? What does "normal" mean to a guy in a wheelchair? "I don't even see the wheelchair anymore," says my friend, Jeff, the ponytailed owner of the coffee shop across the street from the church. "To me you're not disabled."

I know Jeff means well, but darn it, I *am* disabled. Or, more properly, I *have* a disability that significantly defines me now. My legs don't work and my bladder's still a mess in spite of repeated attempts at repair, a colostomy bag collects solid waste and a bag strapped to my leg collects urine. I can never be totally confident that any of these jury-rigged systems designed to keep me going won't fail on me at the most inopportune times—that a flat tire on my wheelchair won't sideline me, for instance, or that a leak from a tube or a plastic bag won't spread a telltale stain on my pants or let loose in the air a toxic odor that qualifies as a weapon of mass destruction. If that's not a disability, I don't know what is. I appreciate Jeff's intentions, accepting me as a person, overlooking my limitations. He meant to pay me a compliment, and that's saying a lot for Jeff—underneath his crusty exterior is an even crustier interior. He doesn't hand out compliments very frequently. And to his credit, I'm partly responsible. I've even contributed to his misperception by hopping my wheelchair up the step into his coffee shop for my daily caffeine fix, rather than demanding of him compliance under the Americans with Disabilities Act (ADA). But would it have been considered a compliment if he had told an African American, "You don't really seem black to me," or a woman, "I don't even see you as a woman anymore"? Why is it considered polite to ignore a disability?

By overlooking my disability, Jeff illustrates the difficulty in rebuilding a shattered life. I'm not the same person I was before. Disability makes a difference. I have a significant disability now and that disability is part and parcel of who I am. That person who used to crank out endless miles on his bike, run and swim competitively, walk around town without a second thought about mobility—that person is dead and gone. His back and pelvis were crushed beyond repair by a Memorial Day drunk driver, and he's not coming back from that bike ride. The person who did return to claim his roles, his family, his job, and his life is an imposter. This new person is a mosaic hammered together from bits and pieces left over from the old life, from new material offered by the perspectives of the people who surround me, from stuff I've created myself through persistence, luck, genetics, faith, and random scavenging. There's a television program called *Junkyard Wars*, in which teams race to construct high-tech machines out of junk they scavenge at a junkyard. In the episodes I've seen, they've built such things as hovercrafts, submarines, airplanes, and dune buggies. What I'm doing is no less remarkable. I'm building a life out of the junk left over after my injury.

But don't conclude that this project is unique to those who have suffered catastrophic injury or illness. We're all engaged in it, all the time. In this, a person with a disability is no different from anyone else. We're all building lives out of the stuff we can scavenge. You play the cards you're dealt, discarding the ones that don't serve you, hanging onto the high cards, and gradually trying to build the best hand you can. And few of us get royal flushes.

There's a story told about violinist Itzhak Perlman. One November day in 1995 Perlman walked onstage at Lincoln Center to give a concert. He was stricken with polio as a child, so he uses leg braces and walks with the help of two canes. The audience waited respectfully as he slowly made his way across the stage, then sat down, lowered his canes, released the clasps on his braces, and finally picked up his violin and prepared to play. But just a few bars into the piece, one of the strings on his violin broke. Everyone heard it snap. And everyone wondered what he would do.

Perlman sat for a moment with his eyes closed, then signaled the conductor to begin again. The audience could see him sweating through the piece, modulating, changing, recomposing it in his head, retuning strings on the fly to pull new sounds out of them.

Asked after this astounding performance how he pulled it off, Perlman said, "You know, sometimes it is the artist's task to find out how much music you can still make with what you have left." Without intending to contradict Perlman, I would add that this is everyone's task.

Another important insight I've arrived at through this experience is that the changes aren't all bad. Just as Jeff errs in ignoring the disability that partly defines me now, others can't see anything else. They look at me and see only tragedy—a man in the prime of his life, physically, spiritually, in terms of career and family, cut down and broken. What a pity. How could God allow such a thing to happen? They look at me and at other persons with disabilities with sympathy. When we persist in accomplishing things—great things or even normal things—in spite of our disabilities, they see us as inspirational. This, too, is an oversimplification of disability. The experience of a person with a disability, like the experience of anyone else, is complex. But with all the difficult moments that call for perseverance, there are also celebrations. There are some very real graces that have been visited upon me as a result of my injuries and disability. I have learned many things and grown in insight and wisdom. Someday I may be able to say that, given the choice, I wouldn't have changed a thing about my life—not even the injury. I'm not there yet, but I may arrive.

This surprising, positive side of disability that I'm discovering as time passes I chose to call grace. Grace is a technical theological concept that means, at its most basic level, "gift." A gift is something good that you receive, not because you earned it or were entitled to it, but simply because it pleased the giver to present it to you. Grace is an unmerited blessing.

Theologian Frederick Buechner talks about grace in his book *Wishful Thinking*:

> Grace is something you can never get but only be given. There's no way to earn it or deserve it or bring it about any more than you can deserve the taste of raspberries and cream or earn good looks or bring out your own birth.
>
> A good sleep is grace and so are good dreams. Most tears are grace. The smell of rain is grace. Somebody loving you is grace. Loving somebody is grace. Have you ever *tried* to love somebody?
>
> The grace of God means something like: Here is your life. You might never have been, but you are because the party wouldn't have been complete without you. Here is the world. Beautiful and terrible things will happen. Don't be afraid. I am with you. Nothing can ever separate us. It's for you I created the universe. I love you.
>
> There's only one catch. Like any other gift, the gift of grace can be yours only if you'll reach out and take it.
>
> Maybe being able to reach out and take it is a gift, too. (33)

Now, disability per se can hardly be interpreted as a good thing. Not by a long shot. The collision that put me in the hospital and resulted in a permanent disability was not an expression of grace, but a consequence of evil. Yet, as we'll see, out of even the most tragic of circumstances tiny seeds of hope and joy and promise may take root and blossom. That's grace.

Actor Michael J. Fox, who at the height of his career revealed to the world that he has Parkinson's disease, talks candidly in his book *Lucky Man* about the grace that accompanied his devastating diagnosis:

> What [the doctor] did not tell me—what no one could—is that these last ten years of coming to terms with my disease would turn out to be the best ten years of my life—not in spite of my illness, but because of it.
>
> Coping with the relentless assault and the accumulating damage is not easy. Nobody would ever choose to have this visited upon them.

Still, this unexpected crisis forced a fundamental life decision: adopt a siege mentality—or embark upon a journey. Whatever it was—courage? acceptance? wisdom?—that finally allowed me to go down the second road (after spending a few disastrous years on the first) was unquestionably a gift—and absent this neurophysiological catastrophe, I would never have opened it, or been so profoundly enriched. That's why I consider myself a lucky man. (5)

This book is an exploration of my attempt to regenerate the pieces of my life, find meaning in the new me who emerges, and discover insights along the way. I offer it hoping that it will be useful to others facing catastrophic change. If it's valuable at all, the value should transfer to anyone who is adjusting to newly imposed limitations, including those who grieve losses in their lives and those who are aging—pretty much everybody, wouldn't you say? Think of this book as a road map, or a travel guide—"Disability on Five Dollars a Day." Not that every person adjusting to change or loss follows the same path—far from it. Each pilgrimage is unique. But the essential features of the journey may be similar enough that following another person's map may be useful in setting one's own course. For whatever it's worth, I'm leaving you a trail of breadcrumbs.

I'm trying to take us to the heart of the meaning of disability. Clearly, having a disability means more than having a physical limitation or imperfection. How is that limitation to be understood? If disability is just a medical problem, for example, like a broken arm or a boil on the skin, then doctors could set the bone, lance the boil, the body would heal, and there would be no need for this, or any other book on disability. Take two aspirin and call me in the morning. Case closed.

Many people, perhaps a majority, would like to define disability in these terms. It's a lot simpler that way, don't you think? Rather than putting in the hard work of understanding the complex reality of disability, one can just wish it to go away! With enough funding and research, maybe we can fix you. This concept of disability has a certain ring of truth to it. After all, think of all the diseases throughout the centuries that were once permanently disabling but now respond to treatment. Perhaps spinal cord injury is like that. Perhaps every illness or defect is like that.

But because not every physical imperfection responds to treatment (critical inquiry may prove to us that such a course may not even be morally desirable!) then disability takes on social and cultural dimensions as well. How does society treat people with special mobility requirements? Is it my responsibility to learn how to open doors and access flights of stairs, or is it society's responsibility to accommodate me? The answer depends on your understanding of disability. If, in spite of the radical differences between people with differing disabilities, you conclude that all people with disabilities share a common experience, then your understanding of disability must encompass a civil-rights framework as well. Disability moves from the medical arena into politics. It becomes a justice issue. Disability takes on moral and theological dimensions as you examine how the biblical world generally regarded human imperfection as a consequence of sin.

In the long run, my goal through this book will be to get beyond the ability/disability dualism. Conventional wisdom says that there are two kinds of people: those with DOT-issued handicap-parking permits, and those who have to park farther away. You either have a disability or you're "normal." I hope we can come to agree that all human abilities can be located on a continuum where infinite shadings of gray eliminate any possibility of black-and-white distinctions.

Is disability an individual or a social concern? Until very recently, I have attacked my recovery as my own personal project. The stronger I get, the better off I will be. It takes a great deal of upper body strength to open doors from a wheelchair (literally and figuratively). I do full body presses every time I transfer into or out of my chair. My goal has been to return as closely as possible to the roles I had before my injury occurred. And the work has fallen to me alone. I didn't expect anyone to share the responsibility. After all, it wasn't Jeff's fault that I was injured. Why should he have to make an expensive accommodation for me? No, I just got progressively stronger and more skilled in wheelchair mobility, doggedly going about my own business and solving my own problems.

Of course, I realize now that even within this personalized perception of recovery, I was never truly alone in the work. It couldn't have been done without me, to be sure, but I was surrounded by family members, friends, parishioners, and others who have consistently picked up the slack for me. My injury and disability have sent ripples far and wide in the communities in which I live and work.

One of the things I have learned along the way is that my experience is shared by millions of Americans, and hundreds of millions of people around the world. When congress passed the Americans with Disabilities Act in 1990, it counted 43 million Americans living with a severe disability. That's one in five of us! In spite of the variety of disabilities we live with, and the severity with which we experience them, still we share some common experiences. We have to claw our way into a world that is arranged and organized for people who can walk and see and hear. We tend to be hired at a rate that lags far behind the general public. We are four times more likely to be poor. When churches post signs that say "All are welcome," they may not be talking about people with disabilities who can't climb their stairs or hear their sermons or read their bulletins. Only in the last thirty or forty years has it dawned on anyone that the disability community, sharing a common experience of stigma and discrimination, can rightly be seen as the largest minority group in the country. That fact certainly needs to be part of any attempt to explore the meaning of the disability experience. When I was struck by that truck and left partially paralyzed, whether I knew it or not, I was enrolled as a card-carrying member of a minority group.

Given the fact that a minority-group model may be helpful in understanding disability, then a society whose constitution guarantees civil rights to all its members has a responsibility to extend certain guarantees to the one-in-five who may need ramps to access public places, specially designed telecommunication devices, and legal leverage in overcoming hiring discrimination. All of a sudden, it's not just my personal struggle to fit into a one-size-fits-all world. It becomes incumbent upon me to help change that world to be more responsive to people with alternative needs. Disability, properly understood, demands advocacy.

Because I'm a pastor, it was natural for me to frame my experience theologically. When sermons called for it, I combed the Bible for clues to help me understand disability. At first, what I found shocked and discouraged me. On the surface, there's not much good news for people with disabilities in the Holy Book. Either disability is seen as deserved punishment for sin, rendering the person with a disability an object of scorn or pity, or it is a medical or spiritual affliction which Jesus, in power and compassion, miraculously heals. For those of us with disabilities who don't feel like we're that much more deserving of divine punishment than our nondisabled neighbors, who haven't been cured of our impairment and don't look for such a cure on the horizon, and who resent being pitied, there wasn't much of a sustaining vision offered. It takes a careful reading of the Bible, taking into account the ancient worldview held by its various authors, to arrive at a helpful understanding. Through painstaking, imaginative reconstruction, a student of the Bible can arrive at a vision of the world as God's radically inclusive banquet, at which everyone—whatever their ability level—is welcome. People with disabilities are more than welcome at that banquet; they are crucial participants. They're offered the best seats! They serve as reminders to the rest of the assembled guests that the body of Christ is a broken body. People come in an amazing assortment of sizes, shapes, and abilities. Lusting after the holy grail of physical perfection and beauty is a dangerous illusion and a deadly sin.

Then the work becomes getting this message out to the churches, many of which are still operating with a first-century model of disability. Churches successfully lobbied exemption from the ADA's requirements for full accessibility. Church buildings are still often the last buildings in town to accommodate people with disabilities. What theology is demonstrated by their actions?

Adjusting to a disability, I'll argue, is like a cross-cultural immersion experience. When you prepare to spend some time living in another culture, you don't just pack up, move, and restart the same life you had before, only in a different place. Unless, of course, you're in the military. But if you live out of the barracks and off of the base you're going to have to figure out the new culture you reside in. You need to be sensitive to how the people in your new culture view life, and, as far as it is in your power, adjust your own assumptions to your new reality. You need to learn the language and figure out how people in your new culture get things done. If culture is like the lenses we look through, then adjusting to a new culture is like putting on a new pair of glasses.

I know about this stuff. I spent six years in Central America. My wife, Ann, and I spent an extended honeymoon of three years in the highlands of Guatemala, teaching gardening and nutrition for the Peace Corps. Then we went to Nicaragua with our children, Ames and Kate, in tow during the early 1990s to work with the Mennonite Central Committee on community development. Each time we moved to a foreign culture, we underwent a quite predictable process of cultural adaptation. What at first seemed an alien and uncomfortable environment gradually came to feel more homey (in an adventurous sort of way).

This book attempts to provide the new arrival to the reality of disability—or the merely curious—a travel guide to this new culture. What are some of its salient features? What are the people like who live there? What have they experienced? How have their experiences impacted their outlook on life? Where are the landmines, the tragedies, and the sources of humor in this strange place? Will you be able to find a McDonald's in this place, or is it black beans and rice for the rest of your life?

This is not to claim that adjusting to disability is necessarily a pleasant experience. Who in their right minds would willingly undergo the pain, inconvenience, limitation, and stigma attached to life with a disability? But the point is, though living with a disability may not be the most pleasant experience one might imagine, it's still a perfectly natural dimension of what it means to be human. It's entirely consistent with the human condition. After all, from age thirty we're all in decline. At one point or another, most of us will slow down, our hair will turn gray or fall out altogether, we'll have to squint more reading the paper, our teeth will fall out, and we'll experience any of a thousand indicators that we are aging and losing functional abilities. Face it. What we're undergoing is the experience of our own mortality. You can't avoid it, and it won't be healthy to try to put it off. A word to the wise: make your house accessible now, while there's still time. You'll appreciate the investment later. As a fringe benefit, I'll be able to visit you.

Change is difficult. Some of us adapt to changes better than others. In 1990 when Ann and I decided to uproot our family from our comfortable life in small-town Iowa and jump into a cross-cultural adventure in Managua, Nicaragua, our younger child, Kate, was just five, and not at all sure she wanted to have anything to do with this craziness. She was not a child who welcomed change; she still doesn't. We tried to convince her how much fun it would be to learn a new language, but she wasn't buying it.

Our day of travel to Guatemala, where we were to study Spanish for six weeks, was long and arduous. With our eight duffel bags and four carry-ons, including one suitcase completely full of Lego blocks—I'm not kidding—we arose at 4 AM, hopped one flight to Philadelphia, another to Miami or Dallas (it's all a blur now, I can't remember clearly), and finally touched down after 10 PM in Guatemala City. Ann and I had been through these airports before. We knew it was wise to be inconspicuous. We wanted to keep a low profile in order to pass under the radar screens of the customs officials, who could, if they so chose, make life a living hell of unpacking and repacking. We could just imagine having to unload our entire three-year supply of clothing and supplies, laying the whole kit and caboodle out on the long tables in the security line at the airport to satisfy the whim of some diabolical customs worker. We strongly cautioned our children to toe the line and follow our lead as we hit the terminal.

But Kate, who had been cooped up in planes and strange airports for the past seventeen hours without an opportunity to take her customary afternoon nap, would have none of it. As we approached the dreaded customs area, she launched a full-blown tantrum. "I don't wanna speak Spanish!" she shrieked at the top of her lungs. All our hopes of avoiding the attention of the ominous customs officials were dashed. We became the only show in town. "Hey, José. Come here and see this little *gringa*. Either she just ate a really hot tamale, or she must really need her nap." Fortunately, the guards were moved by pity and, with understanding smiles, waved us through. They must have had their own five-year-olds at home.

I experienced my own form of culture shock six years later. When I started regaining consciousness six weeks after my injury, I was stunned by what had become of my body. The last thing I remember, I had been on a training ride on my bike. Now I was attached to a hospital bed and I couldn't move my legs. I had lost forty pounds and was tethered to machines and IV pumps and oxygen tubes and monitors. Food was being pumped into my stomach from one plastic bag and waste was emptied into another. A tracheostomy tube in my throat kept me from speaking. They kept asking me what day it was, where I thought I was, and who was president. Horrified, I discovered I didn't have the slightest idea. What had happened to me? What was wrong with my body, my mind, my spirit? If I could have talked, I would have screamed, "I don't wanna be a cripple!" But my vocal cords didn't work and I was too dull-witted, stunned, or medicated, even to be able to conceptualize the lament.

Kate, bless her heart, after some months in Central America, calmed down. It wasn't easy. We tried to put her in school, but at first she fled into her older brother's classroom, and then she refused to go altogether. She learned Spanish sitting on her mother's lap in Ann's private class. There were many tearful nights when she ended up in bed with her mother and me. But gradually she made friends. She learned Spanish. She found ways to get what she needed as a curious, energetic little girl. A flock of little girls down the block from our house adopted her. She adapted to her new culture and became a new person. She became able to look critically at her old culture. When it came time after three years to pack up and return to the United States, she cried and cried over that imminent readjustment.

Now that I have five years' perspective on my injury and disability, I'm calming down, too. I have had opportunity to look around, gauge the lay of the landscape, learn the language, and figure out how to get my needs met. I've made friends and found meaning here. It's certainly different from my old culture, and the going is not always easy. But this place has a certain weird charm of its own. I'm becoming a different person as I adapt to it. I've learned a few things in the process. I'm even able to look at my old culture from a new perspective, opening up insights I never would have had without this experience. It's true that a drunk driver plowed into me at sixty miles per hour, mangling my body and leaving me for dead. But I was no less blindsided by the unexpected grace that has trickled into my life like a gentle healing rain in the years since.

This is my story.

And I'm sticking to it.

Chapter 1

Blindsided
by Grace

On the last day of my old life, if I had thought about it, I would have realized just how idyllic my life was as a pastor in a small Iowa college town, the same town in which my father and his father had practiced dentistry, and in which I had been born forty-two years before. But of course I didn't think about it. We never do. Something has to happen to shake the foundations first. My foundations were shaken at around 6:00 PM Saturday, May 31, 1997.

Images from that day float in my memory like pieces of a complex jigsaw puzzle. Thanks to friends and family members who were eyewitnesses of my day's activities, I have been able to reconstruct the pieces of the day into a coherent picture. My own memory, by itself, was not up to the task. This reconstruction was an amazing process. Even years after the events of that day, people still come up to me with information that helps fill in the gaps. "I saw you ride your bike by my house," one man volunteered, helping me figure out what route I might have taken out of town. "You were at my daughter's graduation party that day. I couldn't believe it when I heard about the accident," a friend reminded me. "If I had accepted your invitation to ride with you," my training partner said, "maybe I would have taken the impact and you would have escaped."

The day was unseasonably hot and sunny for a Memorial Day weekend Saturday. I got up early to run for an hour with a local surgeon and his faithful sidekick, a mathematics professor at Grinnell College. Charlie and Ron, indefatigable, had run every street in Grinnell during these Saturday morning training runs. They had mapped it out and it had taken them months. Now they were training for the Comrade's Ultramarathon, a 52-mile event in South Africa. When I joined them at 8:00 AM they had already put in an hour; they would run for another hour after I quit. I peeled off downtown to pick up doughnuts at the bakery to bring home for my family, who were probably just now waking up. Ann was always much more tolerant of my training obsessions when I returned home from runs or bike rides with doughnuts. After a quick shower I attended the graduation open house for the high school girls. Commencement would be the following day.

My daughter, Kate, had lunch ready when I got home. She had made tuna sandwiches, and we ate them with soda pop and chips on the front porch, rocking in the warm breeze in white wicker chairs. This house was a dream come true for Ann and me. We had been pining to live in such a place for years. It was a Victorian house with fine oak woodwork, built in 1906, just two doors south of the house I had grown up in. When we were first shown this house by the real estate agent, none other would do. It was a house with character, charm, history, and a great front porch.

Old houses have front porches. New ones have back decks. Front porches are unquestionably better in every way. Front porches build community. From a perch on your front porch you can watch your town file by. You can shout greetings at people if you want. They'll salute you back if they feel like it. Some will stop and visit. If you want them to stay you offer them a cold drink. If not, you just talk for a spell and everyone understands it's been a pleasant, unexpected encounter, and they continue on their way.

Back decks separate you from your neighbors. Back there it's just me and my charcoal grill. It would be considered rude to drop in unannounced on a family dining on their back deck. The popularity of the back deck is one of the factors contributing to the decline of this great nation today, in my humble opinion.

Anyway, Kate brought her tuna sandwiches out to the front porch. We had a little picnic. Then I stayed to work on my sermon. The Bible text for the next morning was from Mark, chapter 3, about the healing of the man with a withered hand on the Sabbath. The Pharisees, legalistic literalists, accused Jesus of violating religious law by working on the holy day of rest. Jesus countered, "Is it lawful to do good or to do harm on the Sabbath, to save life or to kill?"

As things turned out, I clearly backed the right horse with that sermon, coming down solidly on the side of Jesus and his Sabbath healing. The next day was Sunday, and teams of doctors would be working around the clock to keep me alive. That sermon was never delivered. I found my notes months later and marveled at how the Spirit must have been moving that day.

But it was just too nice a day to stay inside, even on the front porch of a beautiful Victorian house, and work on a sermon. I set down my notes, trotted down into the basement to change into my biking gear, and headed out into the late afternoon sun for a hard, quick ride. I must have been reveling that day in my conditioning and physical prowess, to have undertaken two workouts on the same day. Coincidentally, that level of conditioning would certainly contribute to my survival over the next few hours and days. It would be four months before I'd come back to my family, rediscover my sermon notes, and find the jeans I'd left on the hook by the basement shower. Instead of pedaling back sweaty, with a sense of accomplishment, refreshed and ready to get back to work, I'd be carried and wheeled into the house, broken and defeated.

Pumping hard, I rode in celebration of power and speed and my sense of control over the environment. Control has always been an issue for me. Ask anyone. It seems to run in my family. I'm most comfortable when I'm in control of my body, of my schedule, of my church, of the events of the day. I try to be gracious about it, but Ann will tell you she can tell when I'm feeling out of control by the subtle signs of discomfort I exhibit. I grind my jaw and my lips narrow down to nothing. Control, I was about to learn, was the first thing that disability robs you of. It's not just a limitation of mobility, speech, vision, or other physical functions. Deep down, disability means a loss of control. When you have a disability you're more dependent on people. People have to do things to help you. You're on their timetable, not your own. Special accommodations must be made for you. The people around you may or may not be willing or able to make them when you desire them made. The worse the disability, the more loss of control experienced. For some people, an itch on the nose is an exercise in powerlessness and dependency. People with disabilities need to learn patience. The world will not respond to their demands as it had before.

But on that day I was in total control. With my head down, I was hammering out the miles on the road, punching through the early summer heat. It was shaping up to be a good summer for my training and racing. A quick check of my computerized speedometer showed that already, this early in the season, I was riding faster than last year's race pace. Imagine that! A forty-two-year-old minister getting stronger by the year! At a time in life when most of my colleagues were growing thick around the middle and slowing down, I was getting leaner and faster! Head down, legs like pistons. This attitude, I was soon to learn, could not protect me from contingency. But it would serve me well in rehab.

Rounding a final turn and heading for home, I picked up a tailwind and accelerated. Twenty-five miles per hour, maybe faster. A final celebration of speed, power, and control.

I had no idea that a changed life was bearing down on me. Several eyewitnesses had seen it approaching and wisely gave it a wide berth. It was a dark Ford pickup truck, driven, apparently, by a man who had started his Memorial Day weekend party early. He was driving as though intoxicated, weaving all over the road and off onto the shoulders. He'd slow to 45 miles per hour and then accelerate to over 70.

The witnesses, seven of them, all reported seeing the same thing. The man on the bicycle was pedaling fast, head down, tracking near the right edge of the paved road surface. The pickup truck swerved to the right, as though intentionally to hit the rider, and blindsided him. They were horrified to see the cyclist fly through the air, landing in the ditch. Later the sheriff would measure 113 feet from the skid marks of my narrow racing tires to the spot in the ditch where they found me. The driver left the scene, failing to acknowledge liability or render aid. I wasn't even a blip on his radar screen. Does he even know what chaos he left in his wake? To this day it frustrates me deeply to have been left on my own to bear this burden of pain, loss, and readjustment, while the criminally negligent driver went on his drunken, merry way. I take some satisfaction in knowing that I damaged his truck. Pieces of his front right headlight and fender were found beside me in the ditch.

The witnesses, stunned by what they had seen, rushed to my side. No one thought to get a license number. The ambulance and local police, racing to the scene, actually met and passed the truck that hit me, but no one had reported the accident as a hit-and-run. They weren't on the lookout for the perpetrator.

But those witnesses—bless them—in spite of that one oversight, clearly saved my life. There happened to be two EMTs among them. They became very nervous when my rapid breathing slowed down, but I suspect I was just catching my breath as I recovered from the exertion of racing.

The first person at my side was a woman about sixty years old, Hildegard Ledbetter. Hildegard and her daughter were, incredibly, crossing the Midwest on rural highways, making their way back to their home in Littleton, Colorado. (Littleton, of course, made the news a few years later as the site of the shootings at Columbine High School.) Hildegard runs a shop that sells religious icons and art furnishings to churches, such things as crosses and communion ware. She was the first to hold my hand. She said a prayer for healing. Four years after the accident she came back to Grinnell to visit me. She said that it had occurred to her while cradling my head that my blood on her hands was like a communion. It was a sacred moment, during which life and death were in balance. That's what communion is. It's when the divine becomes a real physical thing. This was God's moment, not hers or mine. The outcome was God's; whatever grace or evil might follow was a divine mystery.

Amazingly, my glasses were found nearby, with not so much as a scratch on them. I did have to have new lenses made after I was back home, because the impact had caused some minor retinal damage and I needed a new corrective prescription, but I had my old glasses tinted and still wear them as sunglasses. My watch, a twelve-dollar Casio, weathered the crash just fine. The cheap plastic band has since torn, but the alarm on the watch, which is now buried somewhere deep in my sock drawer, continues to chime faithfully every morning at 4:35 AM. My bike, of course, was a sight to behold. The rear wheel was bent double and the frame had snapped. I sent it back to the manufacturer, hoping they would recognize it as defective and replace it, but that never happened. And my bike helmet, shattered into several pieces but recovered by bystanders, now serves as a visual aid when I give bike safety talks to school children about the value of wearing a helmet. "Whenever there are wheels under your feet, there should be a helmet on your head," I tell them. The wise guys among them always counter, "Then why aren't you wearing a helmet when you roll in your wheelchair, Pastor Bob?" The way I drive my chair sometimes, maybe they're onto something!

Things began to move fast. In hindsight, the string of events begins to look like a carefully orchestrated, divinely ordained drama. Grinnell Regional Medical Center, just seven minutes from the scene of the accident (or the crime, depending on your point of view), had just been designated a class III trauma center—one of the first in the state. That means all of the key players, including ER physicians, surgeons, technicians, and nurses, were present at the hospital when I arrived. It was a showcase of readiness. I was the first trauma patient seen under the new classification.

Still, there wasn't much they could do for me. They tell me I was still responsive at that point. Apparently I overheard the ambulance technicians debating my identity, so I told them who I was. Ann was called to the emergency room. I complained to her about discomfort in my back and legs. Could she have them elevated? I could still wiggle my toes then, but that was the last time my toes were able to move under their own power.

The doctors found a gaping hole in my rear end, extending up into my lower back, with my pelvis shattered in what they call an "open book" fracture. They called for a helicopter airlift to a more advanced trauma center in Des Moines, stuffed two hospital towels into the hole in my back in an attempt to stanch the flow of blood, bundled me off into the waiting helicopter, and sat, stunned, hoping and praying for what they knew then would have to be a miracle. They knew me. They also knew the extent of the injuries. This was hard on them.

I learned later that a helicopter had already been called to Grinnell before I got to the hospital, to transport a newborn baby in distress. They sent me on that helicopter, knowing that my condition was extremely delicate, calling for a second helicopter for the infant. Her mother sought me out a couple of years later. The child had died. Was it a fair exchange, I wonder? Did the mother hold me responsible? I couldn't tell. But this is another of the jagged wounds left behind in the wake of this tragedy.

Dr. Greg Timberlake, head of the trauma department at Iowa Methodist Medical Center in Des Moines, received me. He knew right away that he had his night's work cut out for him. There were two marathon races beginning for him. One was to stop the hemorrhage of blood before it became irreversible. That night alone the doctors pumped into my body 57 units of blood to replenish what I was losing. Before it was all over, I consumed another 60 units. My family watched in anxious fascination as an orderly carrying a small cooler and wearing white scrubs and brand new running shoes ran an endless loop all night long from the blood products storage cooler to the ER suite. They thought that one day I might appreciate the fact that a runner was keeping me supplied with blood. They were right.

Dr. Timberlake later confided to me and my family that he had never seen a patient who had lost that much blood recover. Privately, he placed my odds at less than 1 percent. But bless his heart, Dr. Timberlake was a betting man and he took the long odds. He didn't tell Ann how unlikely my recovery would have been. He simply went to work on me as though I would survive. He wouldn't allow talk—not yet anyway—of "pulling the plug."

Dr. Timberlake's stubborn perception of me as a person who was going to recover was in distinct contrast to the perception of one of the nurses who staffed the intensive care unit where I was taken following surgery. Ann tried to post a photo of me at the head of my bed. I had just the week before confirmed a group of eighth grade students in my church. The photo of me and the freshly scrubbed young people was hot from the developer. Ann wanted it there as a reminder of who I was. This is a person, she wanted them to know, not the lump of torn and scarred flesh you see before you. But one nurse intercepted her and made her take the photo home. She expressly did not want to be reminded that her patients were people. Her actions seem odd now, but I can imagine how much harder it would be for them to work on patients they had come to know as human beings—and perhaps later to lose these patients. A surgeon friend of mine tells me that it can be almost impossible for him to operate in cases where he's emotionally attached to his patient. Anyway, the hospital later apologized and said that our treatment by that particular nurse certainly did not reflect hospital policy. On the contrary, they encourage personalizing medical care. Except for that one isolated incident, I'd say they got it right.

I mentioned that Dr. Timberlake was engaged in two distinct races. The second was more bizarre than the first. He was in a race against my body's miraculous power to heal itself. Even as my body was hell-bent on dying—and would have without heroic medical intervention—it was at the same time trying to patch itself together. There was a great deal of work the doctor had to do to ensure that my body would heal in the ways he wanted it to heal. Already that night, with blood flowing out like a faucet and equal amounts frantically pumped in, my body was trying to heal itself. Things were knitting themselves together. Some organs were in the wrong places and some bones were still crooked, but torn tissues were already seeking out and finding and reattaching themselves to other torn tissues. For a while the doctors had an external stabilizing device attached to my pelvis with pins and screws, but when an anaerobic infection set in in my lower left leg, they were forced to remove the device. As a result, my body healed a bit out of kilter. My pelvis has a big crack down the middle and a gap of more than an inch between the two halves. The bone on the left side is punched up about an inch higher than the one on the right, so that when I sit on a hard surface now I list to the left. But, darn it, my body still works! Each organ continues with its assigned task and the blood pumps merrily along. Go figure. God must have been quite a capable creator to have left human bodies with such an effective power for self-regeneration.

I remained in intensive care for six weeks, until the middle of July. I don't remember any of it except for the view I had past the end of my bed, across the room, into adjoining rooms or hallways beyond. I didn't have my glasses, so the world looked as foggy as my brain felt. A person walked through my field of vision, but didn't stop. I couldn't call out. I couldn't attract their attention. I felt very alone. There was a dying helium balloon at the foot of my bed that kept bobbing in minute breezes. I thought it was some kind of creature from a horror film, stalking me.

Dreams kept me company during this time, but they were bizarre, disjointed, imagined realities. They may in fact have been a single electrical pulse that flashed through my mind in the moment just before I woke up, but to me they seemed to last days and even weeks. They all had this in common: In each one I was trapped in an uncomfortable, untenable, threatening situation. Each dream ended when I discovered that I had the power to end it, simply by choosing. Like Dorothy clicking her ruby-slippered heels together, I could depart from Oz anytime I wanted. There was that old control mechanism kicking in! But unlike Dorothy, I didn't land back in Kansas. Not by a long shot. Each time I deliberately ended a dream by decision, I landed in the middle of another one, even more realistic and frightening than the one before.

And then, when I finally escaped the dream world for good and awoke, I was still trapped in the worst nightmare of all. I found myself in a body that only half worked. After that, the dream world didn't seem all that bad.

Piece by piece, through the months of June and July, the doctors removed their equipment. The neck brace came off. Monitors were removed. They weaned me gradually from the respirator. It must have been excruciating to watch, as my body, not used to breathing on its own, struggled for each breath. At one point, perhaps four weeks after I was injured, my body seemed to have had enough. I stopped responding to treatment. I was losing weight. Organs began shutting down. Ann called in some friends of mine to talk and pray with me, though I was not consciously aware of their presence. A resident doctor, Chris Reising, came up with an idea that probably saved my life. He suggested they try human growth hormones, normally used on infants who fail to thrive. The response was immediate. Only days later, around the middle of July, I was transferred out of intensive care into a private room. My personal memories begin here.

As I slowly swam to the surface of consciousness from the depths of my drug-induced coma, the most startling fact of all was that I accepted this new reality with no question, no panic. There was no emotion at all. Blessedly, I was free of pain. Most everything that was going to heal had already done so. But that was meager blessing. My kidneys had long since shut down, due to the excessive volume of blood that had been transfused the night of the injury. Every couple of days I was wheeled down to dialysis, where I remember wonderful nurses and excruciatingly long four-hour sessions waiting for my blood to pass through the machines. I watched my own blood—actually, most of it was borrowed from others, newly transfused—flow out of my body, into the clear plastic tubes, through machines that filtered and scrubbed it, then back into my body to slowly clog with waste again and have to be filtered all over again two days hence. If the port failed or the machines were temperamental, it would take longer. I watched the minutes and seconds pass on the clock on the wall. I planned my sessions, with naps, music, and little mental games. I felt stifled in the still, stagnant hospital air, and demanded that a fan be brought down with me from my room to blow on my face. It was my one source of pleasure. Maybe I considered it a reminder of the wind on my face from biking or running.

Apparently I was quite temperamental for a while. Ann tells me I was not a pleasant person to be around. I can believe it. My friends who visited found me angry and withdrawn. But in my defense, let me point out that they were seeing my raw self, stripped of window dressing and sugar coating. As a card-carrying introvert, I believe that people shield their real selves from outsiders, projecting a facade that the world sees and interacts with. Normally, I put a lot of energy into being sociable and nice. It doesn't come naturally to me, but in my role as a parish pastor, I've had to develop that side of my personality. Now, however, I had no energy to build the superstructure of social graces that make humans palatable to one another. Too much of my unfiltered inner self must have been seeping out, like the blood I had lost. People saw me without my mask.

During this time I was afraid to look under the covers. Ann and the nurses would come and go, bathing me, changing dressings, emptying the colostomy bag, draining some things and packing others. I didn't know and didn't care to know what they were doing. It wasn't my body anymore, anyway. I wasn't particularly interested in getting to know it. It was frightening and disgusting. It was a month after my return to consciousness before I decided to learn to empty my own colostomy bag.

Nights were terrifying. Because I dozed all day (I would fall asleep in the middle of a session with a nurse or physical therapist), I was not sleepy at night. Around 10:00 PM I started to wake up. By midnight I was fully awake, watching the second hand creep around the face of the clock and calculating how long it would be until a nurse would come in with medications or breakfast. By 4:00 AM I would hit the call button, needing reassurance. When Ann slept in the room with me, I was constantly rousing her from sleep to keep me company. A hospital psychologist rigged me up with a tape deck and a relaxation tape, but I couldn't figure out how to run the machine at night. Part of the sleeplessness, I'm convinced, was anxiety. I had been so close to death that I was afraid to close my eyes and lose consciousness again, even if only for a few hours. It was that old fear of losing control coming back to haunt me at night.

Ann had a mantra for me during these anxious nights. "Never doubt in the darkness what was revealed to you in the light." This provided the anchor. I remembered that our lives had been good. Ann made a little list of special moments and places for me to run through in my memory. She reminded me of camping trips to the North Shore of Lake Superior, of romantic picnics, of the birth of our children. There was meaning in our relationship and our shared experiences. I was loved as a husband, father, and minister. The confidence with which we had embraced life was real. It was not to be doubted. I began recounting the evidence of grace that had attended my life before the injury, and reminding myself that nothing had happened to shake that grace.

But a backrub at four in the morning was still remarkably reassuring.

A great project loomed ahead of me, for which all of my physical training on the roads and trails and in the pools had prepared me well. At some point in late July, almost from one moment to the next, I accepted that project. Bring it on! I had to get back to my life, one tiny skill at a time. That's what rehab is all about: putting you back into your old life, or at least as close to it as you can manage. There's a problem with this, as we'll see later. It may be that that old person you're trying to reconstruct no longer exists. But that was the name of the game for my first months and years.

The nurses seemed inordinately proud of me when I started wetting the bed. Personally, it seemed a trivial accomplishment, a disgusting accident even, until I realized I hadn't been urinating at all for seven weeks due to kidney failure. As the kidneys came back on line, dialysis visits were scheduled further apart, freeing up time for bigger things. Like teaching me to speak, roll over, sit up. I once had a dog more advanced in these tricks than I was at that point. One day, six nurses were rounded up. They lifted me out of bed and plopped me into a special reclining wheelchair resembling a rolling La-Z-Boy. I managed to sit up for several minutes before succumbing to nausea and begging to be returned to bed. The six nurses had to be assembled again. They filed into my room and dumped me unceremoniously back into bed. But it was a start. My long journey back to personhood had begun.

It was accelerated when my Bible study buddies, the ones who had earlier prayed over me, sprung me from the hospital one day. We were going to Grinnell to see the musical, *Joseph and the Amazing Technicolor Dreamcoat,* performed by the Grinnell Community Theater. I was supposed to have been in the cast of the play, one of Joseph's brothers, with a solo to sing and a dance number to lead. My daughter Kate and I had auditioned for parts just before my injury. Our summer had been scheduled around rehearsals and performances.

Echoing Ann's mantra that had protected me during the long, anxious nights was Joseph's song from Pharaoh's prison. He sang about hope even though he lay forgotten and alone in the dungeons in Egypt. He claimed God's promise of a homeland for himself and his people even though all the evidence at hand would seem to make that claim unrealistic. It was the most powerful piece of music in the play, and I could picture Donny Osmond, who played Joseph in the Broadway production we had at home on video, belting it out.

Now it seemed therapeutic to get me to a performance. The Grinnell Regional Medical Center graciously donated the use of a hospital ambulance (a $1500 value!). A driver volunteered her time. The Bible study boys (our wives call us the "Boys' Club"—we spend as much time catching up on sports as we do studying the Bible) came to my room and bundled me off. It was a beastly hot day. I wasn't sure I would survive the ride. We rolled into the theater just as the performance began, and they found a place for my cot in the back of the balcony. I missed most of the production because my eyes were full of tears. Kate had kept her role in the children's choir. Many of the cast came up to see me during intermission. That night back in the hospital I slept peacefully, without drugs.

The pace of my recovery picked up after that because I began to take control of it. They pulled my feeding tube with a loud and painful pop, and I tried to keep up with caloric intake on my own. Already Ann was saying I looked like a concentration camp survivor. I lost further ground when I had to eat on my own. I counted every calorie going in, every mouthful of soda and every slice of bread. But I was still throwing up a couple of times a day and losing ground. The doctors were threatening to put the feeding tube back in. That made me more anxious than ever, and so I threw up even more.

What helped me turn the corner was a weekend pass home in late August. During my last month in rehab, the medical team thought it would be wise to have me experience the challenges of life at home, so I might structure my remaining weeks in rehab training to best advantage. Those first weekends were like vacation time—no rehab work, and there were plenty of family members home to take care of me. My brothers continued taking precious vacation time—as they had off and on throughout the summer—to be there when we needed help at home.

That first weekend was special. Although it was August, Ann had spent the day cooking a full Thanksgiving meal. Nothing was overlooked. Turkey, dressing, cranberries, mashed potatoes, green bean casserole, and pumpkin pie. She served me on a new dinner plate I'd never seen before, oversized with writing around the rim: "Today is your Special Day." The first helping she piled on was a frightfully ambitious mound of food for someone who was more likely to barf it up than retain it. But this stuff tasted like real food! I cleaned my plate and held it out for seconds. I consumed more calories that meal than I had during the entire preceding week. That was when I realized I could eat.

I started daily physical therapy the week after my buddies dragged me to see *Joseph*. I hadn't yet met all the requirements for the rehabilitation program—I was still on antibiotics, still considered a medical patient, still not eating enough—but I was insistent, and they figured that my attitude might count for something.

My first few weeks of therapy gave the doctors cause to wonder if I was ready. There was no real progress shown. I wasn't getting out of bed to eat with the other patients. I wasn't making an attempt to dress myself. I suspect I absorbed more nursing care than I was allotted. They began to wonder if I was a bad apple. By the end of each week I would fall back into my bed exhausted, drained, and depressed. I had been in training before, but there was more at stake here and I was starting from way back in the pack this time. I hit the wall, that condition in long-distance endurance events in which the body has no more to give, again and again.

But after a few weeks I began showing progress. I was soon able to lift a broomstick over my head without quivering from the strain. I could catch and throw a balloon—they move slowly and don't weigh much. I learned to transfer from wheelchair into bed across a narrow transfer board. Once in awhile I did it by myself, with great anxiety but a tremendous sense of accomplishment. I jumped progressively higher curbs in my wheelchair, and learned to get up off the floor and back into the chair when my maneuvers failed, which they often did. There was a steeply sloping corridor in the hospital, dubbed the "Purple Mountain" by the rehab staff (it had purple carpeting), where the therapists used to take new wheelchair users to train. My first trip down the hill was a dizzying ride. My first hike up took several rest breaks to accomplish. I learned to navigate escalators in a wheelchair, a move that still makes Ann nervous and brings mall security people running in alarm when they see it. And I learned how to push a grocery cart. A doctor had promised me I'd be back to my church for the Christmas sermon. But my rate of progress accelerated such that by late September there was nothing they could do for me in the hospital that I couldn't do for myself at home. An instructor taught me to drive with hand controls, which I eventually mastered after a first spin that almost dumped the two of us into the Des Moines River. I became nervous as a kid getting his first driver's license when I had to go to the DOT for a driving test and a new restricted license.

That's when I got one of those handicap-parking permits, so coveted by drivers trying to park close to the mall on busy shopping days. I learned, as a matter of principle, to keep the placard out of sight until I needed it to claim a parking spot wide enough for me to transfer into my wheelchair beside my car door. I'm not proud enough of my newly-disabled status to want to flaunt it to the world as I drive.

The entire hospital experience, then, taken as a whole, was a steady march back toward competence, independence, and control. The specialists' jobs were to get me back to my life. Their work implied a promise that I would make it, and I had swallowed that promise hook, line, and sinker. There were always goals and they were always attainable. I always succeeded, and it felt good.

So far, rehab had been a linear process designed to get me back to as close an approximation of my old life as possible. In therapy we kept pushing the envelope of what I could do, to see what might eventually be achievable. Hopping curbs in my wheelchair. Higher and higher lifts from the floor. Transfers into a car. Yes, they had a Chevrolet Cavalier in the little gym on the third floor of the hospital. Some vo-tech students from a local community college had torn it down, passed it up the elevator piece by piece, and reassembled it in the therapy room. They got me upright on cumbersome leg braces and tried to mobilize me on crutches. Kimbra Corte, described by her colleagues and patients as "one of the best gait-trainers in Iowa," worked closely with me on walking skills and advanced wheelchair maneuvers. Six years later, I still count her as a friend and continue to look forward to sharing news and accomplishments with her.

Some of our attempts were dead ends, at least for the moment, but many panned out and opened up new horizons. In some skills I've now far exceeded expectations. In an emergency, I can walk with simple ankle braces and a walker, allowing me access to buses, airlines, and stairs. My basement is an obstacle course of expensive but no longer useful mobility aids that I've long since graduated from.

So the hospital became a can-do place with nothing but reminders of accomplishments surrounding me.

Leaving the hospital was another thing entirely. In the hospital I was constantly reminded of what I'd been able to accomplish, how far I'd come. I regularly turned down assistance from aides whose job it had been to push me to therapy. Now I pushed myself. I'd passed other patients who were still struggling with rudimentary skills. I was a rehab success story, because I was on my way out, back to my old life.

But while the hospital reminded me of how far I'd come, home was a series of brick walls and dead ends, a constant reminder of what I'd lost. When I arrived home for good in mid-September, the new ramp wasn't finished yet, so I had to be lifted up the back stairs. Our beautiful 1906 home, so valued during all our years of married life, had five different levels, none of which was accessible from the ground. Even with a ramp to the back door, I could access only one level, and there were no beds there. At first I slept on the rollout sofa in the living room. No nurses came in the next morning to wake me up, bathe me, change my bandages, dress me, or bring me my breakfast tray. No one in my family would seriously entertain my request to install a call button to summon them for any of these duties so willingly carried out by the hospital staff. It was a rude awakening, I'm telling you.

On that first Saturday morning home, with my wife, my two children, my mother, my two brothers, and one sister-in-law (a nurse) working overtime on my case, it was noon before I was actually up and dressed and ready to face the day. And by then I needed a nap. They had to remove doors into the bathroom, strip off some molding where the doorway was still too narrow, figure out how to transfer me into the tub and get me out again. My two brothers and I were Three Stooges material. At least, in the novelty of the situation, we could laugh about it. I was worried about how funny it would seem a couple of weeks hence after all my relatives had gone home and I had to address the business of daily living for myself.

Even now, as capable and independent as I have become, I am situationally disabled when in new places that are less than accommodating. New settings that aren't fully accessible are not just an inconvenience for me. They are actually disabling. Staying in a hotel room that's not well thought-out, or visiting family members (one brother lives on the second floor and the other keeps moving to tiny houses with narrow corridors and postage stamp bathrooms, and he shares these bungalows with three giant dogs, two cats, a bird, and a pot-bellied pig), or trying to visit parishioners who live in inaccessible homes can reduce me to a helpless cripple—again. "Honey, can you reach me a glass? Can you hand me a towel? Can you get a couple of hefty guys to carry me like a sack of flour up these stairs?" Things as simple as bathroom sinks without a cutout below for my feet and legs make it impossible for me to belly up to wash my face or shave. Mirrors are too high. You can't be too picky about your appearance when you can't find a mirror to use. It's another example of loss of control.

A week after I got home from the hospital I got a phone call from a member of my church youth group. The kids were all down at church and she was wondering if I could come down.

Well, sure I could! I had all the requisite skills, right? I got myself dressed. Couldn't tie my shoes yet, but who would notice? Rolled out down the newly-completed ramp. My car, freshly equipped with hand controls, was waiting in the garage. Getting into the car was a most challenging project, but certainly doable. I transfer into the driver's seat and then begin to dismantle my wheelchair. Mine isn't one of those folding chairs that are most often seen in hospitals. Mine has a rigid frame. Rigid wheelchairs are much better than those old hospital chairs in terms of performance and weight. The one I'm in now, having searched four years for a suitable candidate, is made of titanium, was custom-made to fit me like a glove, and weighs just over fifteen pounds, if you can believe it. But these new chairs come with a price: Not only do they run two to three thousand dollars in price, but they don't fold up into a neat package. I have to lean out of the car, remove the seat cushion and throw it into the back seat, fold the little lumbar back support down, pop the quick release wheels off and put them carefully where the passenger's feet would go, then heft the rest of the chair frame in through the door, over my lap between the steering wheel and my chest—if it will fit; some cars are too small—and dump it in the passenger seat. Now I can accomplish the whole maneuver in significantly less than a minute, but back then it took nearly a half hour.

I succeeded in getting into the car, dragging my chair in after me. I breathed a self-congratulatory sigh of relief, and made ready to start the car—to drive unassisted into my new life of freedom and independence— when I realized that I didn't have my car keys. For situations like this one, I now carry a cell phone, but I hadn't learned that trick yet. No one was home since they were all down at church for the youth group meeting. I kept watch out the rear view mirror for any passersby who might heed a distress call from a cripple trapped in his own garage, but no one appeared. I sat for maybe twenty minutes trying to figure a way out of this dilemma.

And then I leaned my head on the steering wheel and cried.

And after that was over I put my chair together again, transferred out of the car, went back inside, called the church to tell the kids I wouldn't be joining them after all, and went back to bed. You do what you have to do.

One day in late October I felt good. It was a fleeting sensation, to be sure, but it was real and it was so unusual that I marked its arrival. I was driving to the hospital in town, not as a patient this time but as a pastor visiting parishioners. A few blocks from the hospital, I realized that I didn't feel half bad. There was no pain. I was back to doing ministry again. My head was clear. The sun was shining. I said a silent prayer of thanks. As quickly as the feeling came, it disappeared again. Things started to hurt and inconveniences cropped up. But that one pain-free, optimistic moment was enough to convince me that life could be lived again. I was back!

I was blindsided by a drunk driver and have had to face a great deal of uncertainty, loss, grief, and pain. My losses have encompassed more than the use of my legs. I've also lost a sense of self-image that was highly dependent on my physical abilities and appearance. I've faced ongoing health issues and reconstructive surgeries. My life is a daily routine of bowel and bladder maintenance that many would consider repugnant. I do it as a matter of course. I've had to let go of sexual performance and fulfillment, an aspect of my marital relationship I had found essential and miss terribly now that it's gone. My life expectancy, in all likelihood, will be much reduced. Many people who see me roll cheerfully and with determination through my day have no idea what it costs me, what I've had to give up, and how I still grieve.

But whole new realities have also opened up as a result of this life-changing incident. My pace has slowed down and I have been forced to become more deliberate and disciplined. People tell me that I was a decent enough pastor before the injury, but I feel as though I have become more caring and compassionate since the accident. I can empathize more with the trials that all people go through. I see human diversity in a whole new light. I have begun to develop new theological insights. I've had to rethink my understanding of God's role in tragedy and suffering, and what biblical healing is all about. Conventional interpretations of faith and healing no longer ring true for me. New opportunities for travel and adventure have opened themselves to me. I was featured in a television special about the 2000 San Diego Marathon as an elite athlete, and invited for an all-expense-paid weekend in Spokane as a wheelchair participant in the 2002 running of Bloomsday, one of the largest road races in the United States. I certainly never could have competed at that level before! People are interested in what I have to say about adjusting to hardship and overcoming adversity. I'm becoming an expert in the field.

A whole new relationship with Ann and Ames and Kate has opened up. I'm learning interdependence. I'm no longer the guy in charge. I still have gifts to offer, to be sure, but I need help from others now in ways I never did before. I still try to control what I can, manipulating whatever factors in my immediate environment that respond to my demands, but I realize that less of this universe is responsive to my will than I had thought. My household responsibility, now that I'm incapable of mowing the lawn or shoveling snow or doing routine maintenance or cleaning, is to be the family timekeeper. Not that I'm universally appreciated for reminding Ann and the kids when to get up or what's on the calendar for the day, but that's my job and I do it well. It may be a thankless task, but somebody's got to do it. Ann also lets me do the laundry, since she had the washer and dryer moved up into the kitchen from the basement. A recent remodeling of our new ranch-style home included a cutout under the kitchen sink, so now she lets me do the dishes, too.

In spite of my wife's helpfulness in making me useful again, I'm in charge of less than I had imagined myself to be before. I wasn't in charge of my personal safety on Memorial Day, 1997, no matter how accomplished my riding skills were, or of my body's miraculous power to heal itself, or of the community of faith that surrounds me with prayer when I can't even pray for myself. Learning the patience to let go may be the greatest gift to have surfaced from the depths of this tragedy.

There are other fringe benefits. When you roll around in a wheelchair you always have a seat handy. I can roll faster than a comfortable walking pace, and my legs never get tired. I enjoy the benefits of a mechanical advantage. My daughter presented me with a T-shirt for Christmas that reads, "I'm not handicapped. I'm just lazy." In a wheelchair you find yourself at eye level with little kids, who are always fascinated with how you get around. While adults are too "polite" to ask questions, kids will ask you anything: What's that you're riding? A wheelchair. Why? My legs don't work. How come? I was in an accident. Why don't you stand up? I can't. Will you get better? No. Can I have a ride?

And it has helped me to see that my previous understanding of human beings as being divided into two classes of able-bodied and disabled was an illusion based on stereotype and misunderstanding. People live out their lives on a whole variety of different scales of abilities. Though I'm in a wheelchair, I'm still more mobile than some people who walk. Though I'm mobility-limited, I'm gifted in other areas and highly capable on other scales. The more you look around with a critical eye, the more raw human variety you find, and the harder it will be to lump people into any categories at all. We're a marvelously rich and varied stew.

Finding yourself among the disabled, whether having arrived suddenly or gradually, through traumatic injury or gradual impairment, permanently or temporarily, is simply part of the human condition. Life goes on. Maybe not in the same way. Maybe things aren't as simple as they once were, as easy or as convenient or as painless. Maybe you have to incorporate assistive technology to stay in the game. Maybe you won't be able to do everything you did before, and you have to find new ways to be you. Maybe you'll have to reinvent yourself altogether, find a new game to play. However it is that you decide to persevere, it's not heroic, it's not miraculous, it's not inspirational. It's just coping. People are doing these things every day, even those who don't drive around with handicap-parking permits hanging from their rearview mirrors. It's what we do. All of us.

To have realized this is grace. If not for the injury, this grace never would have visited me.

Chapter 2

While I Was Sleeping

*I*t's lonely work, this rebuilding of one's life in the wake of catastrophic injury and disability. There are no guidebooks or instructional videos to show the way. It's up to you if you're going to make something of yourself. Reynolds Price, an award-winning author whose bout with a cancerous tumor on his spinal cord left him with limited mobility and intense pain, makes this point bluntly in his book, *A Whole New Life*:

> You're in your present calamity alone, far as this life goes. If you want a way out, then dig it yourself, if there turns out to be any trace of a way. Nobody—least of all a doctor—can rescue you now, not from the deeps of your own mind, not once they've stitched your gaping wound. (182)

From the beginning, my decisions and my determination have made the difference between life and death, between learning the requisite survival skills or not, between attaining the strength necessary to push wheels all day long or remaining dependent upon others, between achieving a return to a productive life or settling for something easier, something less. My decisions to stop the dreams when I was in intensive care seemed to move me forward. My decision to throw myself into therapy made me strong. I work out regularly and have returned to athletic competition. It has taken discipline and perseverance, and these things have had to come from within.

It was a strangely isolating process. Though I realized intellectually that my family was deeply engaged in my struggle, that literally hundreds of people held me in prayer, that I was surrounded by a caring community and skilled medical personnel, I was constantly and intimately conscious of the fact that it was my struggle alone. The work was always mine to accomplish or put off. Writer Nancy Mairs, who uses a wheelchair due to the progression of multiple sclerosis, writes, "Most of the work of living well and fully in the teeth of pain and uncertainty, as well as social neglect or ostracism, falls squarely on the disabled person herself" (*Waist-High*, 169). I was the one who had to get out of bed in the morning. I had to push the wheels. If there's hygiene to be done, I'm the one to do it. I had to take care of me—all the while struggling to return to a life in which the expectation was that I would take care of others. I'm a parish pastor, after all, not a bricklayer. Of course, it cuts both ways; if I had been a bricklayer, I would have had to find a new career. Caring for others can mostly be done from a wheelchair. But still I've often lamented that I now have two full-time jobs. One is caring for the church. The other is caring for myself.

One day, the hospital called me to look in on Joe, another patient in circumstances similar to my own. These requests come not infrequently, and I respond to them willingly, if sometimes for impure motives. Deep down, I think it helps me feel good about my own achievements when I am around others who are less accomplished. Ann and I found, when we were depressed about living so far from home in Central America, that it always helped to have family visit. In showing newcomers around, we always gained a renewed appreciation for how much we had learned about our new culture and how far toward adjustment we had come. Counseling other people with disabilities gives me the same sort of boost. Joe had been injured in a truck accident about the same time I was. But Joe was depressed and didn't seem to be responding well to treatment.

Sometime later I stopped by Joe's house. He did have the front door ramped, a good sign. I knocked and rolled in, finding Joe in the living room, lying in a hospital bed that looked hugely out of place in the middle of the cluttered little room. The television was on, tuned in to *Days of Our Lives* or *As the World Turns* or another of those daytime dramas—I can't tell them apart. The red flags were instantly raised. While the television is a constant companion and sometimes the only difference between sanity and despair, during the long days and weeks that I have been hospitalized I have always drawn the line at soap operas. If the television is still on when daytime soaps begin, I've always turned it off. I may have lost a lot of things, but I still have my dignity.

But Joe was watching a soap opera, drinking from a can of beer through one of those hospital straws that bend in the middle so you don't have to raise your head too high to get a sip.

Now, before I start sounding too smug here, I readily acknowledge that every injury is unique. Joe may have been responding to his particular circumstances in the only way open to him. He didn't seem to have entered the fray with the same financial, social, and spiritual ammunition that I had. I suspect he was recovering from a pressure sore, the most dreaded complication of immobility, because it entails a long bedridden recuperation. It's immature and simply incorrect to judge one person's trauma and reaction to it by the standards of another's. I should be more charitable, I know.

But God help me, I thought to myself as I sat and shared a beer with Joe and watched the conclusion of another exciting episode of *As the World Turns* in the middle of a perfectly good afternoon while he reclined in a hospital bed in his living room, I'm doing better than you are. It was not a very Christian train of thought, I know, but these things come unbidden sometimes. It's the devil, for sure.

Then, as I popped the tab on my second can of beer, I began to entertain a second line of thought. Why the hell was I working so hard at reclaiming my productive life while people like Joe had discovered a path of less resistance? Maybe God was using my injury to invite me to a life of beer and soap operas, and I was just being too stubborn to recognize the invitation. Maybe Joe was on to something. Your response to loss, injury, trauma, disability, or decline is a very personal struggle. The work it entails falls to you alone—or it simply won't get done. No one is going to adjust to your new circumstances but you. This private battle in which you engage the demons of sloth, decay, and depression is a necessary condition for return to anything resembling a whole and vital life.

However, I often say that every sermon is a heresy, because the preacher always makes one particular point and not its opposite, and usually both are true, depending on the circumstances or the audience. Trust me.

Having made the point about the importance of accepting the personal nature of the struggle back to life, let me also lay claim to the opposite truth. While a personal struggle may be a *necessary* condition for a return to full life, it is not in itself a *sufficient* condition. The more I learn about what was going on around me as I slept the summer away, the more I have come to realize that I was not, as it had seemed, entirely on my own. My injury sent out shock waves like ripples in a pond that ranged far and wide, and eventually marched back to buoy me up in ways I could never have predicted or imagined. Many others were also affected deeply by my injury. They shared the hurt and horror. They also participated in the recovery. I would never have returned to life without their involvement.

Ann and I had an argument about that one day in the car. We were on our way to a career-counseling center in the Minneapolis area that contracts with the United Church of Christ. It seemed, a couple of years after my injury, that I might be a good candidate for their services. A trip there would give me a chance, however brief, to sit back and reflect on my future in light of my new status as a person with a disability. On the drive to Minnesota, Ann asserted that *she* was the one needing the services. *She* was adjusting to a new life, too. Yes, I interjected lovingly, but the injury had happened to *me*, dear. Yes, *dear*, she insisted, but *I'm* facing losses *too*. *Fine*, I said. *Fine*, she replied. And that was that.

Not that I'm surrendering any ground to her here, but I do admit that my injuries and resulting disability have affected many people. It may have been *my* accident and *my* injuries, *my* body that was affected and *my* life that has changed as I learn to live with a disability, but the people around me have had to adjust to losses, as well. Ann and my children and my church members have given up things, too, related to my disability. They're grieving too. They have had to pick up the slack that I left them. Like a spider's web, on which the struggling of a trapped insect in one corner sets off a vibration that can be felt by the spider anywhere else on the web, all of my social entanglements were shaken and still quiver with the impact of that hit I took on the highway five years ago. They'll continue to quiver for some time to come. That drunk driver didn't just bump an individual cyclist off his bike; he plowed into an entire community.

All the factors were in place to see my family and me through this crisis. My denominational health insurance paid out huge sums of money for medical bills. My auto insurance even kicked in, since I was "driving" one of my family's "vehicles" at the time. Imagine that. Donations by the community paid for much of what insurance didn't. Resources of faith, physical conditioning, and previous experiences of loss and tragedy helped Ann and me weather this one together. The precisely appropriate medical personnel assembled to provide care. A small town cared and prayed, set up a blood drive, and sent food over to my family when we needed strength. I happen to pastor a church that had the compassion and the resources to keep my position open for a year, paying my salary and hiring an acting pastor to fill in. Key leadership people who could pull off this delicate administrative feat were in place. If any one of these props had been absent, my life might have taken a decidedly different turn. It was a thing of grace, how carefully choreographed was the response to my injury. I don't see how anyone could have consciously manipulated things to such ultimate advantage intentionally. The miracle that attended my injury, survival, and recovery was this incredible interplay of people, technology, compassion, perseverance, and sometimes sheer dumb luck.

Ames, then fifteen years old, was at his summer job with Grinnell College food service. He was serving a meal to college alumni in a dining hall on the main highway out of town. The ambulance on its way to pick me up sped by, lights flashing and siren screaming. Ames said it unsettled him. He felt it was significant. He anxiously hurried home after work. When he was met at the door of our house by a church member, he knew something had happened.

My mother was also on campus, celebrating her fiftieth college reunion. Word came to her about my accident during dinner. A classmate friend rushed out with her, helped her pack, and got her to the hospital. The entire class supported her through the next days and weeks. They invited Ann and me to dinner five years later on the occasion of their fifty-fifth reunion. The class agent had tears in her eyes as she introduced us.

Ann met me at the Grinnell hospital. Meg, a church member and friend, went with her to the hospital in Des Moines. She would be there for the next several days and nights. Ann's close friends and family and other church members began showing up. Three years previously I had served a Des Moines church as interim pastor. Many of those church members flocked to the waiting room. Several of them, in order to get past the nurses to see me in intensive care, introduced themselves as my long-lost brothers or sisters or as my ministers. If they had been keeping track, the hospital staff may have discovered that my "family members" and "ministers" numbered in the dozens, if not hundreds.

The situation was tense, and my survival was by no means assured. On the third night, Ann woke in the middle of the night strangely at peace. She woke up our friend Tim, the Baptist minister from Grinnell, who was keeping her company at the hospital that night. It was revealed to her, she told him, that things would be okay. Not that she had had any special insight into the outcome of my injuries. Whether I would live or die was still uncertain. Her vision did not blindly ignore either possibility. But, by means of a peculiar revelation, she knew that, whatever the outcome, it would be okay. There would be something fundamentally graceful even about my death, if that were to be the final outcome. This was on the third day, the day Jesus rose from the grave.

Ann inserted herself in the group of doctors and residents as they went on rounds each morning. They would discuss any progress or problems about each patient as they looked in on them. Usually, these discussions are private among medical personnel. But Ann would have none of it.

She's like that. When she and I traveled to Europe with our friend Craig during the summer before our senior year in college, Ann's role was to "insert." On the very first night, when our plane in Des Moines couldn't take off due to mechanical problems, the airline put all three hundred passengers up at a downtown hotel. We sent Ann to the desk through an impatient throng of irate passengers to get our room key. She was back in less than two minutes. I'm not kidding. We got through Europe in half the normal amount of time, with Ann inserting herself all the way.

In the hospital, she made it clear that she was going to play a role in my healing. She wrote everything down. If the doctors had discussed something a week before and had dropped it off their agenda for this day, Ann would bring it up. By the end of it, she knew more about the care and treatment of my condition and injuries than did the nurses. They moved in and out of the picture as their shifts changed. They were not privy to the latest information. Ann was. She was a bulldog.

She did something else that turned out to have been very wise. She took pictures of me. She caught me at every stage of recovery, from the first day after surgery, when it was still more likely that I would die than live, to my successful efforts at shaving and brushing my teeth and surviving rehab. She organized them in an album and presented it to me when I could appreciate it. That album has contributed mightily to my recovery, and shows that she and all the others experienced the whole drama of my injury and recovery. They were there from the beginning. I wasn't. I have no experience of the worst of my ordeal. For good or bad, the memories aren't there. That photo album is all I have to help me experience the depths of my trauma. It reminds me how far I've come. Every time I look through it, I get choked up and the tears form freely. I catch a glimpse, at least, of what the people around me must have gone through. Seeing the pictures helps my healing. It brings me closer to closure.

There's one photo, though, that I can't get anyone to explain to me. In this photo, I'm in intensive care, unconscious and still attached to multiple tubes and monitors, and yet, curiously, I am wearing a Groucho Marx plastic nose, glasses, eyebrows, and mustache. What could possibly account for such a thing? At one point in my recovery, apparently, my family had too much time on their hands.

I need to say clearly here that the people who gathered around my bed in presence and prayer during those first days and weeks had a much more trying experience than I did. While I was blissfully in a coma, my lover and partner for life was confronting the brutal possibility of spending the second half of her life alone. Relying on resources of faith, she began to accommodate herself to the seriousness of my condition.

But our children didn't have the same depth of resources to draw upon. Ames was fifteen, Kate just twelve. It's true they had lived through a number of adventures and trials already. The three years we had spent in Nicaragua had shown them that they could create a home anywhere. Ann and I had had a stillborn daughter when Ames was three years old. He still remembers our grief, but he saw that we pulled through it together. And Ames himself, just after Kate was born, had been diagnosed with leukemia and had undergone three years of chemotherapy and radiation therapy. Significantly, he has forgotten the pain and uncertainty. All he remembers is the loving attention shown to him by his family and the medical staff at the University of Iowa Hospitals.

But all through these events, the basic family structure remained intact. Mom and Dad had provided stability. Now, however, Dad was a vegetable on life support. Kate saw me that first night as I was being wheeled into the operating room. My blood soaked the sheets. It was a traumatic sight. She still can't talk about what she saw or how it affected her. Ames began to find it more and more difficult to visit me in the hospital. Reminders of this near loss were too painful.

Perhaps more frightening even than the thought of losing me entirely was the possibility of an incomplete recovery. At first, as I was waking up, I didn't recognize my own kids. Kate says I pinched her hand so hard one night that she cried. The hospital staff wasn't too sure about me, either. I woke up speaking Spanish. No kidding! No one knows exactly why, but we think it had something to do with a visitor, a UCC minister originally from Argentina, who always speaks Spanish with me when we're together. She paid me a visit, and in my confusion, I must have thought I was back in Central America. My nurses hastily called for a hospital translator.

Even when I came back to English, I was still dazed and confused. One of the stock questions they'll ask to determine your mental state is, "Who is president of the United States?" Don't tell me. I know this one. The name starts with a C. Ames and I had just finished a school project on our favorite president, Jimmy Carter, so that was my answer. It was wrong. "Coolidge?" I guessed. They assigned a head trauma team to my case, and my family was filled with dread.

They all survived the ordeal, as I did, but I can't help but wonder if some of the confidence Ann and I had deliberately tried to instill in our children during their formative years has now eroded.

This has also taken some years off the life expectancy of my mother, Connie. Mom's a heavy smoker. We've tried to get her to quit for years, but she has a stock response to our entreaties. "I've quit twice already," she says. "I'm not going to quit again." The first time was just before my father died of a heart attack at age forty-seven. She went back to smoking after that. The second time was in the week before my accident. "Every time I quit, I run the risk of losing another person I love. I smoke now to keep the rest of you alive!"

My sister-in-law, a nurse in Spokane, Washington, also played an active role. She tried to stay up-to-date with my condition and care, but grew frustrated receiving conflicting information from different family members. Finally, she just began calling the nursing station directly, on a daily basis, to get reports and share advice. That's what got her into trouble. The nursing staff didn't want to be told by a nurse halfway across the country how to do their business. They stopped taking her calls. But they knew they were being watched.

In the central plains of Nicaragua, between a remote dry plain and a wholly inaccessible mountain range, lies the village of Colama. I had been there a couple of times while we were stationed in Nicaragua in the early 1990s, training Anabaptist church leaders in community development. There was a dedicated community leader and Mennonite pastor working in Colama. The first time I visited, the pastor was too busy to meet with me. He was suturing the foot of a boy who had cut himself with an axe. I went back later to celebrate with the village the completion of a water system which pumped fresh, treated water to a faucet at the central square. I wrote an article for *The Other Side* magazine about how successfully this pastor combined an evangelical Christian message with direct service for people in need. He had made a big impression on me.

The trip to Colama was an adventure in itself. It involved a drive into the countryside from Managua. You veer off the highway and follow a rutted road through an immense sugarcane plantation that Daniel Ortega, then president of Nicaragua, had constructed with help from his friend Fidel Castro. It was one of those grand scale projects that have since been discredited, but must have seemed like a good idea at the time. You drive through entire forests of eucalyptus trees that were planted for the sole purpose of providing fuel to fire the enormous sugar mill. After about an hour, if you've found all the right turns in the eucalyptus forest, you find yourself at the bank of a small stream. The road disappears into it and reappears again on the other side. When the water level is normal, you can drive through it, although it's a good idea to send someone ahead on foot to determine the depth. If the water is high, you park the truck at the bank and wade through. Then it's another ten kilometers on foot to Colama. It's worth the visit, if for no other reason than to find that there are indeed energetic, creative people eking out a living at the end of that dusty road.

After the speeches and the commendations to those who had assisted with the completion of the water project in Colama, the faucets were turned on and the children danced in the flowing water. The ladies unveiled a feast of local foods laid out on long tables under the trees. After lunch the pastor and I shared cups of strong Nicaraguan coffee and listened to a distant baseball game on his transistor radio.

Several months after my injury I received an e-mail message from Mennonite Central Committee headquarters in Akron, Pennsylvania. They had received a letter from the pastor in Colama. His church—the entire community, in fact—was praying for me. How could God not have heard and heeded prayers from these earnest Christians?

They weren't the only ones. The annual meeting of the Iowa Conference of the United Church of Christ took place the weekend after my injury. Delegates were stunned by the news that an Iowa pastor had been seriously injured, and they took reports back to most of the two hundred UCC churches in Iowa. Prayer cards began arriving from churches I'd never visited, never even heard of. A Presbyterian church in Wheaton, Illinois, where the mother of my brother's wife is a member, still, five years later, sends me an occasional card to let me know I remain in their prayers. I still hear reports of prayer chains operating on my behalf from places I can't even begin to imagine a connection with.

The Reverend Susan Ingham, executive minister of the Iowa Conference of the United Church of Christ, came to the hospital that first night. She made sure that Ann was surrounded by pastors. There was never a shortage of clergy in the intensive care waiting room. This can be a mixed blessing, however. Large numbers of clergy gathered for any reason in the same place is a recipe for disaster. I'm still hearing stories about the unruly behavior of my support crew, how they commandeered the waiting room television set and took over the choicest chairs. Anyone who could pick up a Bible showed up at the door to intensive care and introduced themselves as my minister, thereby gaining access to see me. On her visit that first night, Susan asked what she could do. She was sent home to prepare to lead worship for my church the following morning.

Many of my parishioners had already heard the news. It was on the local radio station and the phone lines were busy. But many people arrived expecting to hear the first in a series of lazy summertime sermons, on a normal summer Sunday. There was a hushed silence in the sanctuary as people began to comprehend what had happened to their pastor. The chair of our worship committee had already secured a retired minister from the congregation to preach, but he graciously yielded the pulpit to Susan. She had scrounged dozens of votive candles and invited members each to light one as a visible symbol of prayer and support. That night there was a hastily called ecumenical prayer service, well attended, at the Catholic church in town. Local clergy lined up to supply my pulpit through the summer. One of the first in line was the pastor of Grinnell's most conservative church, a man with whom I had seldom cooperated and had very little in common, theologically and ecclesiastically speaking. But bless his heart, Pastor John had found common ground to bridge our differences.

Susan did one more thing for us, all on her own. When I first arrived at the emergency room, my wedding ring and an engagement ring that Ann had made for me herself had to be cut from my fingers due to swelling. Susan took the rings and had them repaired. When I was able to wear them again, there was not the slightest sign that they had been damaged. The repaired rings served as a physical symbol of the rebuilding of my life and relationships.

My church office had already been in transition. Incredibly, we had just hired a new office administrator. Julie, the new employee, had been a childhood friend of mine, another little kid running around the neighborhood when I was growing up in Grinnell. She had married, raised two children, divorced, and moved away. Now she was back, remarried, and a valuable member of our programming staff as a youth group leader. She had spent just two days in the church office with me and the outgoing secretary, learning the ropes, before she was to assume full duties on Monday. Her initiation was a trial by fire. On June 2, her first day on the job, she became the nerve center for the congregation, relaying status reports from the hospital, helping groups within the church communicate with one another, and fielding inquiries from local media. She was the right person for the position at that moment.

We also benefited from a key moderator and head trustee, who happened to be married to each other. Rick, the trustee, was a second-generation member of the church. His mother, still living, is a lively lady and has been a respected pillar of the church for all of her ninety-plus years. Rick's wife, Sue, was moderator, the highest elected member of the congregation. She was competent, detail-oriented, had the time this new responsibility required, and was highly respected by the entire membership. They pulled into their leadership cadre a retired minister, Orlan Mitchell, who had recently moved to Grinnell. He had been one of the executive ministers of the Iowa Conference, charged with the task of financial ministry for the Conference. He served now as consultant to the church leadership. And, of course, Ann was on the team, helping to keep the Molsberry vision before the church. She met with them when she could. A better team could hardly have been assembled.

There was no blueprint for what they faced now. Even after my return from the injury, as I searched the literature available on churches experiencing trauma, there was precious little to be found. It was unclear whether I would survive or not. If I were to live, there was no way of knowing if I would ever recover sufficiently to come back to the church, or how long it would take, or whether I would even want to. They had to make decisions as though this would all work out, with no assurance that it would. Rick riffled through my files first thing Monday morning, discovering to his horror that I didn't even have disability insurance. There would be more of a burden on the church than he had anticipated.

Julie told me later that it was the church's finest hour. Tactfully, she stopped short of saying that this was the best thing that could have happened to the church. People came together in ways they never had before and never would have without a common crisis. Sue says that you could have asked people to do anything, and they would have done it. Meetings were held to make sure the decisions being made were sound and honored UCC policy. Believe me, we have members who would later scrutinize the minutes for the propriety of every single action taken, emergency or no emergency. By mid-July the congregation had met formally to approve a proposal that had bubbled up from all the boards, to the effect that the church would keep me on full salary until at least the end of November, that an acting pastor would be hired in the interim, and that the life of the congregation would move forward. Money was borrowed from our church endowment fund, the guidelines for which we had recently hammered out together as a congregation.

On top of all this, the church was in the middle of a construction project at the time. The church steeple was crumbling after forty-five years. Some specialists had been hired to make minor repairs, but once they discovered the structural decay of the tower they wouldn't even lean their ladders against it. They warned us it was going to come down on our heads with the next good wind. Replacing it was not optional, and the work was urgent. But have you priced church steeples recently? We were looking at a $100,000 expense. With no choice, and on the basis of hurried fundraising, we had moved forward with the work. Now the church was saddled with that little problem on top of this crisis in pastoral leadership.

When I came back in the fall, the steeple was finished. And a lovely steeple it is. It became yet another symbol of the reconstruction of my life. While the church was rebuilding, so was I. I joked with the congregation that I was going to take the following summer off as well, just to see what they would build in my next absence.

Vicki Engelmann was the pastor brought in to provide leadership in my absence. This was a delicate issue. If I were to recover, my ongoing position with the church (not to mention my ego) would be on the line.

If I did not survive, the church needed competent professional leadership in place to help guide the decision-making process. I had known Vicki previously, having stayed in the home of her father, also a UCC pastor. Vicki and I had met just the spring before my injury at a meeting of the National Board for World Ministries of the United Church of Christ. She and I had sat over coffee and plotted getting the Iowa Conference to partner with a church institution in a Latin American setting. In consultation with the board staff, we had decided on the Dominican Republic and determined to bring our recommendation back to Iowa. As an aside, the partnership relationship we envisioned has begun; Vicki and I both continue to serve on the steering committee.

At the time of the accident Vicki was, incredibly, finishing her clinical pastoral education internship as a chaplain at Iowa Methodist Medical Center in Des Moines, the very hospital where the helicopter happened to deposit me for emergency treatment. She was one of the first on the scene when my family arrived at the hospital. She had been on call that night and had gotten word that a UCC pastor had been injured.

Vicki was first tapped as a possible candidate for church leadership as early as that first Tuesday evening, June 3. Sue, the church moderator, paid Ann a visit at the hospital, met Vicki, heard of her connection with me, and asked, "Want to help us out?" At that point her question was just tongue-in-cheek, but shows how sound Sue's instincts were. Vicki immediately volunteered to preach in my place a couple of weeks hence. The church had a chance to meet her, members were favorably impressed, and so the process was begun. The Iowa Conference staff soon added their blessing.

When I was first aware of the arrangements, I was relieved things were being taken care of. But initially I thought it was overkill. I fully expected to be back in the saddle full time by late fall. My assurances put Vicki in a bad position. She had to serve at my whim. Some days I was full of energy and felt in charge again. Other days I found I couldn't even put in an appearance at the office. I couldn't predict my energy level and Vicki couldn't predict what her role might be on any given day. She had to take charge, but she had to surrender her ground when I felt like showing up. But we danced well together, thanks to her flexibility. She was on staff for a full year after my injury; I wasn't back on my own until June 1998. The congregation had had to schedule two more emergency meetings to deal with the extension. We worked out a creative package for continuing to finance salaries for Vicki and me. Honestly, I would have been crushed if the church had not come through for us. But this was a huge investment and risk on their part. They found the resources and compassion to pull it off. I owe the members a continuing debt of gratitude. I've discovered later that many churches simply fire their pastors when they can no longer fulfill the terms of their original agreements.

Another serendipitous outcome of the ordeal began when Meg, the woman who had driven Ann to the hospital that first night, asked what she could do to help. Ann's first response was to say, "Make sure this doesn't happen to anybody else." Meg took her seriously. She formed a committee she dubbed "Road Smart" and began educating every group she could find on sharing the road safely with bicyclists. When I recovered sufficiently I joined the group. We created a flier that was later picked up by *The Des Moines Register* and published in bulk quantities for safety programs across the state that the newspaper sponsors. Meg and I continue to visit with every driver's education class in Grinnell, sharing my story and raising awareness about driving responsibilities.

People like to claim responsibility for their own lives. "You gotta pull yourselves up by your own bootstraps," preach grandparents and conservative lawmakers. And I'll be the first to acknowledge that I never could have reached this level of adjustment without intense inner drive and determination. But the pain of my injuries was shared widely, in some cases impacting others far more than myself. And a small army of those who loved me, who stuck by my side, who paid my salary and my bills, who ran the church, and who prayed, must share the credit for my return to a meaningful life.

The first sermon I delivered to my church upon my release from the hospital was transcribed and reprinted in the *United Church News*, the national newspaper of the United Church of Christ. A year later it won the United Church Press Award of Excellence in the category of first person/autobiographical reflection. I have no idea how widely it has been read and how it has affected its readers. It has been reprinted in at least two other magazines. I hope this book touches even more readers. And not only because I'm earning royalties on each and every copy sold. I hope God can use this crisis in my life to continue to touch other lives. It's yet another grace visited upon us.

It's humbling to reflect on the degree of involvement of all those who surrounded me at my time of need, who picked up the slack when I could no longer function productively, who came up with financial resources to pay the bills and keep ministry rolling along at church, who pitched in with cards, visits, phone calls, chicken soup, and prayer, and who share, one way or another, the impact of what happened to me.

This process has called from me more energy, faith, and persistence than I ever imagined I would have been capable of. If I had known years ago that this great challenge was bearing down the road at me, I don't know how I would have faced it. I think I would have found ways to bail out rather than brace up to meet it. My efforts in response to my injury, I feel in all humility, have been nothing short of heroic.

On the other hand, there is no way my efforts alone could have brought me to this point. Life is a complex interplay of forces that makes each of us interdependent with one another. A trauma like I've experienced makes this truth painfully clear. I don't create my life alone, out of nothing. Only God works that way. My life, whatever it has become or will become, is a unique hodgepodge of my efforts and the gifts and challenges that others bring to me. It's carefully orchestrated but wholly unpredictable. It's a divine mystery.

And a great adventure.

Chapter 3

You Can't Go Home Again

I'm in a truly remarkable career setting. I currently serve as senior pastor of the church into which I was born and baptized. My father was on the committee that started the church preschool, which is still in operation. I was one of the first children baptized in the "new building," which is still referred to by long-term Grinnell residents as the "new building" in spite of the fact that it is now fifty years old. Once an elderly gentleman stopped me on the street in front of the church, demanding to know why I had "torn down that beautiful old stone building."

I'm a third-generation Molsberry in Grinnell. My grandfather came to town in 1924 to open a dental practice. My father took over the practice just before I was born. Then we moved from town in 1967 for Dad to take a position with the University of Iowa School of Dentistry. My brother is a dentist in Spokane. As a pastor, I'm considered the black sheep of the family. But at least I'm back in Grinnell.

Having moved away from Grinnell with my family when I was in seventh grade, I had always harbored a deep nostalgia for my hometown. I reminisced about summer evenings spent roaming the college campus with my unruly gang of friends, collecting golf balls and tadpoles at the country club pond, skateboarding down neighbors' driveways, playing pick-up games of war, tag, and ball, and walking down the alleys to the movie house to see what was playing. My father died of a heart attack in Iowa City before I finished high school. I think that behind my longing to return to his hometown (and mine) was a desire to be close to him again. I had applied for the position as pastor of this church twice previously at moments of pastoral vacancies, before both the church members and I felt it might be a good match.

Everyone warned me, "You can't go home again." I was wary, but charged ahead because I was convinced that they were wrong. I never had the slightest doubt that I could indeed return to the scene of my childhood and, if not relive it, at least touch it and immerse my own kids in the goodness of it.

And I was absolutely right. Enough time had passed that all but a couple of the older ladies in the congregation had long since stopped thinking of me as "Little Bobby." Mrs. Smith, who had caught me peeing in the rose bushes right below her kitchen window when I was five, had passed on. As far as I know, there were no other witnesses to that little crime spree. My leadership style and sense of humor have defused most of the potential landmines normally associated with pastoring your hometown church. It was the best decision of my life to return home.

But, I'm finding, you can't come back as easily from a traumatic injury.

"You don't have to go back, you know." Ann was sitting on the foot of my bed in the hospital, before physical therapy had even begun, and we were talking about recovery options. "You don't have to be a minister anymore. You may not be able to. You may not want to anymore. You don't have to. You can do anything you want."

As far as I can remember, she was the only one, ever, to have opened up that option. But in desperate anxiety, I rejected it. "What else can I do?" I cried. "This is no time for retooling. We don't have the money for me not to go back to work. I have to go back. I have to work my way back to the person I was before." So that became my all-consuming goal, and the message I heard consistently from every other voice within earshot.

And to a remarkable degree, I've succeeded.

Father, husband, pastor, and community leader—all these roles were held open for me, with the expectation that I would come back to them exactly the same person I had been before. It was the responsibility of the physical and occupational therapists to prepare me for that world.

This is the lesson I remember from rehab, which is hammered into the minds of their patients: The world out there hasn't changed to accommodate your new disability. You need to change to adapt to it. You'll encounter stairs, curbs, and parking places too narrow for a wheelchair, ramps too steep, trails unpaved, bathrooms you can't access, shopping carts you'll have to push, narrow airline seats and aisles, escalators, flat tires, stigmas, and countless other obstacles. All these things were out there before you were injured, though you didn't notice them. Now you will. It is incumbent upon you now to figure out how to adjust to it all.

The medical team had done their best to return my body as close as possible to its original configuration. That's their job. If they had been an auto body shop, fixing my car from a collision, I would have demanded my money back. "Come on, guys, the suspension still doesn't work and the axle seems to be broken. I can't drive around in this wreck!" But doctors extend no such guarantees. Not in writing, anyhow.

The rehab team's job was to give me the necessary skills and adaptive technology to exist in a world through which I would now find it more difficult to move. Rehab forced me to recognize my new condition as a disability, and begin to deal with it. That's an extremely important step toward recovery. Some newly injured patients find their therapists' disclosure of their disability too blunt. They're not ready to receive that information yet. But it worked for me. We weren't sitting around in rehab waiting for a cure or waiting for the complete implementation of the ADA to make our lives on the "outside" easier. We had to get on with it. We were being prepared to face the world as it existed, on its own terms.

Church members must have been in collusion with the physical therapy department. They added their own powerful incentive for me to return to my former life. "Bob," they encouraged me, "we need you back." It was an honest expression of their concern, and was meant to motivate me. It worked. It was important for me to feel needed. I needed them and the role they offered as much as they needed me. But their expectations have proven unrealistic. They have led to impossible goals. I am not the person I was before.

I have found it impossible to crawl back into my old skin. It's like a suit of clothes that I have outgrown. A retired pastor in my church, who was a chaplain in World War II, still wears his military uniform on special occasions. But he's a very special guy. I can't fit into my old role.

The very simplest of tasks requires a new creative ingenuity, strength, and perseverance to accomplish. The first line of adjustment was to figure out how to solve the problems of daily living. Journalist John Hockenberry, currently a correspondent for the NBC news program *Dateline*, was injured in 1976 in a car accident when he was nineteen years old. In his fascinating autobiographical book, *Moving Violations*, he writes about his experience in physical therapy:

My body now presented an intriguing puzzle of great depth and texture. . . . The future seemed like an adventure on some frontier of physical possibilities. Each problem—getting up, rolling over, balancing in a chair, getting from here to there—needed a new solution. I was physically an infant endowed with the mind of an adult. . . . Solving each problem offered a personal authorship to experience that had never before seemed possible. (78)

Life in a wheelchair requires careful attention to detail. Just going out for a stroll calls for attentiveness. With my tiny little front wheel casters, I have to watch every crack in the sidewalk or bump in the street and pop a wheelie over them, or else the wheels will dig in and I'll go flying out the front of the chair onto the ground. It happens regularly, several times a month. My first reaction is always to look quickly around to see who might have noticed. Then I have needed to learn the skill of getting up off the ground, and develop the strength to throw myself back into the chair. I don't dare sit on a hard surface—a chair, the beach, the floor—for fear of pressure sores forming on my backside. Pressure sores are awful buggers, involving the breakdown of layers of skin as a result of unrelieved pressure, which may take surgery and months of bed rest to heal. Wheelchair users are excruciatingly careful to avoid the conditions that bring them on. We need to shift our weight and move in and out of our chairs as often as possible. And it's not just for the comfort of our tushes that we sit on expensive cushions. A good cushion can save thousands of dollars in hospital bills.

Weather makes a bigger difference now than it did before; I can't just roll out the door anymore, without giving a thought to the conditions. If it's raining, I get soaked before I can dismantle my chair and pull it through my car door. In the winters, which come around with punctual regularity every year in Iowa, only an inch or two of snow can get me into serious trouble. Sometimes I'm out before anyone has shoveled, and I find it impossible to even get out of my car. Sometimes the sidewalks and streets are scooped off beautifully, only to leave a small icy ridge of snow piled where the sidewalk meets the road surface. That can stop me cold. Carrying a cell phone has reduced the danger inherent in the situation, but it's still a darned nuisance to have to call my family and tell them I'm trapped on the front sidewalk.

Weather made a huge impact on the life of my disabled friend Mary Thompson, a nationally ranked wheelchair athlete who happens to be from Grinnell. Mary found the temperature twenty below zero the day she was released from the hospital two decades ago following an automobile accident. A quick scan of the national weather report revealed that it was eighty degrees in San Diego, so she moved there.

I can't belly up to a normal sink unless there is a cutout underneath for my feet and lap. I can't reach cupboards mounted over the counter-tops. I have to be extremely careful reaching over a hot stove surface or setting a hot pan on my lap. I can't take it for granted that I'll be able to stay in a reserved hotel room, even one that advertises itself as accessible. In one expensive hotel in downtown Chicago, the manager had to show me to three different rooms, each of which he claimed was accessible, until we found one that would actually accommodate me. And in that one, we had to remove the bathroom door from its hinges to give my chair enough room to pass through. I have to dress lying down on my bed, flopping like a recently caught fish on the bottom of a boat to pull my pants up. It's impossible for me to try on clothes in a mall fitting room. Daily living, which most of us have figured out before we're ten years old, becomes an adventure in creative problem solving. The simple task of getting from here to there becomes a project of some complexity. Even crossing the street is something I can no longer take for granted.

Hockenberry makes the same observation:

> Each intersection required a strategy, a calculation of the best approach, and the potential downsides. If the able-bodied hiked casually through the world's physical terrain, I approached it as a golfer playing sudden death on the back nine at Augusta. Where the world was simply concerned with reaching a destination, I was playing each hole for keeps in front of a staring, open-mouthed audience. (1995, 105)

Ann will concur that I tended to be compulsive about things before my accident, but living with a disability has pushed me over the edge. Before I turn out the light at night, I have to go through a complicated routine of hygiene and preparation for sleep. It involves changes of urine bags, alcohol swabs, syringes, diapers, saline irrigation solution, clips, and wet wipes. I have to set out my clothes for the morning within reach, as well as tomorrow's supply of bags and swabs and diapers. If any one step is forgotten or any item that I need is not placed in reach, once I leave my chair for the day, I may have to ask for assistance. Needing help, though, is a violation of the rules of the game. Once while visiting friends, I slept with my room light on all night, rather than call out to the sleeping family to turn my light off after I had completed my bedtime routine. If I fail in my carefully planned and deliberately executed routine, I become disabled. Or at best severely inconvenienced.

It's like starting over at the age of forty-two to learn the things a child learns as part of growing up. How do you cross a street? How do you go to the bathroom? How do you snap your pants? Will I be able to function in this new situation I've never been in before, attend a church meeting, travel to a conference, visit a parishioner at home, cook a meal? You just can't take anything for granted. Activities have to be planned out to the last detail, lest something like a forgotten car key or a curb you hadn't counted on or an unexpectedly narrow doorway thwart your plans. Wheelchair users confront brick walls with regularity. Sometimes you can roll over or around or under them. But sometimes you simply have to accept them as they are and give up. You grieve that loss and then find something new to do. Several times a day people who are adjusting to new physical limitations go through this learning process. Normal activities might still be possible, but it takes a never-ending spirit of adventure. Some days I only have so much energy for this kind of adventure. Some days the game makes a recluse of me, since only at home can I be confident of how well I can function in the space and facilities.

My family had to give up our great old house with all its charm and character. It was no longer practical. I could no longer keep up with the maintenance needs of an older home, and too much of it was too inaccessible. When a 1960s ranch-style home on the edge of town—the kind of house Ann and I vowed we'd never live in—came on the market, we bought it that same day. After some remodeling, it's a dream home in terms of accessibility. But it changed how we think about ourselves and the kind of places we would call home. Sometimes Ann and I feel we've had to settle. One more loss to adjust to in a long string of losses.

Adjusting to life in a wheelchair is not just learning a new mode of transportation. It changes everything. Nancy Mairs says,

> [Disability] does not leave one precisely the same [person] one would have been without it, only (in my case) shorter. It does not merely alter a few, or even a great many, details in a life story that otherwise conforms to basic narrative conventions: the adventure, the romance, the quest. Instead, it transforms the tale utterly, though often subtly, and these shifts in narrative tone and type arouse resistance in both the "author" and the "reader" of the outlandish plot. (1996, 182)

I was a new person, but in the same old skin. It was confusing to the people around me. I felt like a character in a 1950s horror movie whose body had been taken over by aliens. I looked like the same person (aside from the wheelchair, of course, but, as I've said before, after people got used to that, they tended to overlook it), but I was living a new reality. My presence in the church was a case in point. I began attending meetings as soon as I could get to the office. But at first I could only provide presence, not leadership. This presented a problem.

Church members had been struggling valiantly in the midst of an uncertain, anxious situation to keep the church alive. After all their hard work, their extension of compassion and worry, they were understandably tired. Now that I was back there was an almost audible sigh of relief and a general sense among church members that they could finally relax. Everyone took a breather. As a consequence, things fell between the cracks. When that happens, people get frustrated and hurt.

The job of a senior pastor in a large church with many levels of programming is to provide connection and communication between the various ministries. Pastors function like the hub of a wheel, with the spokes extending outward. We help parishioners work together, and we coordinate the program and facilities. I wasn't doing a very good job of that for a while, and nobody else in the congregation recognized the subtle need for this function or knew how to pull it off. As a result, people got hurt. Important things didn't get done. People were stepping on each other's toes. Turf battles developed. Who "owned" the sanctuary during that all-important rehearsal hour before worship, the balcony choir or the children's bell group? Who was responsible for unlocking the doors in the morning and locking them up again at night? Who kept fiddling with the heating controls in the boiler room?

Normally the senior pastor coordinates or performs or delegates these tasks. But now they were beyond me. I was barely keeping up with hygiene needs and daily physical therapy. I was an imposter disguised as their senior pastor. No one would dare point the finger of blame at me, but congregational life was difficult and not much fun for a while. It showed in attendance figures and in the general mood of the church. The responsibility was clearly mine, but my leadership was absent. I couldn't come back as I was before. I have since then returned with more proactive leadership and strength, but my early appearances at church were quite jarring.

The changes are becoming apparent in other social settings as well. My friendship circles are all in flux. Many of my old friends and acquaintances are disappearing from my life. I grieve over the loss, but don't place any blame. In most cases, we just have less in common. We're not doing the same things anymore. It's harder to find things to share. But new friends are appearing to take their place. Thoughtful people are showing up to populate my life. My patterns of movement in town are different. Some of my old haunts are blocked by stairs, so I don't go there anymore. My new habits incorporate different relationships with different people. People who knew me before I was injured tend to overlook my disability more easily. People who came into my life since the injury bring their own baggage about disability.

My physical self-image was another casualty of joining the ranks of those with a disability. Your image of yourself as a physical being is formed from what you see in the mirror, the impression the people around you give back to you, and what's in your head. Some people have self-images vastly out of whack with their actual appearances, but most of us have fairly accurate impressions of ourselves. By the time you reach your forties, you've long since settled most of the "Who am I" questions that begin to surface in adolescence.

My self-image was significantly dependent on my physical attributes. I took pride in appearing athletic, even entering the second half of my expected lifetime. One outspoken lady in a former parish I served took great joy in calling me a "skinny, nervous little fellow." I may have been skinny but I was fit. At forty-two years old, I was slowing down a little and adding girth, but still in the game. I relished my sense of fitness, strength, and conditioning. I competed in triathlons, finishing well up in the pack. How many other ministers in Iowa, or in the entire United States, I wondered, competed in triathlons?

I'm still trying to figure out who I am post-injury. I can still push my body to Mount Everest endurance performances in handcycle races and marathons, but it no longer shows. I sat on the beach in Waikiki, Hawaii, while writing this book, feeling like a beached orca. Photos of me from these days fail to capture the toned and tanned physique I imagine. They show a middle-aged cripple, all lumpy and white. How does that happen? I complained to the photo development store, but they denied responsibility. I used to do one hundred sit-ups before each run. Now I can't do one. The doctors removed the abdominal muscle on my right side to transplant into a wound, and the muscle on the left side has a piece of intestine punched through it for my colostomy. In a day in which it is fashionable to wear your shorts low enough to expose your belly button and the next several inches below, I have to pull my pants way up to my chest, like a 1950s nerd, to cover up scars and stomas and other things people don't particularly want to see. My legs, which used to be like pistons I cranked to bicycle race, are battle-scarred bony sticks with flesh draped around them. I resist wearing shorts because I don't want to frighten the women and children. I have more upper-body strength than I had before, but it's hardly chiseled. I seem to droop.

Now, I realize that all this might have been in store anyway, for a man in his mid-forties, even without the injury, but all this flabbiness at once is a hard pill to swallow. It calls for a new self-definition.

Physical beauty is an emotionally charged discussion for contemporary Americans. Perhaps nowhere else in the world has a culture's image of the perfect, though perfectly unattainable, body been so narrowly defined. Because of mass media, which defines reality for millions, for the first time in history people are looking to images outside of their immediate social circles for their ideal of beauty. We're no longer just comparing ourselves with our neighbors and coworkers and classmates, who may have a crooked tooth or a mild case of acne or who are a little tubby around the midsection. In other words, our models are no longer normal human beings; they're *models!* A svelte body, blemish-free skin, perfect teeth, and styled hair are all prerequisites for living up to today's standard of beauty. There is less and less appreciation for the heterogeneity surrounding us. We're all drawn to emulate cover girls and foldouts, those impossible and often airbrushed creatures who grace movie screens and billboards.

> For decades, nondisabled viewers have been bombarded with almost unattainable media images of physical "perfection" that most of them could never possibly approximate. Magazine, billboard, and television advertisements are basically designed to trigger anxiety in the minds of viewers about their own appearance, and a multi-billion dollar industry has been created to assuage these worries by peddling an awesome range of products that promise to improve attractiveness. (Hahn 1993, 223)

Advertising is designed to make the consumer feel inadequate. How could I possibly measure up to this image of beauty and perfection I see on the screen before me? Beauty products, including exercise equipment and elective surgery, are sold to address this sense of inadequacy. It's a vicious circle. No one succeeds. Even the top models who come closest to the ideal image find that, with age, they fall farther and farther from the mark that they themselves helped set.

Now, I never considered myself a hot item with the ladies, but I once had a perception of myself as reasonably good looking. I found a lovely wife, didn't I? I wasn't entirely shut out in the mating game by the captains of the football teams and the beautifully tanned golf pros. I stole Ann from her musician boyfriend back in high school and haven't lost her yet. Ann, at least, saw me as handsome. She told me so herself. Disability changes all that. Maybe she can see beyond the physical flaws, but many others can't. I would hate to be in the dating game now. People in wheelchairs aren't seen as attractive. They tend to lose their sexual identity entirely. People who drool or stutter or twitch or are fat or bent or disfigured don't appear on magazine covers or centerfolds.

Ironically, I find that women seem much more comfortable around me now than they were before. They approach me readily; they often touch me on the shoulder while speaking to me. Often they stop just short of patting me on the head. A stranger who walked past me at the bus stop the other day touched me on the arm as she went by, commenting on the weather. Why am I getting all this attention? Is it because I'm so attractive? Hardly. I think it's because I'm no longer seen as threatening, sexually. I'm no longer a player in the game. I have become an object of pity or admiration or any of the other labels laid on people with disabilities. But sexually attractive, no.

A little piece of intestine protrudes from the left side of my abdomen, about level with my belly button. That's where solid waste is eliminated from my body. The doctors had to leave me with a colostomy because the sphincter muscles in my anus were destroyed in the accident. There's no muscle tone to enable me to remain continent; they assured me there were no alternatives. So I woke up with a colostomy. I glue a plastic bag over the stoma and try to go about my business. I sometimes get as much as a week out of each bag before I have to change it. For the most part, it's a fairly painless, trouble-free routine, living with a colostomy. But there are the occasional moments when it makes life a living hell. In my research I read of one man, recently fitted with a colostomy, who committed suicide shortly after his five-year-old son called him a "stinker." I once attended a funeral for the wife of an elderly colostomate, who had not once in fifteen years emptied his own pouch. His wife had always performed this routine function for him. Now that she was gone, he would have to check into a nursing home for no other reason than his inability to handle his own hygiene. In hard athletic events, such as marathons and triathlons, my colostomy appliance routinely comes unglued and pops open. I have to make plans to get back home or to my hotel room immediately after the event. Otherwise, people in my immediate vicinity will stand around whispering discretely among themselves, "What's that curious smell?" The chlorine in swimming pools seems to break down the odor barrier the bags come equipped with. I often have to cut my swimming workouts short in order to flee to the locker room to empty the gas that collects during physical exertion. One of my nurses warned me, "Gas has to come out somewhere." The bag fills up like a balloon and I have to discretely "burp" it. The bag comes with a seal like a Tupperware container. It's quite ingenious, really.

Emptying my bladder has become another adventure in science and technology. Most paraplegics use a simple method called "intermittent catheterization." They stick a small catheter up the urethra on a regular schedule which depends on their liquid intake. It's not a difficult procedure. The trick is keeping your equipment sterile, or at least clean. But of course, I'm not most paraplegics. My urethra is described by X-ray technicians as "tortuous." It's intact but so twisted that it's impossible to insert a catheter. For the longest time in the hospital, everyone assumed that I was urinating sufficiently in the normal way, since I was making a mess out of the bed sheets and my clothes. But when a doctor finally thought to check my bladder, it was discovered that I was retaining up to a quart of urine, which, I guess, is a bad thing. A urologist was urgently called for, and I was outfitted with a suprapubic catheter. Now I have a tube implanted in the bladder, exiting out my abdomen (on the other side from the colostomy), which continually drains the bladder. A bag is strapped to my thigh to collect urine.

My method for eliminating urine, like the colostomy, is not as bad as it seems. I wouldn't wish either on anyone, but once you're stuck with them, you find they're manageable. Again, certain situations are more difficult because of them. When I swim I wear a long-legged swimsuit that covers the bag. Fortunately, these long suits are coming into style now. Once the bag starts to fill, I have to get out of the water, heft myself into my chair, roll into the locker room, and empty it before the bulge gets too noticeable. Long distance endurance events take some preplanning. You have to really hydrate, for example, before and during a rolling marathon. I start drinking fluid the night before, and don't stop until I roll up to the starting line. You know what that means. I have a full bladder and a full leg bag long before I'm ready to stop and find an accessible bathroom. Actually, there are no accessible bathrooms for an athlete in a racing wheelchair. So I'm stuck, right? Wrong. My leg bag empties with a little clip. Before I slip my racing gloves on and tighten them up for the last time, I simply flick the clip open. By the end of the race my shoe is full of pee and there's a trail of wet spots behind me for twenty-six miles, but I've solved my immediate problem.

I've undergone four surgeries and several lesser procedures to try to reverse my suprapubic catheter. Dr. Douglas Hussman, a specialist in the neurogenic bladder at Mayo Clinic in Rochester, Minnesota, is trying to build me a new system. He has enlarged my bladder, using a section of my lower intestine as a sort of room addition on my shrunken bladder, then attached another section of intestine from this new bladder to the surface, where it opens into yet another stoma. This one is the size of a button and is located near my navel. If you're keeping count, this makes three new orifices in my gut. If all goes well, I should be able to catheterize myself through this new stoma. The only problem has been that my original bladder keeps springing leaks. I have to keep using the implanted catheter as a backup. The plan is to remove my bladder entirely and use only my intestine as a pouch. We hope to try that next January.

Bladder maintenance has gotten to be something of a hobby with me. In my first months out of the hospital I was incurring urinary tract infections at the rate of about one per month. This was the condition that proved fatal to most paraplegics before the end of the World War II and the advent of antibiotics. For me, a quick fix of Bactrim always straightened things out right away, but the doctors were concerned that I was breeding a super bug that might not be so responsive to the drugs. I started drinking prodigious amounts of water and taking massive doses of vitamin C and cranberry concentrate capsules to acidify my bladder and make the environment down there less hospitable for bacteria. Now I rarely suffer infections. But I have to be vigilant.

I don't particularly enjoy living with a colostomy and having to care for it, or dealing with plastic tubing and bags to keep my bladder drained. You may wonder why I'm dwelling on such an earthy topic. Maybe it's for pity value, you might be thinking. He wants us to know how disgusting his life is. Or maybe he's just trying to shock us with graphic descriptions of a totally inappropriate subject matter for family reading.

No, it's not that. It's just to show how life is reinvented with disability. Living with a disability is like adjusting to a different culture. The habits of the natives of that new culture may seem disgusting to an outsider, but given enough time among them, their habits may begin to make sense. I thought I had potty training down pat by the time I was two. Now I have to learn it all over again. I handle poop and pee all the time; I see it and monitor it. I deal with incontinence and leaks and odor, and I face the uncertainty of accidents. I wear diapers, though I sometimes make Ann run into the store to pick them up for me. Waste management and the resulting self-esteem problem is a common issue for persons with disabilities. Dr. Mark Nagler writes,

> One of the human organism's earliest accomplishments is the control of waste elimination, a function which is surrounded by strong emotional components as a result of North American cultural values and body perceptions. An individual relinquishes these controls with varying degrees of anxiety. . . . Incontinence, through loss of this control, implies a return to infancy. (1990, 171)

This is a serious piece of adjustment work to a man used to feeling physically competent and in control. Not to mention clean and dry.

We all operate out of stories that play in our minds. Who we are depends on the narratives we rehearse. Women operating out of the *Cinderella* or *Sleeping Beauty* or *Pretty Woman* scenario, for example, wait for a knight in shining armor to fulfill their lives. Men who play tapes of

Bruce Willis or Clint Eastwood tend to be the strong, silent types, vanquishing their foes, but leaving battered relationships in their wake.

I grew up with my own peculiar story playing in my mind. I was the reckless adventurer. I would launch myself off any precipice, climb any mountain, ford any stream. A family friend still shows his home movies of a whole tribe of little kids, smeared in mud, flinging themselves off a ten-foot mud bank into a brown river somewhere. That was me. We went camping with three families that, together, accounted for nine little boys. On one trip to a state park on the bluffs overlooking the Mississippi River in Wisconsin, we found a Tarzan vine hanging high over the edge. It was so inviting, I grabbed hold and took a mighty swing. The vine let go and I went flying. I landed in the tops of some small trees that broke my fall. The other kids, including my two brothers, peered over the edge for a second or two, and then burst out laughing and ran away. My dad, wondering what had become of me, later found and rescued me. I climbed two volcanoes in Central America. At the top of the first one, which my friend and I had spent about eight hours scaling, the wind was howling and lightning was playing. We scurried back down. The second one, located on an island in the middle of Lake Nicaragua, was so high and the day so hot, that I had consumed all my water before I reached the summit. Acknowledging that discretion was the better part of valor, I turned around and managed, with the help of some cultivated banana trees that I ravished, to make it to a local *tienda* at the base of the volcano, where I downed a two-liter bottle of coke. If something looked difficult or was reputed to be impossible, I'd try it.

This narrative is no longer true for me. It doesn't work anymore. I can't do those things. I look longingly at distant waterfalls begging to be climbed or ocean waves calling me to play or long roads disappearing into wooded hills luring me to ride or run them. But I can't do that anymore. The adventures I can still manage take such logistical preparation that it's like mounting an assault on Mount Everest just to take a swim. I face life now with a great deal more hesitancy. I have to be very circumspect about what I decide to do, knowing that it will take careful planning and may take more of a toll on my body than I had anticipated. I find myself reluctant to jump spontaneously into things I wouldn't have thought twice about before my accident. I've been burned too many times. I'm getting careful now.

That word, careful, was taboo in my former narrative.

We did take on a great adventure this summer, my family and I. I received a Lilly Endowment grant to cover the cost of a sabbatical from my pastoral duties in order to write this book. Of all the places in the world we might have gone to spend our summer and get on with the writing, on a whim I accepted an invitation from a follow pastor in Honolulu. I got my writing done, but we also explored everything the Hawaiian Islands had to offer in terms of culture and recreation.

I loved the ocean. Ann has a series of photos of me that she took while I was dragging myself across the beach toward the surf. I lowered myself from my chair to the sand, turned around with my back to the ocean, and then pushed myself backwards, inch by inch, dragging my feet and legs behind me. These legs, which used to be my means of locomotion, were now just dead weight along for the ride. The photos made me look like a sea turtle making its way back to the water after laying its eggs. Even the track I left, from my chair to the water's edge, looks vaguely reptilian.

But I love the water. I love the feeling of floating and moving freely. Water equalizes the playing field. No one can tell, when I'm in the ocean or a pool, that I have a disability. For now, at least, I swallow my pride and put up with the inconvenience of getting to the water.

I took surfing lessons with Ames and Kate on Waikiki beach, in a little class with a handful of other students on vacation. I worried the dark-skinned, longhaired instructor to no end. "You okay, Bob?" he kept calling to me over the waves. "Doin' good, Bob? Hangin' in dere, Bob?" But I learned to ride the waves, kneeling on the board like a trained dog. At least I was still in the game.

But the next day I could hardly move. I was physically ill from the exertion, the bruises, and the sore muscles. Whether it's disability or just age, I don't know. But the obvious conclusion one might draw from this little lesson would be the same in either case. I've slowed down. I told my kids in no uncertain terms, next time I latch onto a crazy idea like taking surfing lessons, talk me out of it. I'm not a surfer anymore. What would have possessed a forty-seven-year-old man in a wheelchair to try surfing? Unless it were a need to prove to himself, his kids, and the world, that there's really nothing wrong, that life is just as it was before the accident and before the effect of too many decades of gravity on his body. Why do I need to keep banging my head against that wall?

A more realistic way to enjoy Hawaii at my age and in my condition might involve a nice comfortable beach chair, a cooler of cold beverages, and a comfortable spot in the shade of a swaying palm tree from which to watch my children launch themselves out into the surf to learn new skills and burn calories. Clearly. But after a lifetime of being the one to lead the charge into the waves, of taking the dare and being the first to try any adventure, how do I learn to be this wiser, more sedentary person? What stigmas will I have to overcome in my own mind to become him? Will I like living in his skin?

I did go back to the beach a couple of weeks later. My kids took the boogie board and the snorkel set. I didn't even take my suit. I sat on a park bench in the shade, watching the kids at play and the sailboats drifting by. It was the first time I can remember ever going to an ocean and not getting in. This observation left me with a strangely profound sense of sadness.

Christopher Reeve, the actor best known for his role in the *Superman* movies, is having a hard time adjusting to life as a quadriplegic after an equestrian accident broke his neck in 1995:

> People often ask me what it's like to have sustained a spinal cord injury and be confined to a wheelchair. Apart from all the medical complications, I would say the worst part of it is leaving the physical world—having had to make the transition from participant to observer long before I would have expected. I think most of us are prepared to give up cherished physical activities gradually as we age. . . . The difference is that I would have had time to prepare for other ways of enjoying the things I love to do most. But to have it all change and have most of it taken away at age forty-two is devastating. As much as I remind myself that being is more important than doing, that the quality of relationships is the key to happiness, I'm actually putting on a brave face. I do believe those things are true, but I miss freedom, spontaneity, action, and adventure more than I can say. (Reeve 1998, 271-272)

This is still a touchy issue for me, too. I'm not yet ready to become an observer of the adventures of life that I used to participate in.

Not only are my self-perception and my activity level changing, my future has been altered. Ann and I had shared a secret plan to some day hike the Appalachian Trail. Now, unless they bring the Trail under ADA compliance, that will probably never happen. Possibilities we had talked about for retirement, such as volunteering for another term with the Mennonite Central Committee, returning to Central America, or studying in the Holy Land, will never materialize. One of my biking buddies had talked of riding his bicycle across the United States before he turned fifty. He hit that milestone a year ago, but, since I was in no shape to attempt the ride with him, it didn't happen. I was incredibly fortunate to find myself in a career in which I could continue to function productively. Another patient in the hospital with me had been in highway construction. He is still searching for a new career. But my long-term future in parish ministry is less certain. In fact, my future anywhere is less certain. My life expectancy is almost certainly diminished. Ann has to face the likelihood that she will outlive me by a considerable number of years. This has implications for her retirement and pension, beyond the prospect of spending a large chunk of her life without her life partner. I'm suddenly counting the years, months, weeks, days, and sometimes the hours and minutes until I can comfortably retire. I only hope I can make it to that day and spend some quality time with her in whatever adventures may still be accessible to us at that age.

Vacations have gotten more expensive. We used to be able to load up our tent and camping supplies and spend a week in an exotic location for little more than the price of groceries. Now I need a luxury resort. Not that I'm complaining about having to stay in luxury resorts. It's just that we can rarely afford them. Often our vacations have become staying with family members (in inaccessible, pet-overrun homes). Ann's parents have a small house across the Iowa River from City Park in Iowa City. During the summers they keep the house empty for family picnics and holiday gatherings. We're allowed to use it from time to time, and it does offer the prospect of lazy days on the riverbank, but even that comes at a steep price—no pun intended—for access to the house is up a flight of stairs. The family recently raised the foundation to keep the house above flood level. We lay down a ramp of plywood on the stairs at a 45-degree angle, and I haul myself up using a thick rope. I find I'm good for just two or three outings a day. Then I'm too exhausted to get back up.

Vacations aren't the only things in my life that have gotten more expensive. My whole lifestyle has necessarily ratcheted up a notch. We're not yet sharing the lifestyle of the rich and famous, but the little things all add up to a new level of spending, for which our salaries have not quite kept up. I've mentioned the addition of a cell phone for safety. A reliable car has become almost a prosthetic device as I run errands around town. My condition necessitated a move to a new house and extensive remodeling. I'm spending several thousand dollars a year on medical accessories not covered under insurance, such as Depends, alcohol swabs, hygiene and sanitary supplies, even Band-Aids. Trips to Rochester, Minnesota, to Mayo Medical Clinics leave us with at least a hundred-dollar-a-day out of pocket expense for meals, lodging, and transportation. It's not cheap being disabled.

I think the biggest change I've had to face in all this is becoming intimately acquainted with contingency. I just miss the confidence I used to have. Life used to be predictable, and it isn't anymore. I can't be sure that any proposed activity will work. I can't be sure, leaving the house for business or recreation or any other pursuit, that my body won't betray me in some embarrassing fashion that may require medical treatment or at least a change of clothing.

I'm not only worried for myself. I'm more anxious now about the people I love. When my daughter is late returning home from a date, I imagine the worst. The police in Grinnell recognize my voice on the phone from the late night phone calls. "That's right, Rev. Molsberry. We don't have any record of car wrecks, homicides, kidnappings, or acts of terrorism tonight. Why don't you go back to bed? I'm sure she's okay." When Ann is delayed in returning home from some meeting, I visualize ever more horrifying scenarios. It is hard to be the fun-loving person I used to be. I have to work a little harder at living, loving, and celebrating life. Working hard at living seems to be one of the identifying features of my new life with a disability. Very little comes easily, without a struggle at some level or another. It's a whole new world to explore and conquer.

While the overwhelming sense is one of loss, there are some interesting insights that appear along the way. I am a new person now. The skills I'm learning, in compensating for losses and adapting to a disability, are opening new horizons in my perception of myself and the world. I'm creating a new person! The pride that God must have felt on that seventh day of creation must have been akin to what I feel now, as I reinvent myself every day out of what has been left me after my injury. Like an architect watching a structure he designed take shape, like a writer pecking out the chapters of a book, I'm creating something new. What it will look like when I'm done is anybody's guess. There's certainly no blueprint or recipe book to follow.

Hockenberry writes:

> From the beginning, disability taught that life could be reinvented. In fact, such an outlook was required. The physical dimensions of life could be created, like poetry; they were not imposed by some celestial landlord. Life was more than renting some protoplasm to walk around in. It was more than being a winner or loser. To have invented a way to move about without legs was to invent walking. This was a task reserved for gods, and to perform it was deeply satisfying. (1995, 79)

This daily self-re-creation leads to some powerful insights. The experience that people with disabilities have of living with bodies that are less than perfect may be of worth to society at large. Persons with disabilities may have something of value to offer a culture obsessed with the perfect image. We have a different take on beauty than you do. Perhaps, if you let us, we can remind you of the amazing diversity of human presentation. In the process of reinventing myself—in terms of self-perception, mobility, hygiene, relationships, and perception of beauty—I have inadvertently stumbled upon an important truth. It's a truth hidden from the general population caught up in the illusion of perfection. We're so oppressed by media images of the ideal human type that we are driven to buy crash diets and expensive beauty products, to work out compulsively, and to pay surgeons to suck hunks of fat from our bodies. It's all a vain pursuit of an unattainable and fleeting image. I'm no longer on that treadmill. Because I can't have it anymore, I can see how hollow it is. You can't deny age, decline, imperfection, and mortality. It's who we are. And it's what each one of us has to look forward to.

People with disabilities can play an important role in reminding society at large of the diversity of human form and presentation. Mairs talks about the value of expanding our perspectives when it comes to trying to understand the human condition. Persons with disabilities may have something to offer in the ongoing discussion of beauty, image, and diversity.

> There are rewards for making the world physically and emotionally accessible to all people, including benefits that accrue to society as a whole. The more perspectives that can be brought to bear on human experience, even from the slant of a wheelchair or a hospital bed, or through the ears of a blind person or the fingers of someone who is deaf, the richer that experience becomes. If it is both possible and pleasant for me and my kind to enter, the world will become a livelier place. You'll see. (1996, 106)

Beauty, Mairs implies, may be as much in appreciation of the full range of human diversity as it is in adherence to the narrowest of definitions. It may take a disability perspective to recognize that.

You can't go home again from a disabling injury. You can, and maybe should, try. You might be able to come partially back and fill some of the same roles you once had. Depending on the severity and kind of disability, you may be able to approximate the look and the function of the person you were before. But in the end it's an impossible task. Disability changes everything, from bathroom behavior to dreams, from your identifying narrative to your appreciation of a gentle snowfall. It changes everything because it changes your perception of the world in which you move (or, in the case of the most severely disabled, the world you observe).

But let me share a final thought, which may be the most important observation of all. I've made the case here that, following my disabling accident, I've had to re-create myself as a person. But this is nothing new. The project I am engaged in now, this re-creating of myself with both diminished and newly discovered abilities, is the same project in which each one of us is continually engaged, all the time. It's not unique to people with disabilities. I'm writing about it as a newly disabled person, but the disability hasn't changed my involvement with this universal human project; it has only accelerated it. Having to solve these problems all at once has given me a unique perspective. But the problems are not unique to me. People are always solving the problems that confront them with the resources life has given them. That's the name of the game, the only one we ever get to play. That, in the words of the "Hokey Pokey," is "what it's all about." That's what it means to be alive! People tend to look at those of us with disabilities as heroic or tragic or pitiful, because we face such daunting circumstances. But really, although we've had to learn new ways of doing it, we're just going about the same tasks that everyone else takes for granted. It's called daily living. It's never solved or finished.

As a person with a disability, I have the advantage in this game. And I use the word "advantage" deliberately. My advantage over the nondisabled is that I was forced into a situation that made it imperative for me to reflect on the contingency and variety of life. We're not all the same. We don't all function at the same level of ability. It's a mistake to think that's even possible. I can't go back to being the person I was before this injury took place, but I have a new perspective on life because of it. This new perspective is a tremendous gift. It's a gift that is worth sharing. That's why I'm writing this book.

Maybe your need to receive this gift is why you're reading it.

Chapter 4

More Than an Inspiration

I was sitting in my everyday wheelchair, one hundred yards beyond the finish line of the San Diego Marathon, rehydrated and well fed and bundled up against the chilly drizzle, swapping stories with friends. A presence hovered over my shoulder. I looked up and was engulfed in a sweaty bear hug by a woman runner I'd never seen before.

"You people are such an inspiration to me!" she gushed. Tears were in her eyes.

I was short in my reply to her, less than gracious, I'm afraid, in accepting her admiration. The marathon was clearly easier for me than it was for her. I had long since given up any hope of running 26.2 miles on my forty-four-year-old legs. Twenty years ago I might have, but these days the pounding would have been too hard on my body. Now that I roll in a racing chair, I've got the mechanical advantage of the wheel, and I roll along in a no-impact athletic event. Sure, I was tired and sore, but the woman inspired by my performance was clearly in far worse shape than I. She stumbled back to her support group.

This wasn't the first time, nor would it be the last, that well-intentioned but misguided people would find me a source of inspiration. A year later it happened again at the finish line of a triathlon, at which I beat half the able-bodied participants. A well-conditioned jock came up to me after the race, "Man, if it weren't for you I would have given up. But I saw you out there cranking away, and I said to myself, if he can do it, then I can, too. You people are an inspiration!"

But surely "inspiration" is too facile a label to slap on people with disabilities who may have varieties of abilities, goals, limitations, and gifts. "Persistent" might be more applicable. Or, in my case, stubborn. And that "you people" should raise red flags every time it's heard. What did those two athletes mean? Balding pastors? Fathers of teenagers? People from Iowa?

As my recovery in rehab progressed, I felt the need to get back into athletics. I longed to run again with the college cross-country team, graceful gazelles in their prime. I wanted to stand up to blizzard conditions in my running shoes and nylon suit, to get back to the swimming pool at 6:00 AM on summer mornings, listening to the rooster crowing in the yard next door and counting the laps and the miles as the sun came up.

One way or another, those things were going to be an important piece of my recovery.

At one point in the early days of my hospitalization, a raging infection set in on my left calf muscle. Because of the infection, surgeons had to remove the hardware that set my pelvic bone structure in correct alignment. But the infection persisted. A surgeon called Ann late one night to say he was sorry, there was nothing they could do to halt the spread of the infection. They would have to amputate the leg. He reassured her by saying, "It's okay. He's just a minister. He won't miss it." Ann, bless her heart, screamed at him, "He's not just a minister. He's a triathlete!" And she made them try another procedure and thus saved my leg.

Newly crippled, it was crucial for me to test out my new body and get reacquainted with sports to see what I might be able to do. I tried basketball, just me and the church youth group on the gym floor. But I wasn't any better at basketball after the accident than I had been before. So I gave that up.

The rehab department at the hospital had an old upright handcycle, a three-wheeled machine propelled by arm cranks rather than pedals. The staff hoisted me on the seat and I rolled out of the therapy room and into the hall. The staff ran along beside, imploring caution. I skidded around the first corner on two wheels and accelerated down the straight stretch toward the elevators. The staff was left behind, shouting warnings. I felt the wind on my face.

I had to get me one of these!

I ordered a racing model, paying for it with money raised by a swimathon sponsored by my daughter's swim team. On my first ride I covered just short of one mile, coming home exhausted and concerned that maybe four thousand dollars was way too much to have spent on this impractical toy. But I kept at it, managing to put in five hundred miles of training for *The Des Moines Register*'s Annual Great Bicycle Ride Across Iowa (RAGBRAI) that second summer after my injury.

RAGBRAI is a rolling party of ten thousand bicyclists who ride from Iowa's western border to the Mississippi River on the eastern side of the state each summer. It descends like a flock of locusts upon tiny host communities trying gamely to feed and entertain it. RAGBRAI had been part of my vacation plans every summer for almost fifteen years. I had always ridden it fast and hard, way off the front of the pack. I could crank out an eighty-mile day by 10:00 AM and had prided myself on getting passed by no one during an entire day of riding. Now it was time to see if I could do it by hand.

My kids rode with me that first year, with Ann driving the family minivan to meet us at motels each night. We rode about half of each day, forty or fifty miles a day. It was a certified Great Achievement, duly commemorated in local nightly news features, *The Des Moines Register,* an article I wrote for *Sports 'N Spokes* magazine, and my own annual RAGBRAI sermon. I was, after all, an inspiration. Inspirational stories sell.

I rode it again the following summer, this time in much better shape. A week before this year's ride, a television reporter doing yet another feature about me asked innocently, "So you're planning to do the whole ride this year?" Actually, I hadn't been. But she had lowered the gauntlet and now, come hell or high water, I knew I had to cover every mile.

The 1999 ride will go down in history as one of the most grueling ever. The mileage was long, the route meandered through the "Iowa Alps" in the northeast quadrant of the state, and the heat index hit the 120s. Nearly half the riders at one point or another during the week threw in the towel and hitched rides. But I was determined. Stubborn. Even inspirational. On the longest day, cranking painfully up mile-long grades at less than 2 miles per hour (below 2 mph my bike computer reads zero, which is a very frustrating state of affairs), I was on the road for thirteen hours. It wasn't pretty, it wasn't much fun, but I did it.

There's a great deal one can learn from a week cranking across Iowa. One of the timeless truths that became clear to me is that the snacks are always at the top of the hill. This is a normative as well as a descriptive statement. Food is one of the great rewards of RAGBRAI. With the calories you burn riding all day you can eat six full meals a day and not gain any weight. The towns and farmhouses along the way provide an endless supply of corn on the cob, spaghetti, watermelon, pie, cinnamon rolls, pizza, homemade ice cream, beer, sports drinks, and pork burgers. But don't stop at the bottom of the hill to eat. Do your work first, get to the top, and then enjoy your reward. It tastes lots better on the top of the hill, too, anticipating the next downhill. That's how I've faced all these years of therapy and recovery.

I was also reminded again that I'm not the in-control kind of guy I used to think I was. I used to ride all day without needing to stop, now I needed the help of a whole support crew to get across the state. This year Ames drove the family van and checked in by cell phone periodically during the day. Kate rode at my side and ran for food when we hit the towns. One day I had a flat tire and went through my entire supply of patches with no success. There I sat, in the gravel on the shoulder of the highway, with no means of extricating myself from the situation.

Soon a crowd gathered around me. One cyclist offered to ride back to find a support vehicle. Another rode forward. One tried some of his patches. One guy, a rather portly man as I remember, simply hovered over me and shaded me from the sun. I appreciated his contribution. Finally a sheriff's deputy pulled up in a Chevrolet Blazer. He threw my bike in the back, picked me up and dumped me in the back seat, and drove me to the next town on the route, Roland, Iowa.

Once in town, he parked at a corner, took my bike to a repair stand and carried me into a front yard, setting me in a lawn chair next to an elderly man in overalls.

"This is our mayor," he said. "He'll get you anything you need."

"Really?" I asked the overalled man.

"Sure."

"Well, then. Could you get me a cold beer?"

And darned if the mayor of Roland, Iowa, population 1,002, didn't get up out of his lawn chair, disappear through his screen door, and return with a can of Budweiser for the crippled cyclist dumped on his lawn!

Vulnerability brings out the best in people, both the needy and the Samaritan, and reminds us that we are all interdependent.

A final lesson from that year's RAGBRAI concerns the wisdom of attempting the ride in the first place. Pick your challenges well, I advise. Some are worth conquering; some may not be.

In the early days of automobile travel, all the roads connecting little towns in Iowa were just dirt paths. When it rained, of course, these roads became deeply rutted and all but impassable. Sometimes a sign would appear by the side of the road, "Pick your rut carefully. You will be in it for the next ten miles."

Readjusting to life after disability has been a learning experience of immense proportions. Like an amoeba exploring its environment by pushing out the cell wall in one direction after another, I have tried to return to many different activities. Some things work, some things don't. Some things I do accomplish are too blasted difficult to ever want to repeat again. Just because I can do them, doesn't mean they will ever become part of my life again. Some things just aren't worth it.

During the second RAGBRAI, Ann spent the week visiting her sister near Boston. She spent her days dining on lobster and crab, walking in the woods, listening to the Boston Symphony, and staying in quaint bed and breakfast lodgings. She asks me who had the better vacation. I'm hard pressed to answer.

Competing in the San Diego Marathon was an accident, really. It came along just a couple of months after I had finally secured a used racing wheelchair. My only previous experience in the chair was a five-mile trot in which I won a pumpkin pie for having finished first in my division (there were no other wheelchairs in the race, of course). I had been planning to train for a year or two before entering my first marathon. But we had a vacation scheduled in southern California, and Mary Thompson, my friend from Grinnell who had been injured in a car accident, had moved to San Diego and become a famous wheelchair athlete. She invited me to give it a try, so I signed up.

Training for a marathon in a wheelchair during the winter in Iowa is no easy task. It was difficult for a parish pastor to squeeze in training time around Christmas, for one thing. Church members seem to have other expectations on my time during this season. For another thing, the weather isn't cooperative. I put in most of my training hours on an indoor track at Grinnell College, eleven laps to the mile. Those mind-numbing workouts of two hours or more sometimes added up to over two hundred laps each.

And rolling around in flat circles indoors hadn't exactly prepared me for conditions in San Diego. The first hill, barely a mile into the race, reduced me to a crawl. Bugs on the pavement below me were passing me as they scurried up the hill. The downhills were positively dizzying at 35 miles per hour. And when people tell you that it never rains in southern California, don't listen to them. It makes a catchy song lyric, but it is meteorologically incorrect. The drops began to fall as we lined up our wheels for the start. They didn't stop until about the time that the tired and sweaty woman marathoner embraced me at the finish. I skidded off the slick pavement three times, once careening into a crowd of wet bystanders.

The course and the race were beautiful. After that first awful hill, it wound through the town of Carlsbad, where the Sunday morning crowd was sipping cappuccino at street side tables and a clown dressed in a funny costume was high-fiving the runners. Hugging the Pacific coast most of the way, the course took two detours inland and uphill before a finishing home stretch of five or six miles, flat, fast, and scenic. For two-and-a-half hours I was back in the hard-driving racing mode I remembered from the days before the injury. It was heaven.

But a two-and-a-half-hour excursion in heaven probably wouldn't leave you sore for the next week, which this experience certainly did.

Everything I have accomplished since my injury has been a challenge. From sitting up in bed to finishing a marathon, I've had to get fairly pushy. To get through these challenges I put my head down and charge ahead, doing what I have to do to realize my goals. Outsiders may see this as inspiring. I guess I can't change how other people see me. But that's an overly simplistic reaction to my efforts. They miss what's going on inside. I'm simply doing what I have to do to survive a difficult situation. It's a training ethic. I compensate for impairments in one area by building up in others. My legs don't work, but, by God, my arms sure do. I can't run in races anymore, but I can roll. Isn't that the way everybody deals with limitations and differences in ability? You pick up the pieces of your tragedies, minimize your losses, maximize your assets, and just go on.

I suspect pity lies behind the tendency of nondisabled people to label people with disabilities as inspirational. What a tragic life we must live. People are surprised when they see those of us with disabilities actually accomplishing something. "These people should be in hospitals or institutions or in a sheltered workshop somewhere," they may be thinking. "I'm sure, if it happened to me, that I'd never have the courage to go on like you do. I'm not sure how I could handle it. Boy, do I admire you." Hockenberry recounts how, once, on a commercial airline, a stewardess drew near to him and asked if he had ever considered suicide. What sort of question is that, he wondered, coming from a stranger? What was she thinking, unless it was that people with severe disabilities couldn't possibly be content with their lives, that the only viable alternative—that she can imagine, at least—must be suicide. Mairs writes, "To the nondisabled, despondency and desperation may seem the natural, indeed the necessary, response to pain, fatigue, and debility: it seems so unquestionably awful being who we are that we must naturally seek to cease being who we are at any price." (1996, 167)

Some nondisabled people don't seem to understand that living with a disability is not primarily a tragedy, it's not heroic, it's not even that abnormal. They don't see that, like Itzhak Perlman on stage and the *Junkyard Wars* competitors on television, I'm building a life out of the only pieces I have available. And they fail to discern the even more subtle point that this project—building a life out of the resources at hand—is exactly the same project they themselves are engaged in at the moment.

Many people with disabilities are sought out as motivational speakers. I once competed in a handcycle race in which several of the other competitors earned money to cover race expenses by speaking at schools and conventions. At the time, I remember thinking it sounded like quite a racket, especially in light of the fact that I beat many of them in the race. I've been invited to give talks along the same lines. "Talk to my football players about overcoming impossible odds." "Talk to my Fellowship of Christian Athletes group about how God has helped you accomplish great things in spite of your tragic circumstances." Such invitations make me uncomfortable. I resist being seen as inspirational. There's more to living with a disability than that. My spin to the football team must have disappointed the boys. Instead of firing them up with step-by-step instructions on how to win against an overwhelming adversary, I put it to them that football is *not* life. Life is what happens when you're through playing the game. The kids didn't lose another game that year through the entire regular season, but the coach hasn't invited me back.

Christopher Reeve is something of an enigma for the disability community. He is probably the most well-known and visible example of a person with a disability in the world. He's a celebrity and a quadriplegic. Like E. F. Hutton, when he speaks, people listen. The disability community has been looking for a powerful spokesperson who might make an impact on how society regards people with disabilities. Unfortunately, many people with disabilities believe Reeve is using his influence in ways that perpetuate stereotypical perceptions. Here, in his book *Still Me*, he takes the simple, everyday challenge of living with a disability and casts it as a heroic undertaking:

> When the first Superman movie came out, I gave dozens of interviews to promote it. The most frequently asked question was: "What is a hero?" I remember how easily I'd talk about it, the glib response I repeated so many times. My answer was that a hero is someone who commits a courageous action without considering the consequences. A soldier who crawls out of a foxhole to drag an injured buddy back to safety, the prisoners of war who never stop trying to escape even though they know they may be executed if they're caught. . . .
>
> Now my definition is completely different. I think a hero is an ordinary individual who finds the strength to persevere and endure in spite of overwhelming obstacles. The fifteen-year-old boy down the hall at Kessler who had landed on his head while wrestling with his brother, leaving him paralyzed and barely able to swallow or speak. Travis Roy, paralyzed in the first eleven seconds of a hockey game in his freshman year at college. Henry Steifel, paralyzed from the chest down in a car

accident at seventeen, completing his education and working on Wall Street at age thirty-two, but having missed so much of what life has to offer. These are real heroes, and so are the families and friends who have stood by them. (273)

Pardon me for raining on the parade of the media lovefest that has surrounded Reeve since his accident, but I disagree. People who face difficult circumstances in everyday life, I maintain, are not heroes at all. They are simply ordinary individuals doing what they have to do in order to survive. Besides not being an accurate description of how most people with disabilities feel about their experiences, Reeve's interpretation both diminishes the word *hero* and also diminishes the person who is struggling simply to live out her or his life with the hand dealt. Don't narrow our experience—even if in the process you place it on a pedestal. It may be flattering, but it's wrong. Some people with disabilities may be heroic. But some aren't. Some people with disabilities would crawl (or roll or stumble or shuffle) out of their foxhole, if they could, to rescue an injured buddy. Some wouldn't. So don't be too quick to pass judgment on an experience that looks challenging to you. Do your homework first. Get involved in that life before you make a judgment about it.

That's what is wrong with the major telethons. Have you ever watched one of those things with a critical eye toward the experience of disability that they portray? They never examine the preconceived notion that people with disabilities are universally suffering as a result of their ailments, that their condition is a tragedy to be pitied, that those with disabling conditions who manage to live useful lives are heroic figures for overcoming a terrible situation, and finally, that your tax-deductible dollars can prevent this from happening. Telethons open the purse strings by tugging on the heartstrings. They're good at what they do, and, to their credit, they have raised astonishing amounts of money for their causes. The "Jerry Lewis Muscular Dystrophy Association Telethon," for example, has raised over 1 billion dollars for the Muscular Dystrophy Association. But at what cost? Is there ever the slightest effort made to get behind the stereotype to try to understand the experience of a person with a disability, in all its complexity and ambiguity? The fundraising formula doesn't come close to describing my experience of disability, for example. Is it possible that "Jerry's Kids" might be more than objects of pity or admiration? Jerry's not going to let on, if that's the case, because that knowledge would cut into his fundraising margin. Who wants to give money to a person with a disability who seems to have accepted her or his condition, who's managing quite well with a disability, thank you very much? Many people with disabilities would much rather have the public *understand* their condition than to contribute money to *reverse* it.

We're going to spend more time with telethons in a later chapter. Their impact on common perceptions of persons with disabilities is as damaging as it is pervasive. Let the reader beware, we're also going to narrow our sites on Christopher Reeve again, too. The model of disability through which he understands his life is fertile ground for critique.

Inspiration is an easy, knee-jerk reaction to people with disabilities. Hide behind that perception and you don't have to get your hands dirty trying to discover the rich and intricate complexity hidden there. I have been the subject of no fewer than six local television news features. I was featured prominently in an hour-long program covering the 2000 San Diego Marathon, which played all over the country on the Outdoor Life cable channel. Articles about me have appeared in a half-dozen papers. Each feature had the same exact spin. Each reporter presented my story as an inspiration. Why? Is it a conspiracy? Do they get together and compare notes? Or is it sloppy journalism, slapping an easy interpretation—one that will sell newspapers and television features—of a complex reality? "Disabled Pastor Overcomes Obstacles: He's such an inspiration!" "It's the amazing story of one man's faith getting him through a devastating accident." "This man of the cloth is now a man of the roads." "Riding in RAGBRAI is nothing short of a miracle for this true road warrior." Who do they think I am, Mel Gibson? They never wrote about me when I was nondisabled, even when I did things that I thought were much more heroic. Why not? I worked just as hard then. And I'm sure there are people who, in their daily living, face a more daunting task more doggedly than I tackle marathons. Why aren't they featured?

One woman with a disability, June Price, editor of *Living Smart* magazine, wrote an account of how the media attention on "inspirational" achievements of more active people with disabilities affects her.

> Part of me is in awe of these athletes as they pour forth their last ounce of energy in quest of gold. But another part of me resents that these brawny specimens waste their precious resources on "games" when I need every scrap of my strength just to survive another day! . . . I kept thinking of my many friends for whom reaching to scratch their nose is a monumental task. They don't get high fives or their photos on a bulletin board. . . . What really makes a winner, after all, is not what we can achieve compared to others, but what we can achieve given what we have to work with. (2000, 10)

Price recalls seeing a program about a mountain climber scaling some craggy summit in the dead of winter. It demanded all his effort. His fingers were frozen, arms exhausted as he struggle upward. She writes,

"So? I thought. What's the big deal? Isn't this exactly what I go through every winter when I'm outside in the numbing cold trying to push my joystick?" (10)

I have to admit I'm shamefully flattered by media attention of my postdisability achievements. I don't apologize for it. I think most people would be proud. I'm just surprised by it, and, deep down, more than a little embarrassed. At my first marathon I was invited for television interviews in the motel suite reserved for elite athletes. They even had a sign at the door announcing it. "Elite Athletes." I had known that such watering holes for the privileged gazelles existed, but I had never seen one. And I had surely never been invited to one. There was free food and drink laid out on long tables. International athletes sat around talking and watching television. I had Ann take my picture in front of the sign. I've had that photo enlarged and it serves as an ego boost. But, however much I enjoy impressing people, I realize at a deeper level that this is a narrow definition of who I am. It's not very accurate, either, if you come right down to it. I'm still no better than a middle-of-the-pack weekend athlete. I'm just more competitive now because the field is so limited. There is only one other wheelchair racer I'm aware of in Iowa, and only one handcyclist who can challenge me on the roads. There's no one I'm aware of closer than either coast who does triathlons from a wheelchair. Permit me a little gloating, at least.

It seems as though some people judge my efforts on the basis of degree of difficulty, like figure skating or competitive diving. In these events, the competitors get points for how difficult their attempts are. Two divers are competing. One does a simple dive well. The second diver doesn't perform as well, but he does a more difficult dive. The second diver might just win the competition because of the greater degree of difficulty. At the Salt Lake City Olympic Games, Russian officials lodged a complaint over the scoring in figure skating. It was clear to all who watched that the young U.S. skater, Sara Hughes, skated better than the Russian, but there was some legitimacy to their claim because the Russian skater performed a more difficult program.

What if life were judged that way? It seems like that is how the media and others choose to look at my adjustment to disability. A lackluster sermon last Sunday? That's okay, because you were dealing with a bladder infection at the time and your degree of difficulty was way up there. Your minister never visits you? He's still a great minister, because it's so difficult for him to get around now. Sometimes, I confess, I wish that's how life were judged. Sometimes, in fact, that is the way I find myself rationalizing my efforts. "Bob is getting out of bed now. A hush has fallen over the crowd. He's sitting up. Oh, it's a painful day today. Just look at that grimace on his face. He's toughing it out today. Look at that concentration. It wouldn't surprise me if he were to lie back down today. Another five minutes marshalling his strength and then try again. But no! He's moving. He's moving! He has a hand on his wheelchair. Leaning, leaning, leaning, and—yes!—Bob is up. He has transferred into his chair. And a magnificent transfer it was, too. Considering what Bob must be going through this morning, I'd give him at least a 9.8 for that maneuver. Let's see what the judges have to say."

But life isn't judged by degree of difficulty. Life is judged, if at all, by what you do with what you've been given. Are you a competent steward of the resources at your disposal? Do you give back? Do you dive headfirst into this adventure called life, and surface after with gratitude in your heart? Do you love?

If life were judged by the challenges each of us had overcome, then everyone would be getting extra points for something or other. One person needs glasses to read. Another is short. Others are balding or overweight or suffer from arthritis or are old or young or ugly or too beautiful. One woman struggles in the aftermath of divorce. A man has lost his parents. Every newspaper would be stuffed with features about people doing things that seem heroic to someone else. There wouldn't be any room for real news. We'd all have handicap-parking tags. We'd all be inspirations.

Then where would we be?

Chapter 5

A Pilgrim's Progress

I t has been a great trip, a wondrous adventure, a journey of epic proportions. All my life I have sought Great Adventures. While I was still in junior high, a buddy and I began bicycle touring and camping at state parks across Iowa. Now that I'm a parent, I can't believe my folks allowed Craig and me to take off one day in the summer after our seventh grade year to ride our old one-speed bikes with metal frame baskets seventy-five miles on back highways to spend a week camping at Diamond Lake. Whatever were they thinking? In college Craig and I staged a thousand-mile tour around the Midwest. When Ann came into the picture, we took her with us on a two-month jaunt to Europe, riding the rails, living out of backpacks, and subsisting on oranges and crusty bread. That's where I accepted her proposal of marriage and bought her a diamond. Just two weeks after we got married we joined the Peace Corps and spent three years living in an adobe hut in the highlands of Guatemala. Upon our return to the United States, Ann and I rode our bikes from Iowa to Alabama during the summer before I enrolled in seminary. After the kids came along (we divide our lives into BC and AC—Before Children and After

Children), we uprooted the family for a three-year stint with the Mennonite Central Committee in Nicaragua. It has been a great rollicking ride. Want to see our slides?

Other adventures, unbidden, have sought me out. My father died when I was a junior in high school. Ann and I were on our first formal date, out with my parents at a concert. Dad suffered a massive heart attack and died with his head on her lap. I've mentioned the death of our second child, a daughter, Micah, who was stillborn. And then there was Ames' leukemia. Together we suffered through three years of pain and uncertainty.

But the greatest adventure of all has been adjusting to a disability. Now, instead of measuring our lives BC and AC, we find ourselves marking events BA and AA (Before and After the Accident). I have enough distance on it now to be able to look back and identify some distinct stages in the adjustment process. I suspect they are not unique to my experience, but are shared, to one degree or another, by many people who face catastrophic loss or major change in their lives. During my recovery and adjustment, I found it helpful to read accounts of the experiences of other disabled people as they went through their own adjustment process. It helped me realize that my feelings weren't so unusual. I hope that my account here may be just as useful to those who follow me.

Fairly early on in my hospital stay, I received a letter that made something of an impact on me. I got lots of mail in the hospital. Every afternoon when I returned from physical therapy there was a stack of cards on my freshly made bed. I confess that I didn't have much patience with the sappy Hallmark cards that said, "Get well soon." Somehow, in my condition, that didn't strike me as being very realistic. I much preferred the ones with a little humor, which poked fun at hospital gowns that always flap open in the back, for instance, or inedible hospital food or bloodthirsty doctors. When I started getting funny cards, I knew I was getting better. People didn't have the nerve to send me anything funny when they were still afraid my condition might be terminal. Anyway, one day I got a letter from Keith, the Quaker minister in Grinnell, that, at first, made an even less favorable impression on me than the hopelessly hopeful cards. All Keith's letter said, scrawled across a page of notebook paper in Keith's nearly illegible handwriting, was "Thanks be to God who, in Christ, always leads us in triumphant procession (2 Corinthians 2:14)."

My first reaction was, "What a crock of bull!" It's just this kind of sentimental Christian drivel that drives realistic people away from the church. Here I was, newly-injured, still in pain, still connected to IVs, being fed through a tube implanted in my stomach, and paralyzed, and he's giving thanks for some triumphant parade? What nerve. I put his note down and went on to cheerier things, vowing to give Keith a wide berth in the future.

But that darn note grew on me. As time passed, both in the hospital and later at home, as I succeeded in accomplishing one goal after another and returning to my family and work, I saw the truth in the passage he had selected. A pattern developed; I was on a roll (literally and figuratively). Every day since that first night in surgery, I had been making progress in my recovery. Often it was two steps (so to speak) forward and one back, but there was still a measurable gain against the forces of death and decay. Thanks to God, I was marching (rolling) forward in a triumphant procession back toward life.

Elizabeth Kübler-Ross has spent a lifetime identifying the stages associated with grief and dying. Her research indicates that there are several distinct stages involved when people are struck by trauma or tragedy. We don't necessarily pass through these stages in an orderly fashion, and we may not experience them all, or finish one before starting another, but her findings have helped a generation come to terms with the emotional response to powerful milestones in our lives.

My experience seems to reflect her findings. My first response upon hearing the news that I had been injured, that my legs would no longer work, was, incredibly, no response at all. At least none that I remember. Ann might have a different story. She also says that she had been telling me the story of my injury for weeks, when I would rouse enough to listen. So maybe by the time I was really conscious, I already knew what had happened. I think the lingering levels of medications in my system had something to do with it. But the magnitude of the news was probably the main factor in my numbness. This was too big, too tragic for my mind to grasp all at once. I had my own fish to fry, such as figuring out how to speak with a tracheostomy, learning to sit up, trying to sleep at night, getting my digestive system to work again, filling time in the dialysis unit by pondering the timeless soap opera questions of whose baby Jessica might be carrying and who Brad might be fooling around with. Dealing with the details of my new situation, thankfully, crowded out consideration of the big issue. I was in shock.

As I entered physical therapy and began to wrest back a degree of control, I entered denial. There's nothing wrong with denial. It's a natural stage in the process of coming to terms with loss. It insulates you from the worst of the pain. What the mind can't deal with, it puts on hold. Denial buys you time. Time is the one factor that will eventually heal some of the wounds—not all of them, but maybe some. But because you can't get there all at once, you put off facing the harsher realities at first.

Denial has been something of an ongoing issue for me. Denial can take many forms. One form it has taken for me has been pushing the limits. Some would say I overcompensate. I have attempted to adjust to my new circumstances by constantly working toward a series of ambitious goals. I was never content to be disabled; I wanted to do what a person in a wheelchair was not expected to do, not supposed to be able to do. And it wasn't just for my own satisfaction; it was to show people that I was normal, or even better than normal. It wasn't enough to take up handcycling, I had to ride across Iowa. I train with non-disabled cyclists, trying to build my upper body strength to the point where I can race on an equal status with them. It wasn't enough just to stay fit and conditioned; I had to enter triathlons again. And not just enter them to participate, but compete and triumph over nondisabled athletes. Now I am more than half-seriously considering training for an "Ironman" distance, involving a 2-mile swim, a 112-mile bike leg, and a full 26-mile marathon run. The Ironman Competition is the supreme challenge for any athlete. Only an elite handful of disabled athletes have ever completed one. At a certain emotional level, overachieving is supremely satisfying. At another, deeper level, I suspect it is a minor pathology. By setting myself such ambitious goals, I may be denying the reality of my condition. I may be trying to prove that I'm not disabled at all.

Hockenberry describes several incidents during his recovery that reveal the extent to which he was denying the reality of his new life. Here, in *Moving Violations*, he plans an assault on the Chicago Transit System:

> I thought of how I might ride the CTA elevated trains when I returned to school in Chicago. . . . There were stairs, endless, filthy, rickety stairs, and narrow turnstiles leading up and down to tracks and street. I insisted that all of my physical therapists listen in elaborate detail to how I was going to board the trains. It was easy enough to explain. I would roll up to the stairs leading to the platform. I would get out of my chair and sit on the second step. I would fold up my chair. I would tie a strap around the chair and attach it to my wrist. I would begin to climb the stairs one at a time on my backside. At the first landing I would haul the chair up by the attached strap, then repeat the process until I was at trackside. Then I would unfold the chair and hoist myself back into it. (71-72)

Hockenberry actually tried this stunt once, after he had successfully completed a course of physical rehabilitation and strengthened his upper body sufficiently. He did it once, but not twice. He realized quickly that such feats, while possible, were not a realistic part of his new life.

Denial, for him, consisted in behaving as though he weren't disabled. "My friends would offer to help. 'We'll just lift you,' or 'I'll push you up the ramp,' or 'Why doesn't someone go into the store and get what you need and you can wait here in the van?' It was always simpler to utilize the combined effort of the group in getting where I was going, but I would have none of it. . . . In those first months, I insisted on doing everything solo, playing all eighteen holes without a handicap" (105). That's what makes his book so enjoyable to read. He gets himself into some unbelievable predicaments, all in the name of passing as nondisabled. Unfortunately, what is revealed when you read between the lines is that Hockenberry is unwilling to realistically accept his limitations. His denial of disability becomes an obsession. In a strange twist, he becomes oppressed by his need to deny limits. In this, he's a pro without equal.

Physicist Stephen Hawking faces what must be a hugely challenging life as he deals with amyotrophic lateral sclerosis (ALS). He is surrounded by technology that provides mobility, breathes for him, and allows him to communicate, albeit very slowly and deliberately. But he rarely talks about his condition. He's all business. Asked recently how his disability affects his life, he answered:

I guess we're all pretty disabled on the cosmic scale. What difference is a few muscles more or less? Disability does not really affect my consciousness. I see it as an inconvenience like color blindness. (Kahn, 41)

Hawking's response is exactly the line I'm pushing in this book, but to hear it from one with as severe a disability as Hawking has is, to say the least, surprising. His interviewer, a man also suffering from a progressive neuromuscular disability and wedded to wheelchair and respirator, was incredulous. "How then do I respond to Hawking's claim? With disbelief. He must be in denial. How can his inability be only an inconvenience?" (Kahn, 41). Dropping your pencil is an inconvenience. Getting a hangnail is an inconvenience. Living with ALS has to be somewhat more than inconvenient, wouldn't you agree?

Christopher Reeve may represent denial from the opposite extreme. While Hawking regards his disability as a minor inconvenience, Reeve seems to see his as a defining feature. Reeve's message is that the only hope for a person with a disability is to be cured. Somewhere between these two poles must lie the truth.

On the other hand, both Reeve and Hawking may be responding to the difficult conditions in their lives the only way they know how. What works for me may not be the answer for you. Difficult though it may be not to judge an individual's reaction to his or her disability, each person's pilgrimage through this uncharted wasteland is going to be an individual journey. Permit us our little quirks. For some of us, it's all we have left.

Another expression of denial in my life may be the quality of my relationships with other people with disabilities. I find myself uncomfortable around other wheelchair users (unless they happen to be the super-crips who compete in marathons and triathlons. Then I perk up and tag along to see what I can learn from them!). I have long since dropped out of spinal cord injury support groups. I have the feeling that people look at such groups and think, "Look, they let the cripples out for a field trip." Which is exactly what we did during rehab. The staff would drive us patients around town in a special handicap van and we would visit grocery stores, museums, airports, and other places where we could practice independent living skills. I was uncomfortable in those groups then, and I'm even less favorably inclined toward them now. I do not like to be seen in the company of other people with disabilities. I never drive with my handicap-parking tag visible. When it came time to order a special handicap license plate for my car, I deliberately ordered the tiny sticker that you affix to your existing plate (designed, I suppose, for the recently disabled) rather than the disability license plate that features a prominent wheelchair symbol. It sometimes misleads parking police, especially when I also neglect to hang my tag on my rearview mirror, but the local authorities know my car by now, and others who squint real hard can see my license plate sticker. I go to great lengths to disguise the fact that I have a disability, at least in settings where I can successfully pull it off. I have removed the push handles on the back of my wheelchair. I'll go out of my way to let the world know that I'm in control and need no assistance. Disability activists call this behavior "passing." Passing is resisting being identified as disabled even though you are. It's attempting to function in the world as though your disability did not exist. Radical disability movement advocates are critical of people with disabilities who try to pass as though they had no disability.

Barry Corbet, who writes the monthly column "Bully Pulpit" for *New Mobility* magazine, describes the game we play to hide our condition:

> It's generally considered bad form to speak of our losses. One of the tricks of living with a disability, Nancy Becker Kennedy once told me, is to make it look so good that everyone else will want one. We work hard to convince nondisabled people that our lives are just fine, thank you, because we don't want their pity and we don't want them deciding we might as well be put out of our misery. We keep our sorrows close to the vest. (2000, 4)

In my hometown I move about as easily as I did before my injury. That's by design. I haven't holed myself up in my bedroom, nor have I become militant about the civil rights of people with disabilities, demanding that stores build ramps and widen doorways. I don't want to call attention to myself as disabled. I just fit in. I'm one of the few local residents who is an active wheelchair user. I harbor a somewhat smug sense of pride in being able to drive, access inaccessible places, and function as the able-bodied community functions. For now, I'm strong enough physically to pull it off.

Now, to a certain extent, there is nothing wrong with this. This was, after all, the goal of the physical therapy department. I'm a physical therapy success story. I function successfully in a world that doesn't always extend me hospitality. My determination has made me quite skillful in overcoming problems associated with using a wheelchair. But there's a thin line, in the words of Gary Karp, "between challenging yourself within reasonable boundaries and acting against your self-interest because you don't want to define yourself as a person with a disability" (166, *Life on Wheels*). Am I pushing against the world to deny what I've become? At what point is my ambition overcompensating for what I have lost? At what point does it become counterproductive—or dishonest?

For me it has felt necessary at least to explore these limits. I have to push myself to see how much I can get away with, to see how close I can return to my "normal" life. To feel good about myself, I may even have to exceed those limits. It just might be necessary for me to compete in that Ironman triathlon, to see if I can do it, to be able to *say* that I did it. It's important to me to prove something to the world and to myself. But I'm already beginning to discover, through grueling experiences like RAG-BRAI, that the cost of this effort may be too great to sustain for long. Sure, I can do these things. But is it worth it? With time, maybe I can ease off and relax into a more comfortable and realistic assessment of the reality of my situation. I'm a person with a disability. It's okay.

Medical cure is often seen by the nondisabled as the obvious solution to my predicament. Well-meaning people are constantly offering me reassurance. "You'll get up and walk again, Bob. You'll see. One day you'll be running again." In the end, that's another form of denial. Just the other day a man sent me a Web site for an organization dedicated to finding a cure for spinal cord injury. He assumed I'd be interested. A stranger in a church I was visiting grabbed my hand and said a spontaneous prayer for healing, which she interpreted as "leaving this wheelchair behind and walking with the Lord." All I had to do was "get rid of the negativeness in my heart." What led her to believe that my prayer was to walk again? Actually, I'd much rather have sex again than walk, but I didn't feel it appropriate to share that with her. And where did the "negative heart" comment come from? A conservative Christian who attended a wedding I performed assured me that if my faith were strong enough, I'd walk again. "God will perform a miracle in your life." I informed him that God already had performed that miracle. I'm alive! It would be rude of me to ask for another.

No, I've never been stuck where many people—with or without disabilities—are stuck, waiting around for a cure. My denial has never taken that form. I'm quite content to believe the DOT when they define my condition as "permanent, non-expiring." I'm ready to get on with my healing through adjustment, not cure. The problem with seeing salvation for the disabled only in terms of a medical cure for their condition is that this model identifies people with disabilities as imperfect people. I don't feel I'm less than a person in this disabled body. Putting life on hold until a cure is found reduces us to medical patients, not full persons with business to take care of, families to love, and adventures to live.

Grief is an emotion that accompanies any loss, however great or small, and is another stage in the adjustment process. Grief is what you experience when a loved one dies. You also experience it when you lose a valued object, when you undergo a career change or a divorce, when you move, when you graduate or retire, or when your abilities begin to decline. Grief is part of the adjustment process when you lose the use of your legs. Something has died, and we mourn the loss.

It wasn't just the loss of my legs that led to grief. It was loss of control of my situation and environment. I had never been a hospital patient before. In my pastoral visits I had often wondered how I would hold up if I were ever hospitalized. I could never see myself using a bedpan. Now the nurses had taken away the last shreds of my dignity. They pulled back my covers as though they, not I, owned the body beneath. They washed my private areas and took care of my waste elimination. I peed on one of them, quite unconsciously I'm sure, when she lifted me like a sack of flour into the rolling shower chair.

I experienced grief at odd little times over the course of my recovery. When I regained consciousness, I still had the same self-image that I had going into the accident. I asked the hospital to install a trapeze over my bed so I could lift myself out of bed for transfers. When I discovered, to my shame and horror, that I could barely lift my arms to reach the bar, let alone use it to lift my body, I grieved over the loss of strength. At one point in my rehab I was convinced that I could stand, using leg braces, between the parallel bars, and swing my way along them. When I failed, I went back to bed devastated. I grieved when Ann had to leave my side and get on with the business of the church. At first, she was with me around the clock. But she was also trying to direct church business in my absence, and she had to run a week of vacation Bible school. When she left, I was crushed. I felt abandoned. Later, I thought I could come back quickly to managing my church. But I found that I lacked the energy to follow through on projects and take charge of much of anything. Heck, I couldn't even manage my own care. How was I to run the church? I grieve still over things I can no longer do and roles I can no longer fill. Each of these challenges brought a sense of loss, and was followed by grief.

I had never been one to show emotion easily, but now I found that tears came frequently and unbidden. I was embarrassed to watch movies with my family. By the end I'd be blubbering and sniffing. I was completely undone by that part in Disney's *Beauty and the Beast* when Belle is bending over the wounded beast and expressing her love. I'm sitting in a dark movie theater full of little kids, and I'm rubbing tears out of my eyes and trying to stifle sniffles. How strange is that? At odd moments during the day, when it took longer than expected to transfer into the car or as I put my hand on the doorknob, making ready to roll out the door to the office, I'd stop and sigh with the sadness of it all.

Grief wasn't confined to a distinct stage in the process of adjustment. It wasn't the case that I did my grieving, got over it, and went on to something else. Grief as a primary response does fade into the background, but it's never entirely gone. I sit in the shower and look sadly at my scarred body, bristling with tubes and bags. I drive by inviting trails with the realization that I will never run or hike them. I watch the college cross-country team lope by on the street in front of my house, knowing that I'll never again run alongside them. I see a distant mountain or waterfall and know that I can never climb it. I'm on the boardwalk, gazing hungrily across an expanse of beautiful beach at the surf breaking gently on the shore, and I can't get across the sand to splash in the waves. At one low point I was noticing homes along a drive that I would never be able to access. Not that I'd ever want to knock on some stranger's door and ask to come into their home, but the realization that I couldn't do it even if I wanted to hit me hard. Go figure. Grief has become a constant companion on my journey.

But as grief became a more comfortable companion and more manageable, another emotion swelled to take its place. You can maybe guess what that was. Anger showed up next, with a vengeance.

Not that I didn't have ample reason to be good and steamed. After all, some bozo ran over me and drove off without a care, leaving me with the consequences and medical bills. In an original version of my first sermon after my injury, I let my anger slip into the text. "Then," I wrote, "the driver of the pickup that hit me, *may he rot in hell*, left the scene, rolling merrily on his way." This version was transcribed and circulated to six thousand readers among UCC members in Iowa. That "rot in hell" line earned me a stack of critical mail. "How could you, a minister, say such a thing?" the sweet little old ladies demanded to know. I answered in defense, "I was angry. It's okay to express anger. And, in my theologically trained opinion, the driver who hit me really does inhabit hell." I'm not sure my response smoothed any ruffled feathers, though.

Clearly, what I needed to do was forgive the jerk who had hit me. Anger and forgiveness go hand in hand. Forgiveness tends to reduce the anger and speed the healing. It means letting go of the hurt, and in the process the victim can stop being a victim and get on with his or her life. Unfortunately, forgiveness is easier to advocate than accomplish.

According to a resource published through the Presbyterian Peacemaking Program by Richard L. Killmer, forgiveness can be seen as a process by which a person who has suffered an offense moves through a) a recognition of the negative impact of the offender's behavior, b) taking charge—moving from victim to actor, c) recognizing the offender as a child of God, and d) telling the offender that he or she has hurt us, but offering forgiveness (Killmer, "Forgiveness"). The goal in this process is not only the healing of the victim, but of the perpetrator as well. The end product is a restored relationship.

But what if the offender isn't sorry? What if he doesn't even claim responsibility? Even if it's only the victim acting unilaterally, forgiveness can still be liberating. After teaching a class at my church on forgiveness, I wrote a letter to the guy who ran over me, and sent it to my local newspaper, the *Grinnell Herald Register* (April 6, 1998). They ran it, with my picture, on the front page.

I address myself to the person driving the dark pickup truck which hit me last May 31 while I was bicycling east of Grinnell on Highway 6. I want you to know that you changed my life. I'm confined to a wheelchair now, and still healing from broken bones and internal injuries. I experience varying degrees of pain virtually all the time. I'm angry.

But I also want you to know that I'm prepared to forgive you. With the help of God and my church members, I'm finding the strength to take this in stride and go on with my life. Life may be changed, but it's manageable. Anger has been a great motivator, but it will never lead to healing. I'm going to have to forgive you in order to be whole again.

How are you doing? Are you having trouble sleeping at night, holding inside your guilt? Are you in need of some healing, too? I can help you there. Come forward. Confess what you've done. Say you're sorry. I'll forgive you and you can then see if you can forgive yourself.

The sheriff's deputy assigned to my case tells me that you may only be guilty of two serious misdemeanors: leaving the scene of an accident and failure to render aid. See, the law doesn't even hold you responsible. But if you'll accept moral accountability for your actions, you'll find that you can put this incident behind you and go on with your life. Just as I'm trying to go on with mine.

I look forward to hearing from you.

And then I waited by the door for the perpetrator to show up, wondering if I'd embrace him or punch him if he presented himself. He didn't, of course, but the exercise was therapeutic.

In reality, I was never very angry with the driver himself. That was too big a thing to be angry about, and too pointless. I have never dwelt on that incident. My anger found expression in the little things. I was mad at the situation.

It wasn't fair. I felt like I was constantly in the slow lane while everyone else went whizzing by on either side. I was both frustrated with my burden and resentful of everyone else who moved more quickly through the day. My hygiene routine is a burden every morning when I get up and every evening before I go to bed. It doesn't matter if I'm too tired to perform it. I have to take care of urine and colostomy bags. I have to drag my sorry butt into and out of bed and go through the athletic routine that is getting dressed and undressed. I get wet in the rain and bogged down in the snow. My family is down the stairs watching television together and I'm stuck here in bed. I hurt and I'm sore and I want my body back, the one that responds to physical training and doesn't look like some freak thing that scares children and old women. I want to be able to swim without being betrayed by embarrassing bulges and leaks under my suit. I'm sick of wearing diapers.

Whew! Glad I got that off my chest. I feel a little better now, thank you.

There is a condition recognized as disability fatigue, described by Nancy Lane as "an inescapable burden which comes from living with a disability *and* needing to fight for equal opportunity, educate, explain, demand rights, and never having a rest from the effects of the disability itself" (1999, 179). Living day in and day out with this fatigue tends to make one mad.

Anger is underrated. Often people dealing with disabilities are justifiably angry, but unable to express it. People are put off by angry crips. Being able to express anger leads toward healing. It's okay to be mad. Job got mad—even mad at God. He not only got away with it, but his anger cleared the air and led toward a more intimate relationship with God. Even Jesus got mad. He was angered by injustice and thick-headedness.

He tore into the money changers who had set up shop in the temple. He yelled at his disciples, and at God. Anger can be a creative force for change.

One of the fringe benefits of being mad is that anger is a great motivator. I was able to accomplish great things during my angry year. Have you ever noticed how Olympic weight lifters begin their presses with an explosive grunt and a burst of energy? Or how football players bang their heads against their lockers to induce a state of brute anger before a game? It's the same thing preparing to face the day in a wheelchair. As a parish pastor in a small town, I couldn't take my anger out on the people around me (although Ann and Ames and Kate may disagree). And I always knew it was not helpful to harbor anger at the driver who hit me and drove away, though I have wished misfortune on him more than a few times. My anger came out in useful ways. Anger drove me to powerful workouts in the pool and on my handcycle and racing wheelchair. Anger assisted me in making difficult transfers from the wheelchair into the bathtub. It helped me toss my chair into the car and get around. It's like a turbo boost. It helped focus my concentration on a hard driving determination to get done what I had to do. For some time—come to think of it, I still say it—my mantra was, "You do what you have to do." I say it to myself as a command. "Put your head down, buck up, and do it."

Anger motivates, but it's exhausting. It got old after awhile and turned inward. During my first year after the injury, I was mad. During the second year, I was depressed. I found it harder and harder to get out of bed in the morning. I don't think I was as present to my family as I had once been or wanted to be again. Those tearful moments that had been occasional became more and more a regular thing.

Ann and I talked about our losses. She was grieving, too. She had lost me as a sexual partner and a full-fledged companion. It changes a relationship when one partner becomes dependent and the other as a caregiver. My depression was bringing her down, too. I needed someone outside our immediate setting to confide in.

Bruce, a pastoral counselor and a former bicycling friend from Iowa City, became an important ally for a while. I went to see him, to share what I was going though. I didn't have very many sessions with him, but it was a relief to be able to talk through my frustrations with someone whose reactions could be more objective. My family doctor saw me and we talked about depression. He pointed out that there are two kinds of depression. One is chemical, a physical imbalance in the brain. The other is situational, when a person is feeling blue about a current state of affairs. It could be as serious as a death in the family or as simple as a rainy week. We both reckoned that my depression was of the latter type, and that time and counseling would help, but just to be on the safe side, and because doctors receive prodigious amounts of free sample drugs they need to give away, he prescribed an antidepressant. He said that if I didn't notice any flattening out of my affect, my depression was most likely situation-dependent. The drugs had no effect.

After a few months I stopped going to my counselor friend. I didn't need him any more. Now we see each other socially, and it's much more pleasant. Some time later, when I would stop to think about it, I noticed that I was not as discouraged as I had been. More things in life seemed interesting and achievable. I was becoming more engaged and more in control back at church. Physically I was more accomplished and in less pain. There were still challenges ahead, but they weren't so intimidating. I wanted to grapple with them. I think I had survived my blue period.

All of life is an adventure. Just getting out of bed in the morning is an adventure. What will happen to me today? What will challenge me? What will I learn? What new thing will come my way? It may be all the more so for people who enter the day with a disability. Corbet writes,

> Lionel Terray, a famous French mountaineer, called his chosen sport "the conquest of the useless." People with disabilities, I submit, are engaged in the conquest of the ordinary. We find adventure in reaching the unreachable object, in scratching the unscratchable itch, in making the impossible transfer. We find it every time our adaptive equipment breaks down or an attendant flakes out. We find it in confronting patronization and discrimination, in righting wrongs, taking stands, and rousing the courage to be who we are. Adventure stalks us, insists that we participate. Like it or not, most of us get all the adventure we can handle. Of course we don't often choose our adventures, but does anyone? We like to think we do, but the best adventures befall us, not we them. (2000, 4)

It's an adventure just being part of the human drama. We live within the limits we were born with, but seek out love and fulfillment, which, when found, plug us in to that which is beyond limit. We all do it, but those who live with disabilities may find their adventures begin a little closer to home.

I guess what's still out there waiting for me on my pilgrimage from injury through uncertainty is acceptance. Who can say whether I've arrived or not, or whether anyone ever arrives? It's hard for people to accept who they really are in an advertising-driven culture that fuels its economic engines by creating consumer needs. A woman who subjects herself to an expensive and risky medical procedure designed to remove wrinkles, a just-average golfer who buys a five-hundred-dollar driver, a balding, over-the-hill executive who drives a Porsche convertible—are we ever really satisfied with who we are? Isn't there always a better state that we're longing for? (When you're from Iowa, lots of states seem better.)

If I could be miraculously cured, stand upright with no further complications from my fractured pelvis or friable bladder, if the colon could be reattached, would I go for it? Darn straight I would! I'm no idiot. A life without disability would be preferable. It would eliminate many of the problems I have to deal with on a regular basis. Who would prefer to be crippled, for God's sake, if the slate could be wiped clean? In fact, I'd swap you five years of whatever life expectancy I may have left, and throw in the possibility of ever walking again, for just one more opportunity to make love with Ann. Make it a rainy night, with the kids away. Accept my disability if I had a choice? Not on your life!

But have some gifts appeared as a result of—not just *in spite* of, but also *because* of—my injury and subsequent disability? Yes. And is life—just as it is, with no miracle cure on the horizon—manageable? Yes. And is it—just as it is—a good life?

Let me think. This is an important question. I want to give it the attention it deserves. First of all, I'm alive. That's a good thing. I'm sitting in Hawaii for the summer with my family, on a sabbatical from my parish ministry duties, exploring the secrets of these exotic islands, investigating new cultural perceptions, and writing a book about adjusting to disability that a publisher actually seems interested in. My wife loves me. My kids are turning out to be interesting, responsible people. My church supports me. I'm wiser than I was before about the nature of life and loss and the human condition. God has clearly smiled on me and continues to do so. Is it a good life?

Darn tootin'! Michael J. Fox considers himself a lucky man for having been diagnosed with Parkinson's. I consider myself gifted for having been made aware of the blessings that followed my injuries and disability.

Radical theologian Mathew Fox was once officially silenced by the Vatican and later released from the Dominican Order because of his outspoken opinions. He wrote in his book *On Becoming a Musical, Mystical Bear* that life is not so much a problem to be solved (a response typical of the western, scientific, post-Enlightenment mind) as it is a mystery, before which we should stand (or, in my case, sit) in awe. Things aren't to be fixed; they are to be accepted, with grace and gratitude.

Acceptance is getting to the place where you can value your current condition, whatever it may be, in spite of its limitations. It means incorporating into your self-understanding an honest image of yourself as a person with a disability. Having a disability may be a damned nuisance, it may be embarrassing or painful, but it's your life. Whatever its features, it is a gift from God. Acceptance is being able to say, "Thank you. It's enough."

Chapter 6

A Cross-Cultural Safari

I've been on extended cross-cultural excursions several times in my life, and I've learned a thing or two about adaptation. I'm not talking about adventure racing in exotic foreign countries or mountain climbing in Nepal. I'm not talking about Club Med hopping your way around the Caribbean. I'm not even talking about being transferred from one overseas U.S. military base to another. No, each of these adventures allows you to carry your culture with you. They don't change you culturally. They don't make you redefine yourself at your core level. But Ann and I have had the opportunity to live for extended periods of time in foreign cultures, working with local people, living side by side with them, and learning from them. Over the years I've learned some valuable lessons about adaptation to new situations. I never dreamed these lessons would help me adjust to living with a disability.

In the summer of 1976, fresh out of college, Ann and I were married in a lavish Catholic version of *My Big Fat Greek Wedding*, went on a romantic two-week honeymoon camping trip (for which Ann has still not forgiven me), and packed our duffel bags for a three-year stint with the Peace Corps in Guatemala. In preparation,

I got my hair buzzed to a length that would not become popular for another three decades. Ann packed only the essentials, including the new cast iron skillet she was reluctant to part with for three years. Our discussion over the contents of her bag was our first argument as newlyweds.

My initial foray into a new country and culture was less than auspicious. We spent a few days in Miami for staging and getting acquainted with the other volunteers who would be in our group in Guatemala. For Ann and me, coming from the heartland of Iowa, Miami was already a foreign country. The city was big and fast and intimidating. The people spoke foreign languages there.

We flew with our group to Costa Rica for three months of language and technical training. We had volunteered for the "School Gardens and Nutrition" program, and the Peace Corps administrators in Washington, D.C., were happy to have us because, on paper at least, we looked like the perfect candidate couple. Ann was a certified home economics teacher and I had grown up in Iowa. Iowa, in the Washington mindset, was synonymous with farming. I neglected to include on my application form that I lived in a town, was the son of a dentist, had grown up across the street from a college campus, and had never in my life set foot on a farm or planted a garden. I didn't even like vegetables. But they sent us anyway, and proceeded to train us.

It was near midnight when we arrived in La Guacima, the rural area we would call home for the next three months, following a harrowing drive in a rattletrap school bus down serpentine streets and roads. It was sweltering in the bus, and we were exhausted from stress and a long day. Wanting to make a good impression, I grabbed an armload of suitcases from the back of the bus, made my way forward, and proceeded down the steps. I stepped off the bus into the night, and immediately disappeared from sight. I had fallen flat in a ditch, buried under a hundred pounds of luggage. I hopped up and brushed myself off, praying that no one had seen me. It was dark, after all. Who could have noticed? I thought my subterfuge was successful until our colleagues presented me with an award at the end of training, "For the man who has climbed from the gutters of La Guacima. . . ."

After a midnight briefing in one of the sultry, smelly former chicken coops that were to be our classrooms, they bundled us off in the bus again to a flea-infested hotel in the city for a few hours of sleep. Our director's last words as he left us in the lobby were, "Oh, I forgot. Don't drink the water." We spent the night huddled on the bed, afraid to get undressed, uncertain whether or not we should even brush our teeth.

The next day was the day from hell. We went right to language class, where we spent the entire morning trying to repeat back to the instructors their Spanish-accented gibberish. Lunch consisted of a rice dish washed down with pink room-temperature soda pop. And then, now that the day had heated up nicely, they put us out in the garden and told us to dig. At the end of the day, they piled us in the back of a pickup truck and took us down the road to meet our host families, with whom we'd be living for the next three months. One by one, our friends were dropped at homes that became progressively less and less appealing as we got farther and farther from the training center. Finally, Ann and I were the last ones in the truck. They left us at the front door of a simple farmhouse. A Costa Rican peasant family was standing in the doorway, smiling and blabbering in some gibberish that they seemed to think had some meaning. Later, of course, we learned that it must have been Spanish. But for now it was incomprehensible. We stood there dripping sweat, physically and emotionally depleted, our teeth unbrushed for the past forty-eight hours, unable to communicate. How do you say, "Mommy, I want to go home!" in sign language? All we could do was point to our stomachs, the universal sign for hunger.

Every morning we were expected to report to the training center by 7:00; it took us nearly an hour to walk there. Showers were a brutal plunge under an icy, well-fed faucet in the dark of the morning before sunrise. Privacy for the newlyweds consisted of a curtain over our doorway. The food provided by our family was unrecognizable and bland. Lots of rice and gristly meat. Occasionally Ann and I snuck out to a market to buy imported jelly for our morning toast, but we would find tiny finger marks from curious tasters in the jars, which we had stashed cunningly in our bags. One day, to get away from the regime of training and lack of privacy with our family, we took a blanket and spent the morning fooling around down by a little creek on the family's farm. When we next returned to the center, the training staff called us in for a meeting. We learned a new word: *renegar*, from the word for "renegade." It seems we had gotten ourselves a reputation as outlaws, just for escaping for a few hours of comfort and intimacy.

It was tough because everything was strange and it all came at us at once. One of the most abrupt lessons we learned from our family via sign language had to do with bathroom etiquette. It seems you can't flush used toilet paper in rural Costa Rica. The plumbing won't handle it. You're supposed to put your used toilet paper in a can by the john and a family member will take it outside every day and burn it. Can you imagine how difficult it is for North Americans to get used to handling, collecting, and disposing of used toilet paper? We weren't brought up for this.

Our Peace Corps training resembled army boot camp. I think our director was an ex-Marine. In boot camp, the new recruit is shorn not only of his hair, but also of all his preconceived notions and familiar routines. He or she is thrust into an unfamiliar context in which the drill sergeant defines the new reality. Soldiers need to learn to follow orders, so independent thinking is gradually worn down and replaced with a new set of values. In Peace Corps training, our familiar patterns of behavior were stripped away and we were thrown into a new, alien, culture. It was sink or swim. But there's no better way to learn Spanish, or Central American culture.

Later on in our lives, in preparation for other cross-cultural living experiences, we were introduced more gently to cultural sensitivity. Both Habitat for Humanity International and the Mennonite Central Committee, with whom we trained and worked in the early 1990s, provide volunteers with an intensive process of cross-cultural adaptation. They take very seriously the need for travelers to understand the differences between the home culture and the new host culture, and to realize that different does not automatically mean bad. In adjusting to a new culture, you need to begin to see life through the eyes of the people from that place, and to appreciate that perspective. Too often North Americans on vacation travel with preconceived notions and belligerent attitudes. We have created for ourselves an unsavory reputation, I'm afraid, as "Ugly Americans." Americans are often seen by the rest of the world as insensitive and uncaring about foreign customs. When we traveled in Europe, we discovered that many Americans stick a little Canadian maple leaf pin on their lapels or backpacks to disguise their true nationality. They found they were treated much better that way.

One of the cross-cultural exercises that Habitat for Humanity uses to prepare its international volunteers begins by dividing the volunteers into two groups. Each group is given different, secret instructions. One group is told to exhibit behaviors associated with introverted personalities. They are allowed to speak only when spoken to, they prefer to mingle only with their own kind, and they address one another formally, using "sir" or "madam." To add another wrinkle, in their "society" men are the weaker sex. They need to be chaperoned by the women and are forbidden to talk directly to "foreign" women.

In the other simulated society, men and women are equal, they are informal in interactions, outgoing, and very sociable. They earn points by the number of "foreign" interactions they can initiate. You can imagine what happens in the game when the two simulated societies mingle. People from the first culture regard the others as rude, intrusive, uncivilized. People from the second culture tend to see the first as uptight and incomprehensible. Neither group would be able to function effectively in the other's culture without first figuring out the unstated rules by which social interactions were carried out, and approaching the game with some sensitivity toward and appreciation for the foreign culture. As the anvil salesman advised Professor Harold Hill in *The Music Man*, "You gotta know the territory!"

Once our defenses were sufficiently broken down and our eyes opened to the possibilities of cultural differences, we were able to learn a great deal about the traditional peoples of Central America. We successfully completed the training program in Costa Rica and were deposited in our work sites in Guatemala. One of the most striking features of traditional Guatemalan peasants is their tendency to accept their fate with resignation. It drove us crazy at first. We were there to introduce much-needed change, but they didn't want to change. "*Es costumbre*," was the pat response to any question. "It's custom." Why do you do things your way rather than our, more efficient way? "*Es costumbre*."

But when we began to understand why these people were so resistant to change, their lives began to make more sense. Guatemalans have a much more organic relationship with their environment than do North Americans. For us, the environment is raw material to manipulate in order to meet our needs. We call it a natural resource, something for us to use in order to enhance our status or estate. But Guatemalans take the environment as given. They feel it is their responsibility to adapt themselves to the environment, not the other way around. It's too risky for a subsistence peasant to experiment with new technologies. The price of failure is too high. That's why their traditional indigenous culture is so remarkably tenacious. Farmers plant, women sew, and children learn just as generations of their ancestors had done before them. That's very different from North American culture, where the growing up involves deliberately rejecting your parents' values in search of your own identity.

Incidentally, once we learned the ways of traditional Guatemalan society, we discovered why we were having so much trouble getting local families to plant gardens. Our Peace Corps program was designed to train school children how to plant gardens and use the new vegetables in their families' diets, in hopes that they would take the lessons home to their parents. The plan was that each Peace Corps volunteer would visit ten schools. Each school might have fifty students. So by the end of the first year we should have family gardens in five hundred homes across the region. Yeah, right! In reality, we probably had fewer than eight or ten families experimenting with gardening. Our lessons never seemed to get taken home by the students. Upon reflection, it was clear why. We were doing it backwards! In traditional society, children learn from their elders, not the other way around. Once we figured that out, we abandoned the schools, moved out of the village into an adobe hut next door to a respected rural community leader, and began to introduce our technologies exclusively through him. Then we began to see results.

While independence and ingenuity are highly prized by North Americans, they are discouraged by and even dangerous to Guatemalan peasants. Community is everything. Community entails survival for the individual or the family. When a man in a traditional indigenous Guatemalan village starts to "get ahead," that is, when he starts making money or amassing real estate, there are mechanisms in place to cut him down a notch. It's simple, really. The richest man in town is elected mayor. It falls to the mayor to host fiestas for the village and to provide infrastructure and services needed by the inhabitants. By the end of his first term in office, he is no longer the richest man in town. He may, in fact, emerge from office a pauper. Maybe we should try that system here. At least it would weed the scoundrels out of politics. Barbaric as that system seems to North Americans, it works for Guatemalans. It enhances the survivability of the community.

Traditional cultures mystify most North Americans. You try to communicate with peasants, and they won't even look you in the eye. They agree to do something, but the task never gets done. Are they lying to you when they say they'll do it, or does "si" not mean "yes"? Relationships seem more important than efficiency. You try to be clear and direct, and it seems to offend them. They smile at you and laugh with you, then later it seems like they're insulting you behind your back. They never show up on time. Is it laziness? I once hiked fifteen miles over rough, mountainous trails to a village where I was supposed to give a demonstration on raising rabbits. The first participant showed up four hours late, just when I had given up and was about to leave for the hike back out. I'm the kind of guy who feels late when I arrive on time. I need to be there at least five minutes early to feel comfortable. The relaxed sense of time and punctuality in rural Guatemala almost killed me. It seemed disrespectful. Sometimes clothing that we North Americans feel perfectly appropriate in is seen by traditional people as obscene. In places in Africa, for example, it is more acceptable for a woman to bare her breasts than it is to wear shorts. Shorts expose the thigh, which is considered erotic. Shaking hands, touching, and embracing are all loaded gestures, depending on the location. Personal space, that bubble of empty space we maintain around us when we're with others, is a cultural variable. North Americans tend to feel crowded by French and Italians, for example, who need less of that cushion of space than we do.

The meaning and impact of all these interactions, and countless others that may only surface after they have been violated in one way or another, need to be carefully examined before wading into a foreign setting. Too often we simply dismiss differences as shortcomings, oblivious to their meaning in cultural context.

Traditional societies have a much different sense of the value of material possessions than North Americans, and of generosity with these possessions. The first impression that many North American young people have when they are taken to Mexico or Central America for a whirlwind week of mission and service is the glaring poverty of the people in comparison with North American standards of living. It's not uncommon to find entire communities of people living without what we would consider the basic necessities of life, such as running water, electricity, and television sets. We're appalled by the poverty we see and motivated to try to alleviate it in some way. We are moved to raise money for them or build them houses or provide food.

What these dedicated adventurers often fail to notice is how happy and generous the local people might be, even in the midst of what we'd see as abject poverty. My work in Nicaragua often took me into the *campo* for several days on end, teaching community development techniques in small villages and rural areas. I would stay in the home of a rural pastor or community leader, sleeping in a hammock alongside other family members, sharing their simple fare of rice and beans, and bathing in the creek with the men of the village. These trips were often filled with days of celebration, camaraderie, and sharing. The people I visited were universally more eager to share with me from their meager possessions than I was to share with them out of my bounty. Sometimes we'd be caught up in fiesta mode and spend the whole night laughing, eating, and visiting with the neighbors. I learned that there's a simple joy involved in the lives of traditional peasants that can only be appreciated once you enter the culture and allow yourself to be transformed by it.

How does all this relate to the discussion of disability? Incurring a disability is like waking up one morning in a foreign country where you can't speak the language, can't drink the water, can't even brush your teeth. Adjusting to life with a disability is like adjusting to a foreign culture. It's hard. You're surrounded by landmines and you know nothing of the lay of the land. What's it like to have to be confined to a wheelchair? All your life you had been brought up to regard the residents of this strange land as backward, impoverished, limited somehow. It would be tragic to have been born one of them, without the blessings and opportunities you take for granted. In fact, you have even donated to charities that promised to help alleviate the suffering of these poor creatures, to give them a helping hand to pick themselves up out of their misery. You have been moved to pity at the sight of them and the thought of what they must go through every day. You have admired their spirit in surviving their ordeal and persevering in spite of the odds against them.

And now, all of a sudden, you're one of them. The horror.

In shock, you desperately seek ways to get out of there and back home where it's safe, normal, and comfortable. But you seem to have misplaced your return ticket. Newly disabled, you seek out miracle cures, hoping against hope that your arrival in this place signifies a brief sojourn, not a permanent change of address. Maybe it's just a three-hour cruise. You're praying that you're not marooned here with Gilligan and the Professor and MaryAnn for the duration of the series. If modern medicine falls short, perhaps your rehabilitation program can help you approximate your old life. But, you'll soon find out, you can't go home again.

Everything is so strange, and it all came upon you all at once. You were independent, but now you can't do anything for yourself. You can't even get out of bed. You used to be in charge of your schedule. Now the nurses and rehab team tell you where to go, when to go, and how high to jump. The food is unrecognizable. They've taken your clothing and you find you're naked under the sheets, or all wrapped up in a twisted hospital gown. Even later, when you're mobile in a wheelchair, clothing fits funny. Clothing wasn't designed to be sat in. Ever seen a model sitting? It's hard to feel sharp and confident when your pants are rumpled and your shirt is twisted around sideways.

Whatever you thought you knew about bathroom etiquette, forget it. You have to learn new ways to drain your bladder and your bowels. And if you were squeamish at the thought of handling and disposing of your used toilet paper, you haven't seen anything yet. Now you'll carry your waste around on board with you in clear plastic bags wherever you go. You used to pride yourself on being clean and hygienic. Two showers a day on the days when you worked out. Now an odor seems to follow you wherever you roll. A shower is a major production these days.

From time to time in Central America, Ann and I found ways to get away from it all. The jelly during training in Costa Rica was one trick. The blanket by the creek was another. Quick trips to the city to eat ice cream or score a Big Mac, or even a vacation trip home over Christmas helped make our cross-cultural adventure manageable. Sometimes all our Peace Corps friends would gather at our house for volleyball tournaments. The beer and the memories of life "back home" flowed freely. But I quickly found that no breaks were permitted from disability. There was no propping my wheelchair in the corner and walking around for a few minutes, just to get the kinks out. I can't sneak out at night and run barefoot, unseen, through the neighborhood. At first I could do that in my dreams, but by now even the dreams of walking and biking and having a normal sex life have faded into distant memory. We were told in Peace Corps training that when you finally begin to dream in Spanish, you've learned the language. I don't dream in "ambulatory" anymore; now I dream in "disability." I'm here for good. I might as well learn to speak the language, get familiar with the currency, and figure out how the natives function. That's when the adventure begins, and the grace becomes visible.

Living with a disability, I'm learning tolerance. Since I've had to become more tolerant of my own limitations, I've found that skill is transferable as I deal more tolerantly with others. I've always tended to be critical and judgmental of others, but now I find I can accept human idiosyncrasies and vulnerabilities in ways I had little patience for before. I'm finding I can make connections with people in hospital visits and pastoral counseling sessions in ways I couldn't before my injury. In short, while the limitations of this new life are more manageable than I ever would have imagined, there are also fringe benefits no one could have foreseen. You don't know these things until you arrive and look around, unbiased, at the landscape. Being allowed to experience this gentle new reality is another of the gifts of grace.

Adapting to disability is much the same experience as adapting to a foreign culture. Living with a disability is not an unmitigated tragedy; it's simply a new way to order your life. There may be pain and stigma and uncertainty involved, and you become intimately acquainted with vulnerability and imperfection. Also, don't count on bringing the same degree of independence with you that you might have enjoyed before. But don't write off the experience as a universally bad thing. It's a mistake to think there are not valuable lessons to be learned here.

People who look upon the experience of disability from the perspective of the dominant culture (nondisabled) are often as insensitive to it as the Ugly American who travels the globe without ever leaving his or her culture behind. You've seen them on the veranda, wearing Hawaiian shirts and Bermuda shorts and black shoes and socks, sipping Mai Tais and complaining too loudly about the locals. Tourists can be embarrassingly insensitive toward the cultures in which they travel. The nondisabled can be just as insensitive in relating to the culture of disability. Nondisabled people are often quick to organize a telethon or find a cure for us or admire us as inspirations, but can just as easily dismiss us as freaks.

But I don't want to allow my life to be the object of hasty generalizations by those who are not intimately acquainted with it. Just as within the meager (by our standards) and simple existence of Central American peasants there is love and joy and hope and celebration, so within a life marked by disability there are positive features. Disability is not the defining aspect of any life. Disability is just one condition among many that contributes to the richness of living.

Chapter 7

The Bible Tells Me So.

One day, after I had been out of the hospital for a couple of years, I was asked to counsel a new rehab patient. "Sam" had recently ended up in a wheelchair. For years he had been suffering from a degenerative neurological disease. It had been getting more and more difficult for him to walk; now he had given up on it entirely, and he was in physical therapy to learn how to use a wheelchair.

Sam was a man of uncommon strength of faith. He was not content to let the medical world treat him and pronounce his fate. He had been praying fervently for a cure. His church had surrounded him with prayers for recovery. Sam had been to prayer services designed specifically to heal him from his affliction. They had tried laying on hands. He told us that he had even tried exorcism. But the progression of his disease continued unabated, just as the doctors had predicted. Now he was in tears as he spoke to us. His theology seemed as crippled as his body.

"I read the Bible," he confided. "I've prayed for healing. People who come to Jesus in faith are healed from their diseases and afflictions. I know it says that if you have faith like a mustard seed you can move mountains.

But I can't even move my toes. What's wrong with me? Why can't I get out of this chair?"

Ann and I have been to that place many times. You go to draw water and find the well is dry. We sometimes think we've experienced more than our share of hardship. In 1983 we had a daughter who was stillborn. Right up to the day of delivery, everything was fine and we felt blessed to be welcoming a second child into our family. But on my way into the hospital room to see Ann after she had stopped in for a quick checkup (her instincts warned her that something was wrong), I saw written on the chalkboard at the nurses' station outside her room, "Fetal Demise." The baby who had died in the womb was delivered naturally and we named her Micah. Then we went home empty-handed while other mothers were leaving the hospital with squirming bundles of new life in their arms. A woman in my church delivered a healthy daughter that same day. Watching that girl grow and mature has been a sacred journey for us.

Then, just three years later, when our firstborn was five years old, he was diagnosed with leukemia. Our lives took another nosedive. Ames was eventually cured and has gone on to live a fairly routine life, but his illness coupled with the loss of a beautiful daughter threw us into a tailspin of critical reflection. Why us? What had we done to deserve this? Where's the fairness in this world? Where's the evidence of this compassionate God we had heard so much about—whose praises it had been my job to sing week after week in my Sunday morning sermons?

After struggling with these questions on and off for years, Ann and I have arrived at an understanding that works for us. Our faith makes room for the occasional disaster. That's why my injury never caused a crisis of faith. It caused lots of other crises, but not of faith. Neither Ann nor I have stormed at God because of my injuries and disability. We have not found ourselves floundering theologically. It shook us up, to be sure, and called for deeper reflection as we moved toward understanding and acceptance, but the foundations were not shaken. They had already been laid on the bedrock of human contingency, not on the sand of wishful thinking. We felt we had something to offer Sam from our bag of tricks.

Sam's lament was, "Why?" If a person of faith can't expect to have prayer answered, then what good is prayer? And by extension, what has my life been based upon all these years? Sam was in a serious quandary.

The book *When Bad Things Happen to Good People*, by Rabbi Harold Kushner, has been a tremendous resource for Ann and me through some of our most difficult times. Kushner's response to the question of evil and suffering in the world is, first of all, not to answer it as if it were simply a request for information. Too many people get tangled up in trying to find a rational explanation. You run into too many dead ends that way.

Not all sentences that end in a question mark are really questions. Perhaps questions asking for reasons behind our calamities are more like laments than requests for information. When Jesus called from the cross, quoting Psalm 22, "My God, why have you forsaken me?" perhaps he wasn't so much asking for information about why things had turned out as they did, as he was simply crying out of his pain and frustration. Perhaps there are no rational answers to questions like Sam's, although struggling with them may help lead us to a deeper awareness of the contingency of all life. Disability may be the best lesson available on contingency. To paraphrase a popular bumper sticker slogan, cleaning it up slightly for a family and Christian readership, "Disability Happens."

Kushner says, "Insurance companies refer to earthquakes, hurricanes, and other natural disasters as 'acts of God.' I consider that a case of using God's name in vain. I don't believe that an earthquake that kills thousands of innocent victims without reason is an act of God. It is an act of nature. Nature is morally blind, without values. It churns along, following its own laws, not caring who or what gets in the way. . . ." Furthermore, laws of nature "do not make exceptions for good people" (1981, 58-59).

Why did this terrible thing happen? People around you, not recognizing that you need sympathy more than theology, try to be helpful by offering their versions of an explanation. This was the tactic of Job's so-called friends who rallied around him in the face of his trials. One answer often given is that it was somehow your fault. Maybe you should have done something to prevent it, or maybe you did something wrong that brought it on. Maybe it was a secret sin or fault of yours. Maybe you're too self-righteous. Maybe your faith isn't sufficient for God to want to help you. God is bringing you down a notch and any protestations of yours to the contrary only prove the point. Your suffering is deserved.

In nearly every talk I give now about adjusting to disability, someone in the audience will invariably ask me, with a slight edge to their voice, "Why were you out on a highway riding your bike in the first place?" The obvious implication of the question is that I was somehow to blame for my calamity. I think that finding someone on whom to place the blame helps make the universe seem a little safer for the questioner.

But blaming the victim isn't helpful in the long run, because relatively innocent people really do get hurt sometimes. Bad things do happen to good people. Those who are injured may not be any more deserving of suffering than those spared. Contributing to Sam's deep suffering was a relentless suspicion that he was somehow the cause of it. The victim of suffering is convicted by his own theology.

Or maybe what you experience as suffering isn't ultimately suffering. If you could only see the big picture, goes this argument, you'd see that it's all for the best. According to this theory, suffering is like looking at the back of a tapestry, where you see only loose strands and random stitches. If you could see the other side you'd see a beautiful pattern. When we get to heaven and receive our reward we'll see that it has all been worthwhile. But let's follow this argument through to its logical conclusion. Can it be true that every child abused, every bride killed in an accident on her way to her own wedding, every man who dies of a heart attack just after he retires from a life of hard work, every innocent bystander cut down in a drive-by shooting, are all pieces of God's plan for a beautiful world?

I don't buy it. These rationalizations may be intended to be comforting, but they deny a basic teaching of the Bible that life—this life in the here and now—is a gift from God and designed to be enjoyed. It's not a way station on the road to something better. This is the life that God sent Jesus to share with us in all its abundance.

So maybe suffering is redemptive, another theory goes, and is visited upon us to make us stronger. After all, God never gives us more than we can bear. It's a test. You have the resources to pass it. The obvious critique of this theory is that some people don't pass. Some people face trials so severe and crippling that they are broken in the process. As a training technique, brutal contingency leaves something to be desired.

The genius of Kushner is his suggestion that all these rationalizations about suffering are designed more for the sympathizer than for the victim of tragedy. They help keep in place an orderly, structured universe in which God remains benevolent and in charge. Unfortunately, they put the burden of responsibility on the one who suffers calamity and, in the end, provide answers that fail to ring true. Hence Sam's discomfort.

What was the cause of Sam's suffering, if not God? Why was I run over by a drunk driver, if not for some reason? The answer to both questions has to do with the nature of the world God created. It's not finished yet. It's not perfect. We're created flawed, vulnerable, subject to temptation and decay. We are mortal. That's nothing to grieve over. That's just the way the gift is packaged.

Every tragedy we experience might not have proceeded from the hand of God. God did not set a degenerative neurological disease loose in Sam's central nervous system. God did not run me down with a pickup truck. God was not behind the decision of the driver to get behind the wheel drunk, plow into a cyclist on the side of the road, and then drive away. "Listen, buddy, I have a pastor I want you to run over today. Now have a few drinks and start driving!" That is a ridiculous notion! Sometimes the decisions we make bring us closer to God and in line with God's will. But other times we deliberately turn away from God. And then all hell breaks loose. Contingency and free will make for an extremely messy world. But would we have it any other way?

I was asked by a young minister, "So what do you pray for in these times if you don't pray for healing and restoration?" I'm not saying I don't pray for such things. I'm just saying those prayers seem to be fading in importance as I adjust to life with a disability. God is not Santa Claus. Even Santa doesn't bring everything you ask for, especially if your parents aren't rich. Better to pray for understanding, acceptance, God's compassionate presence, comfort, assurance, and the peace of Christ that passes all understanding. Kushner says that this prayer frees God up from being the cause of your calamity to being the one first on the scene to provide comfort. That's what God does best.

A little girl was late coming home after school. Her mother asked her where she'd been. "Oh, my friend skinned her knee on the way home and I had to help her," replied the girl.

"How did you help her?" her mother asked. "Did you take her home, or call her mother? Did you clean the wound or put a Band-Aid on?"

"Oh no," she said. "I just sat with her and helped her cry."

Sometimes that's the best thing to do. I think that's how God enters our pain and transforms it into healing.

The Reverend Dr. James Forbes, senior pastor at the influential Riverside Church in Manhattan, was asked by Bill Moyers during the days immediately following the terrorist attacks of September 11, 2001, to provide a word from God for the occasion. He said, simply, "God's heart was the first to break. God was the first to shed a tear." Our God is a God of compassion. The word *compassion* comes from two words which, together, mean, "to know suffering with." The Hebrew word for compassion is derived from the word "womb." God, who gave us birth, suffers with us.

Ann and I no longer ask "Why me?" That's begun to feel like a selfish question. A better one, in a world in which imperfection (not to mention free will) is an integral part, is "Why *not* me?" Who would we rather wish our random calamities on than ourselves? Who has more resources to deal with the vagaries of life than we do? With our support networks, healthy family systems, insurance, church support, financial resources, physical conditioning, spiritual resources, and education, who on God's green earth would be a better candidate for what has happened to me, than me? One of the ways Ann puts a stamp of understanding on this whole thing is to point out that all our lives we have been preparing for this very thing. We're carefully trained athletes toeing the starting line at the Olympics of Suffering. We're PhD candidates in the field of trauma, receiving our diplomas after years of study and hard work. In fact, don't stop there. Look at all the players who contributed to the outcome of this adventure. All the doctors, all the medical technology, all the church leaders, indeed, all of creation, has been jockeying for just such a thing to take place (see Romans 8:22). We all played our roles magnificently!

Of course, this is not to suggest that God allowed this calamity to take place just because God knew we could deal with it. All I'm saying is that, in the case of my disabling accident, God has helped us identify and make use of resources we had available to cope with what otherwise might have been an unmitigated disaster. We look to God to help pick up the pieces of life.

I'm not sure if this spin on things was helpful for Sam or not. I don't know if he has revised his personal theology as a result of his experience of disability. He may not have been looking for new information or a new outlook at all. But at least he had an hour to sit and share his story with a couple of people who knew where he was coming from. We sat with him and helped him cry. Maybe that was enough.

But remember, my spin on disability is that disability is much more than tragedy seeking understanding. Even having found a satisfying theological handle on suffering and trauma, I soon found it would be necessary to dig much deeper to find biblical and theological resources for understanding disability as a human condition. This proved much more challenging.

Being a parish pastor, I had to continue to preach. In my first sermon back from the hospital I tried to give the Definitive Answer to the question of disability. I knew it was a tall order, but I couldn't back down from the challenge. The congregation would want to know how I was processing this experience. I didn't feel I could let them down. It wasn't a bad sermon, really, given the circumstances. I had been released from the hospital just two weeks previously. I was up and functioning for only a few hours a week. I was still trying to get a handle on what had happened to me and who I was now as a person with a disability. The sermon came off better than I might have hoped. But I soon came to realize that it was a shot in the dark, a sort of shotgun blast from the hip.

I'm a preacher who preaches from experience. Some of the traditionalists in seminary warn you not to do that. To their credit, it is a risky enterprise because one tends to rehearse tired old stories out of one's personal past. Some experiential preachers even use their own children as cute and embarrassing illustrations for sermon messages. Far be it from me to engage in such tactics. To be honest, though, I should point out that my daughter sits in the back pew with a friend because she's been embarrassed so many times. And Ann herself gets knots in her stomach every Sunday morning, wondering what family secret I'm going to reveal on this day. Because my son's away at college, he's usually fair game.

But I digress. In those early months I was sharing lots of material in sermons from my unique perspective as a newly disabled pastor. There were interesting insights about how a person in a wheelchair disappears in a crowd, how I'd never seen the barriers that exist for people with disabilities, about how some individuals continued to connect well with me while others seemed to have drifted away. It was remarkable how often I could weave in at least a mention of my disability. It was hard for me to do otherwise. That was what was foremost on my mind at the time. Only a few of my parishioners—that I know of, anyway—got fed up with my endless tales of "Now that I'm in a wheelchair, I've noticed . . ."

But one Sunday came a moment of real concern, and I was forced to examine what the Bible had to say about disability. The lectionary passage assigned for the day was the tale from Mark chapter 2, verses 1-12, in which Jesus is teaching in a crowded house and a paralytic is brought to him for healing. The house is so full of people that in order to get the paralyzed man to Jesus, his friends have to make a hole in the roof of the house and lower the man through it down to Jesus. The rest is history. "Jesus saw their faith and said to the paralytic, 'Son, your sins are forgiven. . . . Take your mat and go to your home.'"

Now, this presented me with a problem that I had never encountered before as a nondisabled pastor preaching this text. I had always used healing narratives like this text to illustrate the power of faith and Jesus's miraculous ability to heal, and I'd left it at that. Praise God! Now, however, it didn't seem so simple. What does forgiveness have to do with healing? What does healing have to do with disability? How are disabled persons portrayed in the Bible? This became something of an existential quest, as you might imagine.

My current, all-consuming project is to adjust to my new condition and learn to incorporate my body's new limitations into a healthy self-image. Hope for healing is not a healthy part of that task. Are there any disabled folks in the Bible who find wholeness, acceptance, and salvation this side of healing, or is their salvation always tied to healing? Contemporary minority groups ask the same sort of question. Do African Americans have to play white in order to succeed in the current economic, political, and social climate? Does a woman have to act like a man, whatever that means, in order to advance to the top levels of corporate America? Can I find wholeness within my broken body, or does wholeness entail getting fixed first?

Think of all the persons with ailments of one sort or another who show up in the pages of the Bible and in the company of Jesus. Can you think of even one who goes away content—secure in his or her relationship with God and with the community of the faithful—but without having been cured of the ailment? Lepers are cleansed. Bleeding is stanched. Blindness is eliminated. The deaf recover their hearing. Even the dead are brought back to life. Bodies are "normalized." If you're looking for healing, look no further. The biblical stories are beacons of hope and inspiration. If, however, healing is not part of your agenda, what is the value of these stories? Nowhere do you read of biblical characters accepting and adjusting to life's little idiosyncrasies. That's just not part of the biblical narrative. The "flaws" are always removed first. Intuitively, that seems like a great and benevolent thing. But what does it say about people whose flaws don't seem to respond to petitions for healing, or who don't regard their idiosyncratic bodies as flawed?

These were tough questions. I had never explored them before. They had never occurred to me. I didn't feel confident to answer them on my own. In study groups within the church I met with a strange resistance when I shared the discomfort I was feeling. It seemed that I was the only one bothered by the inconsistencies between my experience and biblical truth that seemed so apparent to me. I did some research among theologians and scholars in the cutting edge field of Disabilities Studies and was startled to find only a handful publishing anything in the field useful to me. This was nearly untouched territory! In the new field of what some call "crip-lit," there are only a few theologians asking difficult questions of the Bible from a disability perspective. Very few authors are reflecting deeply enough on their experience of disability and writing well enough about it to make reading their work a fruitful enterprise. Fortunately the field of Disabilities Studies is expanding and rapidly becoming a mainstream field of study. More theologians and biblical scholars are working to find a message in scripture beyond the simplistic "Jesus heals! Praise God!" cheer.

Guided by the results of some of these studies, here's what I found in the Bible about disability. I warn you. At first glance it's not very helpful. Many people living with disabilities have abandoned the Bible and their churches because of what they see as outdated perceptions of disability, and because many churches have refused to make physical and spiritual accommodations for them.

Initially, an uncritical perusal of the Bible leads to the unmistakable conclusion that disability is seen as a manifestation of personal sin, either an indication of moral depravity or a result of it. This represents the "moral model" of disability, which has had a powerful influence through much of history. In the Hebrew Wisdom literature, physical imperfection and moral imperfection go hand in hand. In the book of Job, for example, which was in its original form a simple morality tale, Job's friends are insistent that Job has brought his problems upon himself through some sort of wickedness. Eliphaz warns, "The eyes of the wicked will fail. . . . Who that was innocent ever perished? Or where were the upright cut off? As I have seen, those who plow iniquity and sow trouble reap the same. By the breath of God they perish" (Job 11:20, 4:7-9). And later, "Surely the light of the wicked is put out. . . . By disease their skin is consumed" (18:5, 13).

The book of Proverbs is chock full of pithy little sayings that warn of divine retribution for wickedness:

The fear of the Lord prolongs life, but the years of the wicked will be short. (Proverbs 10:27)

The righteous are delivered from trouble, and the wicked get into it instead. (Proverbs 11:8)

Whoever is steadfast in righteousness will live, but whoever pursues evil will die. (Proverbs 11:19)

Be assured, the wicked will not go unpunished, but those who are righteous will escape. (Proverbs 11:21)

At times Jesus seems to buy into this world view, connecting sin with disability, by forgiving the sins of the afflicted person before healing him or her. His first comment to the paralytic lowered through the roof in Mark 2 is, "Son, your sins are forgiven." Not so much as a "How are you today?" or "What seems to be your problem?" or "What's life with a disability like for you?" Challenged by the religious authorities in the crowd, he responds, "Which is easier, to say to the paralytic, 'Your sins are forgiven,' or to say, 'Stand up and take your mat and walk'? But so that you may know that the Son of Man has authority on earth to forgive sins"— he said to the paralytic—"I say to you, stand up, take your mat and go to your home." "Go and sin no more," are the familiar words by which Jesus often concludes the healing ritual, the implication being that sin has caused the impairment, repentance and forgiveness have cured it, and staying on the straight and narrow will keep one from further ailment. It was a common understanding of suffering in the ancient world.

Because of their implicit relationship with sin, people with disabilities or physical imperfections were kept segregated from community cultic activity. There was fear that their presence would defile the Holy. In the Holiness Code in the book of Leviticus strict guidelines are laid out. "No one who has a blemish shall draw near, one who is blind or lame, or one who has a mutilated face or a limb too long, or one who has a broken foot or a broken hand, or a hunchback, or a dwarf, or a man with a blemish in his eyes or an itching disease or scabs or crushed testicles" (Leviticus 21:18-20). Such flawed persons would pollute whatever they touched. If I had been a biblical literalist, I would have had serious adjustment problems in reentering parish ministry after my injury, seeing my permanent disability in light of these texts. I have at least three strikes against me. The accident left me lame, I'm blemished by skin grafts and scar tissue, and my testicles were crushed as I flew over my bike handlebars. It is fortunate I'm not a biblical literalist.

In the story of the Good Samaritan, contemporary readers are incensed at the behavior of the priest and the Levite, who pass by the wounded traveler without offering aid. But in the context of purity laws of the first century, their behavior makes sense; touching an injured, bleeding person would have defiled them and excluded them from important temple activities until they had been cleansed.

In several of the healing narratives in the New Testament, Jesus does move beyond the simplistic Hebrew identification of sin and sickness. But his alternative understanding of disability is hardly more helpful than the traditional understanding. In the ninth chapter of John's Gospel, Jesus's disciples bring a blind person to him for healing. They ask, from within the traditional school of thought, "Who sinned, this man or his parents, that he was born blind?" In this case Jesus rejects cultural assumptions about the causes of disability. "Neither this man nor his parents sinned; he was born blind so that God's works might be revealed in him" (John 9:2-3). Jesus's response reveals that he has moved beyond a traditional understanding of disability as the consequence of sin. This we celebrate. But the fact remains that blindness is still seen here as an opportunity by God to "fix" a human "flaw." What "works" does Jesus refer to? God's divine authority and intention to heal the sick, those who deviate from the norm, of course. The question "What about people who are blind and remain that way?" is never asked.

Jesus, in fact, is identified by his healing ministry. John the Baptist sends his disciples to Jesus to discern if he is "the one who is to come" or if they are to wait for another.

> Jesus answered them, "Go and tell John what you hear and see; the blind receive their sight, the lame walk, the lepers are cleansed, the deaf hear, the dead are raised, and the poor have good news brought to them. (Matthew 11:4-5)

In other words, we know Jesus is the Messiah because he leaves a trail of people healed of their afflictions in his wake. This brings us back to the question raised by Sam earlier: What of those who come to Jesus and remain sick or disabled? Jesus's most common healing technique involves the personal faith of the person afflicted. If it's not forgiveness of sin that has brought about the healing, it is the faith of the blind person, the hemorrhaging one, the leper, the lame one, or one who is ill. "Your faith has made you well; go in peace, and be healed of your disease" (Mark 5:34). Sam's lament is, "I've tried to live a good life, I've prayed for healing, my church has prayed for me, and still I'm not healed. What's wrong with me?" When the mechanism for overcoming illness or disability is seen to be the faith or repentance of the afflicted person, disability becomes a personal responsibility. If you are not miraculously healed, it must be your fault. You're still sinning, unrepentant, or your faith is insufficient.

In fact, the whole biblical understanding of healing as the appropriate course of action in the case of persons with disabilities is suspect for readers with a contemporary understanding of disability. The error may arise from the traditional tendency to lump disability with illness. Illnesses we do hope to recover from. But disability is another category entirely. The Bible makes no such distinction. The prevailing first century understanding of disability traces its roots to an ancient worldview. Jesus, at least as he is portrayed by his first-century biographers, is prevented by his cultural blinders from stepping outside the moral model of understanding disability.

Another problem in trying to use the healing narratives to illuminate the contemporary experience of disability is that the experience of the disabled person, in all its richness and ambiguity, is simply never the point of the biblical story. The stories are about Jesus, not the disability experience. Those of us living with disabilities can either continue praying for deliverance from our afflictions and wondering why our prayers are never answered, or we can change our perspective and get on with our lives. Choosing the latter, it would seem that we would have to look elsewhere than in the Bible for useful resources. Many people living with disabilities have made that move.

But wait. Before we entirely reject the Bible as a resource for understanding disability, we should note that the Bible offers other perspectives on suffering and disability. In the story of Job, for example, suffering seems to be accepted as a temporary test which, if passed successfully, will earn the afflicted a ticket to heaven. Job is counseled by well-meaning friends to submit to his suffering in silence, as a test from God. "God will not reject a blameless person, nor take the hand of evildoers. He will yet fill your mouth with laughter, and your lips with shouts of joy" (Job 8:20-21). The book of Lamentations advises patience in the face of adversity. "The Lord is good to those who wait for him, to the soul that seeks him. It is good that one should wait quietly for the salvation of the Lord. It is good for one to bear the yoke in youth, to sit alone in silence when the Lord has imposed it. . . . For the Lord will not reject forever. Although he causes grief, he will have compassion according to the abundance of his steadfast love" (Lamentations 3:25-28, 31-32). Isaiah prophesies the coming of a suffering servant who would bear our punishment for us, through whom we would be saved. "It was the will of the Lord to crush him with pain. When you make his life an offering for sin, he shall see his offspring, and shall prolong his days; through him the will of the Lord shall prosper" (Isa 53:10). In Jesus's story of the rich man and Lazarus (Luke 16:19-31), Lazarus submits to trials of poverty as a test by which he wins his reward in heaven. "I consider that the sufferings of this present time are not worth comparing with the glory about to be revealed to us," writes Paul in Romans 8:18.

Embracing suffering, adversity, and disability as a trial from God, sent our way to test our faith, or to strengthen us for greater things, or through which we earn our heavenly reward, has been a common reaction to hardship through the ages. These strategies find support in the pages of the Bible. But again, they are hardly helpful for those who hope to find wholeness and peace within their condition in the here and now. This facile interpretation has been manipulated to counsel passivity and acceptance in the face of social injustice. It has provided rationale for the ownership of slaves and the subjection of women through the ages. It has been applied to keep disabled persons in social and theological isolation from community. It has been used as a tool of oppression. It's also, I believe, a misreading of the value of our present earthly life.

Disability appears in another form in the pages of the Bible. If the disabled can't be cured, at least they should be given alms. Charity for the needy was an identifying feature of ancient Hebrew ethics. Hospitable treatment toward the marginalized was a hallmark of Israelite society. The weakest members of society, often identified as the widow (women who were widowed had no legal rights, no property, and no easy means of support), the orphan, and the sojourner, were always guaranteed the right to a living in Hebrew covenants. The prophetic witness consistently lifted up this expectation. Jesus made serving the poor and oppressed a central tenet in his ministry. In fact, as you feed and clothe "the least of these," you do so to Christ himself (Matthew 25). Charity toward those "less fortunate" is not optional in Judeo-Christian ethics. It is a requirement.

Public and private charity in the United States, based on biblical principles, has funded a great deal of social good in terms of medical care, scientific research, public assistance, housing, employment, and education. But charity by itself can never lead to full inclusion in the community. Charity is not justice. The prophet Micah clearly saw the distinction, asking "What does the Lord require of you but to do justice, and to love kindness, and to walk humbly with your God?" (6:8) Direct service always has a role in Christian ministry. But social policy must also be addressed. As long as persons with disabilities are seen only as unfortunate individuals in need of pity, charity, and social services, they will be separated and objectified, not included as full participants in God's realm—objects of a telethon perhaps, but not full participants.

So where's the good news in the Bible for people with disabilities? Is there any? Are people with disabilities only seen as objects of pity, charity, or scorn? Are they acceptable in God's realm only after they have been "normalized," only after their bodies have been fixed? Or is there any place where the blind, the lame, the disfigured, the mentally ill are loved and received just as they are? Where can Sam go for words of comfort? Clearly, we need new symbols.

In our quest to reinterpret what we find in the Bible concerning disability, we must understand first of all that the Bible was written by specific historic individuals in a particular context, each of whom was writing from a specific worldview. Unfortunately, the worldview reflected in the Bible is more than 2,000 years old and in need of critique. In assessing the Bible's understanding of disability (as well as its understanding of science, medicine, astronomy, geology, homosexuality, geography, and other fields), the reader must understand that we are dealing with an ancient understanding of the natural world. We need to get at the theology behind that worldview, without getting distracted by prevailing cultural paradigms, if we are going to benefit from what the Bible might have to offer.

We also need to be more careful than we have in the past in choosing biblical narratives to illuminate the meaning of disability. In the post-Enlightenment civil rights model of disability that I'll be exploring more fully in the next couple of chapters, according to which inclusion has replaced healing as the indicated treatment and desired outcome, biblical healing narratives become irrelevant. They may be useful as inspirational words of hope, but they are not helpful for those of us who choose to see our disabilities as an integral aspect of our identity.

The Bible gives ample grounds for accepting disability as a natural feature of the human condition. During the six days of creation, when God made the earth and all that inhabits it, nothing was pronounced "perfect." At the end of every day, God said, "It is good." Not perfect. If it was good enough for God, it should be good enough for us. Shot through human existence are weakness, pride, self-centeredness, vulnerability, frailty, even mortality. Short of God, there is no perfection.

Theologian Walter Wink goes as far as to assert that our modern pre-occupation with perfection or normalcy is oppressive. "The idea of normalcy . . . is not only at the root of the mistreatment of people with disabilities. It is a pathological notion that creates illness, persecution, and the rejection of our God-given uniqueness" (1993, 2). He points out that because each of us exhibits "imperfections," it is impossible to divide the world into disabled and nondisabled. Disability becomes an expression of diversity.

Jennie Weiss Block, in her book *Copious Hosting: A Theology of Access for People with Disabilities*, explains why the cult of perfection has such a powerful hold over people today. "We cling to the cultural norms of attractiveness, self-sufficiency, and productivity to avoid coming face to face with two of our great fears: we are not perfect and we are not in control. Disability brings the eschatological horizon into sharp focus" (37). Our drive for perfection, aside from being a sinful enterprise and ultimately doomed to failure, is too powerful for our own good. And our understanding of "normal" is too narrow.

Americans have strayed far from the truth of this insight. We are surrounded by models and media images that bombard us with the message that perfection is achievable. It is within our grasp if only we purchase this advertised product or undergo this recommended procedure. We buy medications to alleviate unpleasant feelings and beauty products to make us look younger. We become obsessed with exercise to slow the aging process and voluntarily submit to the surgeon's knife to remove unwanted fat or wrinkles. You can even take fat out of your butt and inject it into your lips if you are so inclined and have the money. Are we advanced or what? But each of us will ultimately fail in this endeavor and end up sadder, poorer, and more disillusioned. Some of us may get close to the ideal for a while, but you can't maintain it for long. Gravity will have the last word. That's the way God intended it. "We have this treasure in earthen vessels" (2 Corinthians 4:7). Thank God for lumpy, crippled, blind, deaf, short, and fat people to remind us of the diversity and contingency of creation.

Indeed, many New Testament narratives celebrate the raucous exuberance of God's diverse world.

Indeed, the body does not consist of one member but of many. If the foot would say, "Because I am not a hand, I do not belong to the body," that would not make it any less a part of the body. And if the ear would say, "Because I am not an eye, I do not belong to the body," that would not make it any less a part of the body. If the whole body were an eye, where would the hearing be? If the whole body were hearing, where would the sense of smell be? But as it is, God arranged the members in the body, each one of them, as he chose. If all were a single member, where would be the body be? As it is, there are many members, yet one body. The eye cannot say to the hand, "I have no need of you," nor again the head to the feet, "I have no need of you." On the contrary, the members of the body that seem to be weaker are indispensable, and those members of the body that we think less honorable we clothe with greater honor, and our less respectable members are treated with greater respect. . . . If one member suffers, all suffer together with it; if one member is honored, all rejoice together with it. (I Corinthians 12:14-24, 26)

Instead of scouring the healing narratives for good news for people with disabilities, let's explore the stories of God's radical hospitality. In discussing biblical hospitality, Jesus gives detailed instructions about the invitation list. "When you give a luncheon or dinner, do not invite your friends or your brothers or your relatives or rich neighbors, in case they may invite you in return and you would be repaid. But when you give a banquet, invite the poor, the crippled, the lame, and the blind. And you will be blessed, because they cannot repay you, for you will be repaid at the resurrection of the righteous" (Luke 14:12-14). Finally the disabled are valuable in their own right! Jesus is singling out here precisely those who were excluded by the Leviticus Holiness Code. He's inviting them as special guests at God's banquet. It turns out the Kingdom of God is ADA compliant!

This radical hospitality, and not his works of healing, are Jesus's unique contribution to first-century theology. There were plenty of faith healers around, plying their trade. The hallmark of Jesus's ministry was breaking down the barriers that separated and oppressed people, making insiders of those who had previously been excluded. He was not worried about being contaminated by having direct contact with women, Samaritans, sinners, cripples, tax collectors, demons, or even the dead. He extended the realm of God's hospitality outside the customary boundaries, inviting the last in line to enter first.

Often God chooses flawed people as instruments to accomplish the divine will. Moses had a speech impediment. "O my Lord," he protested when called from his sheep at the burning bush, "I have never been eloquent, neither in the past nor even now that you have spoken to your servant; but I am slow of speech and slow of tongue" (Exodus 4:11). Jeremiah complained that he was just a boy when he was recruited as a prophet (of course, he would grow out of that). Isaiah's lips weren't clean. Jacob was a pathological liar. All these people were unexpected, flawed human beings. But they were chosen to carry out God's will. Like Shallow Hal in the recent popular movie, God's vision extends beyond the outer skin. When the prophet Samuel, for example, is searching for Saul's successor to anoint as king, he examines each of Jesse's sons in turn, finding some handsome, viable candidates for the royal position. But God warns him to look beneath the surface. "The Lord said to Samuel, 'Do not look on his appearance or on the height of his stature, because I have rejected him; for the Lord does not see as mortals see; they look on the outward appearance, but the Lord looks on the heart'" (1 Samuel 16:7).

Paul himself, a powerful instrument for the spreading of the Gospel, was apparently not a perfect human specimen. "Friends, I beg you," Paul wrote to the Galatians, "become as I am, for I also have become as you are. You know that it was because of a physical infirmity that I first announced the gospel to you; though my condition put you to the test, you did not scorn or despise me, but welcomed me as an angel of God, as Christ Jesus" (Galatians 4:12-14). In fact, Paul, in an apparent reversal of the Leviticus tradition, finds his power to witness in his very weakness. "[Jesus] said to me, 'My grace is sufficient for you, for power is made perfect in weakness.' So, I will boast all the more gladly of my weaknesses, so that the power of Christ may dwell in me. Therefore I am content with weaknesses, insults, hardships, persecutions, and calamities for the sake of Christ; for whenever I am weak, then I am strong" (2 Corinthians 12:9-10).

Even within Jesus's healing narratives, with some careful interpretation, we can catch a glimmer of hope. There is sometimes a dimension to healing that moves beyond simple medical cure to point toward wholeness for persons with impairments. In most of the stories, the happy ending is not just a restored physical state for the individual in question, but a restoration to family and community. Healing as Jesus practices it involves more than a medical miracle. It sets society straight. The moral of the story of the paralytic lowered through the roof has as much to do with the inhospitality of the crowd around Jesus and with the supportive (if somewhat overzealous and destructive) circle of friends, as it does with the paralytic's supposed sins, forgiveness, and subsequent restoration of mobility. Jesus scholar John Dominic Crossan writes about Jesus's healing of a person with leprosy in Mark 1:40-44.

> I presume that Jesus . . . healed the poor man's illness by refusing to accept the disease's ritual uncleanness and social ostracization. Jesus thereby forced others either to reject him from their community or to accept the leper within it as well. . . . By healing the illness without curing the disease, Jesus acted as an alternative boundary keeper in a way subversive to the established procedures of his society. Such an interpretation may seem to destroy the miracle. But miracles are not changes in the physical world so much as changes in the social world. (1994, 82)

When Jesus cures ten lepers, their first appearance is in the temple, from which they had been exiled since the onset of their disease, for ritual cleansing. Restoration to full community life and breaching the boundaries set up by society is part of the structure of healing for Jesus.

In fact, let's just cut to the chase. Who is it we worship in this Christian faith? We worship a God who became imperfect in a human body in order to show perfect compassion. God is one who suffers with us, the first one to shed a tear in the event of human tragedy. As part of this divine, compassionate project, this God who created a world good (but not perfect) became part of this world himself. "The Word became flesh and dwelt among us." God became human in a particular person, a person who, like the rest of us, walked around in flesh and blood with wrinkled, chapped skin and fragile bones, in a body that was not a perfect instrument. Jesus's power to save is derived from his very brokenness. "Look at my hands and my feet; see that it is I myself," he told his disciples after he was resurrected. That resurrected body was not free from blemish. Those hands and feet had been pierced by spikes as Jesus hung on the cross. "Touch me and see; for a ghost does not have flesh and bones as you see that I have" (Luke 24:39).

The most powerful symbol we have by which to remember Jesus is the sacrament of communion. The words with which he instituted this sacrament were, "This is my body, broken for you." Early Christian writers saw Jesus as a fulfillment of Isaiah's prophecy:

> He had no form or majesty that we should look at him, nothing in his appearance that we should desire him. He was despised and rejected by others; a man of suffering and acquainted with infirmity; and as one from whom others hide their faces he was despised, and we held him of no account. Surely he has borne our infirmities and carried our diseases; . . . and by his bruises we are healed. (Isaiah 53:2-5)

As we sit at the communion table, sharing the sacred moment in which Christ becomes body and the body is broken, we become one in the Spirit of God. At the very heart of our Christian faith, at the most sacramental moment, the diversity of the body is upheld and all people—crippled, blind, poor, or "normal"—are saved. We find salvation as we are, in whatever condition or ability, unconditionally. When Hildegard Ledbetter held my bleeding head in her hands at the side of the road and thought of the sacrament of communion, this is what she had in mind.

Nancy Eiesland, professor of ethics and society at Emory University, has given us a useful new symbol. She coined a term for God that helps open up possibilities for a theology that liberates rather then oppresses persons with disabilities. She understands God as disabled. "In presenting his impaired hands and feet to his startled friends, the resurrected Jesus is revealed as the disabled God. . . . God is in the present social-symbolic order at the margins with people with disabilities and instigates transformation from this de-centered position" (1994, 100). The upshot of this new way of conceptualizing God is that "full personhood is fully compatible with the experience of disability."

That's the answer we've been looking for! A major shift has taken place here as new symbols and theological insights relating to the issue of disability are discovered. Where once disability was seen as a problem of sin or healing or charity or virtuous suffering for the individual, now it takes on social dimensions. The issue becomes one of inclusivity. We become not only interested in exploring the process by which the paralytic was healed by Jesus, but the social dimension of why it was so difficult for the man to gain an audience with Jesus that his advocacy group had to lower him through a hole they cut in the roof. Two thousand years before the ADA, Jesus parted the crowd to accommodate a cripple. Once disability is seen not just as an individual's affliction, but as a condition defining a minority community, like race or gender or economic class, then theologies of liberation can be brought into play to help with the interpretation.

Liberation theology, a phenomenon of the last half-century, has arisen as different social, racial, and ethnic groups have taken to reading scripture from their own personal contexts. This enterprise is legitimated by the fact that our faith is a historical religion, based on people and events that took place in a particular historical context. God worked God's purposes out in history, revealing Godself in flesh and blood as a real person, located in a particular time and place. Over the centuries, biblical interpretation has tended to be the private enterprise of a very narrow class of scholars, generally wealthy white male Europeans, who have consistently produced a fairly narrow theological framework. It has, not surprisingly, tended by implication to support the status quo. People in power tend to compose ideologies designed to keep them there.

All of a sudden, groups who felt themselves on the margins of society, such as women, the poor, Latin Americans, Asians, Africans, African Americans, and Native Americans, began reading the Bible from the vantage point of their own experience. And they found some radically new themes in the texts. Just as persons with disabilities can discover value and meaning in life as they adjust to their new condition and culture, a member of an oppressed class reading the Bible from his or her perspective may discover themes of liberation and hope that are only available to their eyes. One thing that became clear in their reading is that, as mentioned earlier, God has consistently chosen outsiders—powerless, unexpected characters—through whom to act. Look no further than Joseph, Jacob, Moses, David, Jeremiah, Mary, Paul, and Jesus himself for examples. Not one of these figures would have been the expected candidate to have been chosen to carry God's message. Maybe these contemporary groups with "outsider" status actually have an advantage over the more established, centrist groups, in biblical interpretation.

When my family and I lived in Nicaragua we were recipients of a great blessing. We got there just in time to experience the tail end of the contextual theologizing that had grown out of the Nicaraguan revolution of the 1970s and 1980s. In fact, the biblical explorations of base Christian communities had helped fuel the revolution and eventual overthrow of the dictatorship of Anastacio Somoza in 1979. As simple peasant people read the Bible, they conveniently glossed over the historical gulf between Jesus's time and their own, and read themselves into the narrative. The project worked because it was such a good fit. Jesus was a simple working-class kind of guy. So were they. Jesus spoke in parables about peasants and farmers and fishermen. They saw themselves in the stories. Jesus became one of them and made salvation and liberation something attainable at last.

The art and music of the revolutionary period illustrated this. A unique style of primitive painting emerged at this time. Many of the scenes that appeared on canvas depicted stories from the Bible. But they would place Jesus in contemporary settings in the Nicaraguan countryside, surrounded by peasants in traditional clothing. Actually, that's what the Europeans had been doing since the Middle Ages, so there was nothing new here. A famous painting of the Palm Sunday procession into Jerusalem depicts Jesus surrounded by supporters waving signs that read, "Down with Somoza." You and I know that no one at the time of Jesus's arrival in Jerusalem had any foreknowledge of a twentieth-century Nicaraguan dictator, so, historically speaking, the painting's accuracy must be questioned. But the painter wasn't trying to recreate a historically accurate scene. He was depicting in a stunning way a metaphorical truth about the presence of Jesus in a contemporary struggle for liberation. A painting of Jesus's betrayal shows Somoza's despised national guard leading Jesus away. Other paintings place historical revolutionary figures such as Che Guevara and Agusto Ceasar Sandino (a Nicaraguan freedom fighter) among Jesus's disciples.

Local musicians developed a whole opus of contemporary music for Catholic Mass. One of our favorites was "God Is God of the Poor," in which Jesus is portrayed in intimate terms as a common day laborer. He's one of us, and he lives today just as surely as he did twenty centuries ago.

He is "the laborer God" and "the worker Christ" who walks hand in hand with the poor.

What surfaces from the work of contemporary liberation theologians is the possibility that God may have a preferential option for the poor and oppressed. Just look at how many of them play key roles in Scripture, and at how Jesus continually assaulted the barriers that kept them excluded from power and fulfillment. Themes of justice, liberation, inclusion, and peace jump off the pages when you begin to interpret Scripture from the context of the disenfranchised. This has made a real contribution to biblical research.

In the final analysis, when you read between the lines, moving beyond simple rationalizations of a primitive people trying to account for suffering and disease in their world, you find the central nugget of truth in the Bible, a truth that can set persons with disabilities free from oppressive, disabling theologies. The great insight of the Bible is that all human beings are flawed and in need of redemption through a power greater than themselves. We are saved not by our own abilities but by God's grace. In fact, reliance on human ability is the greatest stumbling block and the greatest sin a person can encounter. There's more material in the Bible condemning pride than there is condemning greed, lust, heresy, sexual impropriety, and all the other sins combined.

In this, people with disabilities may actually have an advantage. People with disabilities know they are dependent. They experience it daily in mobility, access, visibility, communication. We need technological assistance to get around, to walk, or to roll. We need devices to communicate, new languages, or understanding family members. We may need audio technology in order to read or assistance in overcoming obstacles. We need ramps and wide doors. We have to ask our children to reach our cereal bowls from the cupboard. In accepting this vulnerability we may be light years ahead of a general population obsessed with independence, flawlessness, and perfection.

One declaration of the World Council of Churches states, "Churches without persons with disabilities are disabled churches." It can make that surprising claim because in God's sight there is no such thing as a reduced or disabled human being; to the degree that we overlook that truth (perhaps because there are no disabled persons in our immediate field of vision and we consequently continue to apply society's stereotypes defining the disabled?) we miss God's vision for the church and the world. Wink writes, "Not only are [people with disabilities] to be included in the festal celebrations, but they are to be given preferential attention. The last shall be first. But this means also that the very basis of human fellowship before God has been altered. Only when the previously excluded are in gathered can the feast commence. Only when the pernicious ideal of normalcy is destroyed can normal life begin" (1993, 4).

According to God's vision, the church is not a private club for the "perfect" specimens among us, for the actors and models and athletes with washboard abs and perfect teeth and great hair. It's a veritable freak show with reserved seating for misfits and outcasts, gimps and cripples and blind and deaf, widows, orphans, and sojourners, gay and straight, rich and poor, fat and short and ugly and old, and any other marginalized group you might identify. It's a celebration of human diversity. In the sacrament of baptism, the rite of passage by which members are brought into the community of the church, candidates are not asked if they can walk up the front stairs into the church, or if they can read the bulletins, or hear the words of the sermon. They are asked only if they desire to serve God.

The next time you need a lesson on dependency, vulnerability, diversity, community, or hospitality, ask a cripple. At the very least we make a great visual aid.

The Disney animated movie *Lilo and Stitch* premiered in Honolulu when we were there on sabbatical. It caused quite a stir. Set in Hawaii, it's the story of a destructive little alien named Stitch who finds a home with a dysfunctional Hawaiian family consisting of just Lilo and her older sister, Nani. The movie gets the Hawaiian concept of *ohana*, or family, right. At movie's end, Stitch sums it up: "This is my family. I found it all on my own. It's small. And broken. But still good. Yeah. Still good." Churches can/should take a lesson from this movie.

New symbols *can* be found to give people with disabilities a sense that they belong. For people like Sam, who have been disillusioned by oppressive theologies, there is new hope. Unfortunately, the church has not yet consistently applied these new symbols as they relate to the disabled. In many places the local church is the last building in town to be made accessible to persons with disabilities. Government buildings have ramps and other accommodations. Stores offer assistance and increasingly boast accessible restrooms. I can even get in the bars. Increasingly, urban transit systems work for persons with disabilities. But often the church entrance sits on top of an impressive stack of stairs. If I can get inside, I find that the bathroom doors are too narrow for me to use. Many times the sanctuary has no cutout for wheelchairs. "You can sit in the back if you like," offers an usher, "or sit in the center aisle." They'll assure you that they have made accommodations, but the rickety chair lift at the front steps doesn't work for someone who needs his wheelchair to arrive at the top of the stairs with him in it. Once, at a regional church meeting, I had to drain my leg bag into a bottle in the church nursery; it was the only room I could access. When bars and theaters provide better hospitality than churches, something is wrong.

Churches distinguished themselves in 1990 by successfully lobbying exemption from the Americans with Disabilities Act. It seems that compliance would have been too expensive for them. In truth, many church buildings are historic, built long before people were concerned about the independence of disabled people. And have you priced an elevator lately? They cost more than the entire annual budget of many churches. But what institution should be more fervent in its hospitality than the church? Churches should have been leading the charge in adopting the ADA. They certainly would have if they had been motivated by faith rather than finances.

The United Church of Christ, to its credit, has an active committee at the national level currently known as Disabilities Ministries. Committee members seek to have a voice on each of the national expressions of the church, keeping them aware of disability issues. Commendable. But there is yet more work to be done. One issue that long concerned committee members was the structural "location" of the committee, and what that revealed about the church's understanding of disability. Before a recent reorganization, the United Church of Christ housed disabilities with Health and Human Services ministries. It is now housed with ministries that deal with racial and ethnic minorities. The implication of this change is significant. The earlier structure saw disability as a medical issue. Now people with disabilities are seen as part of a social, cultural, political, or economic minority.

The church should be the one institution among all other human institutions where those who are traditionally confined to the periphery of society can find a voice, and, as it were, room at the table. After all, that was Jesus's project. He dedicated himself to the demolition of social barriers that excluded, among others, the poor, the ritually unclean, the ill, the outcast, Gentiles, and women. After some initial disappointments in biblical exploration that yielded evidence of a primitive and damaging worldview, a wealth of useful, empowering symbols can be discovered. The church has not always been very imaginative or energetic in applying these new insights when it comes to dealing with persons with varieties of impairments and disabilities. In this, to its shame, it is not much distinguishable from society at large. But the church has a higher calling, a responsibility to learn about—and from—people in and beyond its walls who are finding meaning, purpose, and wholeness in bodies that are less than perfect.

Walter Wink concludes that such people may have an essential role to play in the Realm of God.

Those who are more obviously disabled or who have been forced by life to come to terms with their disabilities have a prophetic task to play in awakening the rest of us to the uniqueness of who we are under God. This gift must be given unapologetically and even aggressively. It is not in order to render sympathy to you whose disabilities are more extreme than ours, but to discover our own most divine possibilities, that we turn to you for guidance, leadership, and wisdom. Perhaps this is the preeminent gift you have to give to God, and to the world. (1993, 6)

If disability is the gift that, in the words of Michael J. Fox, "just keeps on taking," it's also the gift that keeps on giving, as the stories of people with disabilities help transform the lives of all of us. Grace abounds.

Chapter 8

Disabled by Definition

The invitation, per se, was not particularly remarkable in any way. It was clear in its intent and straightforward in content. "Come talk to my class about the meaning of disability." A high school teacher wanted me to visit her life-skills class and talk about my experiences so that the students might have an appreciation for the varieties of challenges faced by people with disabilities. I get these invitations from time to time. People want to hear about my injuries, how they limit me, and how I have "overcome" those limitations.

What was interesting about this invitation was its timing. I had to postpone my lecture to the class about adjusting to a disability because I was going to be away, competing in the San Diego Marathon. Do you see the irony here?

It causes one to wonder, just what *is* the meaning of disability? How is it to be defined? What constitutes a disability? What are the criteria you might use to decide? Who is authorized to make that decision? If some people can be said to have disabilities, does it follow that everyone else is nondisabled? These questions are as important as they are perplexing. Each one leads not to a closure on the line of inquiry, but opens the door to more and more confusion. At the end of the day we may be further from an understanding than we were at the start. Don't get your hopes up if you're looking for a quick answer.

I told the high school life-skills students that the word disability itself would seem to have something to do with abilities or the lack thereof—with being able to do something or not. So I asked them who among the class ever had, or ever thought they might or could, run a marathon. When no hands went up, I informed them of my recent third place finish at the San Diego Marathon (I didn't go on to explain that there had only been three wheelchairs in my division. No sense in giving more information than necessary). So on the scale of abilities involved in running a marathon, who is able and who is disabled?

Think about other abilities or impairments. Who can dunk a basketball? Who has ever shot a hole in one? Who can swim a mile? Who can stand up in front of the student body and give a speech? Who's earning straight A's? Compared with Michael Jordan and Tiger Woods and the other gifted individuals who can do these things well, the rest of us are impaired, disabled, if you will.

My point with the class was that everything that humans do requires a specific set of skills and abilities. Some of us have those skills, some of us don't. Some of us have them in spades in one area of endeavor but not in other areas. Where I've always had a disability when it comes to dunking a basketball, I suspect that Michael Jordan could be considered disabled in the field of preaching.

Even those outstanding individuals who set records in their particular field face limits in that very area of expertise. What's the world record high jump? More than seven feet? Beyond that you bump up against the limits of human performance. In every field there are human limitations. The fastest mile run by a human is currently around three minutes and fifty seconds. Until recently, it was believed that a four-minute mile would be the absolute limit of human speed. Better conditioning, training, and nutrition keep lowering that "absolute." It may be impossible to predict how low the times will go, and how fast the human body can run. But no one doubts that there are such limits. I predict, for example, that there will never be a two-minute mile. There are absolute limits to human performance in every discipline. The fact that we can't predict where those limits will lie doesn't change the fact that there are limits. Limitation is part and parcel of the human condition. Get used to it. Does that limitation imply a disability?

Furthermore, those athletes who are currently setting the records will one day slow down or lose their competitive edge. It's called aging. Gymnasts peak at age sixteen. I got really excited when, at the 1984

Olympic marathon, a relatively obscure thirty-seven-year-old Portuguese runner named Carlos Lopes set a new world record. Imagine that! Thirty-seven years old and still setting world records! At that point, I was not yet thirty-seven. Hearing of Lopes's achievement gave me hope that I, too, still had time to set a world record. But alas, it was not to be. I passed thirty-seven without ever having set a world record. Very few people my current age set records in anything.

But consider this: human performance alone is not the exclusive determining factor as we weigh what people can accomplish. We consistently incorporate the use of adaptive technology in areas where we find ourselves deficient. Gymnasts wear a specially designed glove that helps them grasp a parallel bar. As a result, they can perform routines that are much more demanding than their barehanded predecessors could perform. We use calculators to figure sums. Have you ever seen a grocery store cashier try to figure change when the cash register is down? How many of us wear glasses? In primitive times, diminishing eyesight would have been a matter of life or death. If you couldn't see game, you couldn't hunt. You couldn't avoid larger creatures who were hunting you. Without 20/20 vision you wouldn't last long. We wear shoes to cushion our stride when we walk and because our feet are too delicate for pavement. When their teeth wore out, our ancestors used to starve to death, but we seek out dentists to build us crowns, caps, and dentures. Hearing aids help us function socially when our hearing declines. Some people use canes or walkers or wheelchairs when, for whatever reason, walking becomes too difficult.

One of the things that separates us from the animal kingdom is our use of specialized tools that help us overcome physical deficiencies. We use knives or scissors to cut tough things that we can't tear by hand. The wheel was invented to help us carry heavy things and travel great distances that would have been impossible otherwise. We've got the wing and the jet engine. We wear clothes and build houses to shelter us from harsh environments where our pitiful covering of body hair is inadequate. Every single one of us uses technology all the time to overcome weaknesses and deficiencies and limitations of the body. You could say that my wheelchair, the assistive technology I came home from the hospital with, rather than being a sign of stigma or limitation, is precisely a defining feature of what it means to be human. I am a user of tools. Hear me roar!

So why does the use of one particular assistive device, say, a wheelchair, qualify one for a handicap-parking tag, when another, say, a pair of glasses or a down parka, doesn't? It's hard to pin down the notion of disability.

Let's try another line of inquiry. Attitude has a significant impact on what it means to be disabled. Yet another invitation from the Grinnell school district put me in front of a whole building full of middle school students on "Accentuate the Positive Day." I started out by asking the students who was having a bad day. Half the kids raised their hands. Then we brainstormed about what causes a bad day. Answers ranged from a broken pencil to a broken relationship, from the death of a parent to a bad hairdo. There were as many causes of bad days as there were students. But what breaks down one person may not even faze someone else. For some people, a paper cut may be the last straw. For others, a broken leg is taken in stride, so to speak. What's the difference? Attitude. *You* decide what brings you down. *You* determine whether you're having a good day or not. It's a matter of choice. So, to a certain extent, the definition of disability depends on your attitude. Do you choose to be limited by your biological condition, or do you choose to take it in stride and go about your day?

Unfortunately, damaging misperceptions about attitude and disability are commonplace. The most insidious of these is that disability will respond to will. If you have the proper attitude, you can overcome it! That unrealistic expectation was Sam's problem in the previous chapter—that faith can make you well. "If anybody can beat this thing, Bob, you can. I've seen your perseverance. You'll be walking again. No, you'll be running. I know it."

Ask David Hasselhof. Now, I don't normally watch *Baywatch*, I swear, but one day I when I was high on pain medication I was channel-surfing and I caught part of an episode in which the lead character, played by Hasselhof, was injured and in a hospital. I don't know what had happened to him, but he seemed paralyzed below the waist. His doctors and friends were convinced that, if he put his mind to it, he could move his legs again. When he was unable to do so, they shook their heads and walked sadly out of his room, as though he had let them down. What it took for him to rouse himself from his paraplegia was some bad guy threatening his friend. He had to get out of his wheelchair and fight back. What an inspiring story!

Not!

No, where attitude enters the picture in a healthy way is not whether you can somehow reverse your disability, but how you adjust to your disability. Are you going to let it define you, or are you going to embrace it as just another feature of your personality? And how about those around you? Do they see the disability as the thing, or can they accept it as just one piece of the constellation of features that make you who you are? Charlton writes:

> Having a disability is essentially neither a good thing nor a bad thing. It just is. This intrinsic "neutrality" of disability is the primary aspect of all

the contradictions bound up in the condition of disability. . . . By mini-
mizing, patronizing (hero worship), and often eradicating the essential
neutrality of disability, the dominant culture trivializes the intrinsic complexity of disability. . . . In the real world, some people with disabilities
have a generally good life and others a generally bad life. . . . Some of the
people with disabilities living a good life do so in spite of their disabilities;
others may be living a good life because of their disabilities. (1998, 167)

Mary Thompson chooses to see her disability as an asset. Her motto
is, "I had to break my neck to see the world." As an elite world-class racer,
she has competed in more than one hundred marathons. Number 101
was the one in which I also raced in San Diego. At one time she held the
quad women's record at the Boston Marathon. She has been all around
the world competing, her trips and equipment paid for in part by sponsors. If she had not been injured as a teenager these opportunities would
not have been open to her. Chances are, her horizons would have
remained much more parochial.

Allow me to elaborate on the issue of the relative advantage or disadvantage of having a certifiable disability through what I pray you'll find a
fascinating, and hopefully not entirely irrelevant, digression. Digression is
the spice of life. Trust me, we'll find our train of thought again.

In the summer of 1999, just two years after my injury, Ann and I took
our youth group and a few interested, adventurous adults from our
church on a work and mission trip to the Yucatán Peninsula of Mexico.
Such trips are the hallmark of our youth ministry. We believe they show
North American kids who, let's face it, tend to be rather self-absorbed and
materialistic, a whole new reality. Their eyes are opened to the world
beyond the local high school and mall, and they get an opportunity to
participate in productive work that benefits others. Having a big exotic
adventure to prepare for also gives the youth group cohesion and
momentum for the entire school year preceding the event.

We had already taken this same group of kids to Atlanta, Georgia, to
work for the Salvation Army, and to Saint Louis, Missouri, to volunteer
with the United Church of Christ Neighborhood Houses, working for a
day camp for inner city kids. A similar trip to Chicago had been scheduled
for the week of my injury, but that was another casualty of the accident.
The youth group and leaders spent the week working on a Habitat for
Humanity house in Grinnell. At least that's what they told me.

We had long been hoping to take this seasoned group of young people on a trip outside the United States. But could I, newly disabled, still do
something like this? After all, it takes boundless energy to keep a youth
group running smoothly when you're out beyond the kids' comfort zones.

Hard physical labor and the stress of group dynamics make for a long week under any circumstances. Add to that the cross-cultural stress and the unknowns surrounding my physical condition and accommodation needs, and you have a recipe for a potential disaster. Would I be able to get around in a foreign country? Could I find accessible accommodations? Would taking care of myself preclude helping take care of the group? What about a medical crisis?

Notwithstanding all these concerns, a project too good to refuse fell into our laps. We signed up with Intercambio Cultural de Yucatan. We were going to Mexico. *Ole!* Intercambio "exchange" is a program run by the campus ministries of the University of Illinois at Urbana-Champaign and the University of Indiana. It takes a group of between thirty and fifty youth and adults to the Yucatán each summer for building projects with Presbyterian churches, medical clinics, or orphanages. This year's project would involve roofing a new wing on a small church in a working class neighborhood in . . . Cancún.

Now, I know what you're thinking. A project in Cancún will be a glorified spring break. Party time! But let me set the record straight. Cancún does have a strip of glorious white beaches, hotels, nightclubs, and tourist shops. And, I'll confess, we did avail ourselves of their temptations from time to time. But we were there to serve with hard-working Mexican families who find themselves economically exploited by the tourism industry. Seasonal layoffs by the hotels devastate poverty-stricken families who flock to the area in search of work. We were there to support the churches that minister to such needs.

The Intercambio program was enticing because their people handle all the arrangements and had a track record of a dozen years of successful leadership of these trips. All we had to do was pay our way and pack our bags. The six years Ann and I had spent in Central America previously put us at perfect ease about the culture. My only concern was going back into primitive conditions with a disability. After all, the reach of the ADA doesn't extend south of the border.

With great fanfare and more than a little trepidation, we set out for our Mexican adventure. The logistical support provided by Intercambio was impeccable. Jack Diel, the fearless leader (who promises that one of these years he would definitely bite the bullet and actually try to learn Spanish) handled all the arrangements and shouldered any emergencies. I could sleep at night. We had communicated to him all my special needs and Jack's local contact, an experienced group leader and Presbyterian minister, Ramon Celis, found me a modest, air-conditioned motel room just a block from the church where the kids were sleeping in hammocks strung up in Sunday school classrooms. Ramon had prepped the hotel management, and they had already removed bathroom doors that were too narrow for my chair and had found a lawn chair for use in my shower.

The roofing project was excruciatingly difficult. It involved, first, placing massive concrete beams over the cement block walls of the three rooms we were to roof, then passing specially-made concrete blocks one at a time to volunteers on the roof who placed them between the beams, then mixing and passing cement, bucket by bucket, up to the roof. This thinned-down cement mixture is poured on top of the blocks, forming a solid—and very heavy—cap. Temperatures soared near one hundred degrees every afternoon.

Clearly, my contribution would be limited. I tried pulling myself up a ladder at the work site, but found there was little I could do once on the roof. I nailed some boards together for cement forms. But I didn't want to spend my days back at the church washing dishes. So finally we hit on one task that I could do. I was the guy who sat at ground level to catch the five-gallon buckets as the kids emptied them and tossed them over the edge of the roof. It became a great game for them. They called it "Nail the Pastor with a Bucket." After the first day at this job I spent two hours on my lawn chair in the shower scrubbing dried cement off my wheelchair. There are still chunks on the chair in hard-to-reach places.

I was also in great demand as a piece of recreational equipment. In a game called "Bowling with Bob," which we invented on this trip, the kids would set up ten of those five-gallon plastic bottled water jugs like bowling pins on the floor. I was the ball. The kids would roll me at the "pins" from the other side of the room.

During several of the days when the students were working, I led a workshop for local Presbyterian pastors on church-based community development. Concluding my work in Nicaragua five years previously, I had developed and written a Spanish language manual for church leaders introducing a biblically based process of community development. They had never seen anything like it. In the five years since we left Nicaragua, my manual had gone through two additional reprints and had been translated into Portuguese and Haitian Creole. The Mennonite Central Committee graciously gave me all the copies they had left to share with the Mexican Presbyterians.

I was also invited to preach in town one Sunday while the rest of the group went out to a rural village for an overnight stay. No one thought the village stay would be a good idea in a wheelchair. I didn't want some monkey to roll off in my expensive chair during the night.

The upshot of all this is that my initial fears evaporated; they had been absolutely groundless. With a little foresight and preplanning, my experience in Mexico was more than manageable—it was fun, comfortable, and productive. Even the flat tire I incurred one night dining at a fancy restaurant was no deterrent. I simply cleared the table, flopped my wheel on it and patched the tube, replaced the tire and pumped it up with the little bike pump I carry, and I was on the road again before you could say *"Otra cerveza, por favor"* (another beer, please). The hotel zone, crowded with sunburned tourists, upscale hotels, and souvenir shops, was actually more of a challenge for wheelchair users than the working-class neighborhood where we were based. Out there curbs, stairs, and crowds were everywhere, and no one would give you the time of day, let alone offer to assist a cripple in a wheelchair.

In fact, in Cancún, my mobility impairment was less handicapping than the language barrier was for the rest of our group. This is an essential point. Let me put it another way. My being in a wheelchair was not as serious a handicap in Cancún as was the disability of our youth in not being able to speak the language.

One of our adult leaders, a well-adjusted, resourceful high school social studies teacher named Bob, got sick and had to be hospitalized for a day during the trip. We put him in the Baptist Hospital. The hospital was a cut above anything else available in Cancún, but it was a far cry from a U.S. hospital. The patients' rooms were bereft of electronics, including call buttons and televisions. The beds were bare cots. No one in attendance spoke English. Bob was clearly out of his element. It didn't help that once, when he dropped his bedpan on the hard cement floor, making a terrible din, no one came to investigate. In addition to feeling ill, Bob was suffering from culture shock. He was very grateful when I could pop in during the day to keep him company.

Disability took on a whole new meaning in that context. My gifts in one area more than made up for my deficiencies in another. Who was disabled in Mexico? Not me. I was fully functional. It was my church members, unable to communicate, who found themselves handicapped. So I ask you again, just how do you define disability?

The ADA defines disability as "a physical or mental impairment that substantially limits one or more of the major life activities of such individual." This definition would seem to imply, and common perceptions agree, that disability refers to something concrete and physical, some condition, medical or biological in origin, that limits a person in an abnormal way.

Under this definition, in 1990 about 43 million people in the United States were considered disabled. Current estimates place that number as high as 54 million, which makes people with disabilities the largest minority group in the country. However, there is no agreement as to what conditions should be included in such a tally. Some analysts count those with AIDS or who are HIV positive. Most definitions do not include people who suffer from arthritis, a potentially crippling condition. What level of severity gets you a ticket to this exclusive club? A rough estimate is that one in five have some sort of disability. Disability is the one minority group that anyone can join. It's an equal-opportunity recruiter. Economic class or status count for nothing. Most people don't come knocking by choice, but most people will eventually join at some point in their lives. The boundaries are quite porous. Some people apply for membership and then turn around and withdraw, some several times.

According to the book *Disability and Culture* edited by Benedicte Ingstad and Susan Reynolds Whyte:

> A preliminary common-sense definition of disability might be that it is a lack or limitation of competence. We usually think of disability in contrast to an ideal of normal capacity to perform particular activities and to play one's role in social life. . . . Disability is used to refer to limitations resulting from dysfunction in individual bodies and minds. . . . [T]he core meaning for most of us is a biopyschological one. Blindness, lameness, mental deficiency, and chronic incapacitating illnesses—these are prototypical disabilities. (Ingstad and Whyte 1995, 3)

But Ingstad and Whyte also recognize the cultural implications of disability. Their definition continues, "But the significance of a deficit always depends on more than its biological nature; it is shaped by the human circumstances in which it exists." The distinctions are fuzzy.

A whole series of problems surfaces when you attempt to define disability simply in terms of a physical flaw in someone's body. First of all, if disability were simply a deviation from the norm, by implication you should be able to establish objectively by some standard what the norm is and what constitutes a deviation from it. The underlying assumption is that there is an ideal or normal state of the human body. This is an illusion.

In the United States we are constantly bombarded by media messages urging us to conform to a narrow and restrictive definition of "normal." The ideal of beauty and performance is narrowly defined for us by the images we see. We're told that attaining this image is vitally important. You won't get the job or the girl or the car or the house or ultimate happiness if you can't measure up. The composite drawing includes washboard abs and perfect teeth and big hair and blemish-free skin and an anorexic figure.

In reality, no one lives up to this ideal. No body is perfect. It is revealed that even the models on the magazine covers have had their photos digitally retouched to make them look slimmer or more muscular or more beautiful. Madison Avenue steps in and snares us. We crave the look we see in the media. Someone is eager to sell us what we need—the product or food or exercise video or corrective surgery—in order to bring ourselves up to that standard. In just four easy payments!

What they're selling us, my friends, is snake oil. In reality, there is an infinite variety of bodies, abilities, and continuums of competency. It becomes impossible to determine where the "norm" ends and the "deviation" begins. Don't let this little news flash get around, though. If the truth were known, a lot of sales people and inventors and industries would be out of business. In fact, the entire U.S. economy would crumble in a heartbeat, so dependent is it on creating and advertising superficial "needs."

Second, even if the preceding concerns were set aside and we could agree, for the sake of argument, that one could identify a norm and then determine what would constitute a deviation from it, it would still be true that such deviation is not necessarily disabling. It depends, as we will see in an upcoming chapter, on the cultural context. For example, a facial scar is considered disfiguring in Western culture. Among the Dahomey in Africa, facial scars are considered signs of status. Another example: the Maasai tribe in Kenya has no word for "disability." They recognize incompetence and variance in human abilities, but they incorporate these varieties of traits into community life. Among the Maasai the only truly disabled person is one isolated from the community. In the Western world, where people are oppressed by an emphasis on slenderness, fat is considered unattractive. In Polynesia it is beautiful. Cultural variables raise just one more problem in trying to define the concept of disability.

Is a physical disability limiting? Does it handicap or disable? Like every other question in this chapter, that, too, depends. In some societies, specific physical impairments limit one's potential and participation. In others, they may not. In the United States, up to two-thirds of disabled persons are unemployed, not because they don't want to work or can't perform meaningful tasks, but because society has been slow in removing barriers to their full participation. Either they can't get to the work place, they can't get in the front door, or no one will hire them. I haven't been in the job market since I've been in a wheelchair. Because of horror stories I've heard about pastors with disabilities being fired from their churches or never getting an opportunity for an interview, I'm not excited about getting into it. (That's why I'm being so nice to the members of the church I currently serve. I'm hoping to hang onto this job as long as I can! If any of them are reading this, they're really swell people!) These stereotypical attitudes that exclude people with disabilities may not be intentional—I don't know many mean-spirited people who deliberately set up barriers to people with disabilities—but they are pervasive and powerful nonetheless. It's also sometimes very expensive to tear down the physical barriers that keep people with disabilities from full participation. Funds for an elevator could always be used elsewhere. But whatever the reason, social barriers and attitudes place limits on people with disabilities. I find that unless I'm very assertive, a store clerk or waiter may address my son or daughter instead of me. "What does he want?" they ask, giving me scarcely a nod of acknowledgment.

Tell me, is it just me or are the counters at pharmacies unusually high? I'm lucky if I can see the top of the pharmacist's head. Unless I cough or toss a bottle of aspirin over the top, no one knows I'm waiting for my drugs. What's with those things, anyway? Are they for security purposes? I suppose they'd come in handy as a security barrier if someone rolled a live grenade into the store, but to my knowledge that isn't a big risk in the drug store business. Rolling up to the impenetrable counter at the back of the pharmacy, I feel like a child begging for a favor.

Once I spent a weekend on an organized bike ride with a blind woman, Deb. She rode on the back of a rusty tandem bike I had borrowed for the occasion. At check-in the first night I stood behind Deb as she waited in line for her room key. The receptionist looked over Deb's shoulder and asked me, "Can I help her?" I said, "Don't look at me. She's the one who wants to check in." Except for children, who stare at me unabashed, people who see me in my wheelchair tend to look away. Are they embarrassed, disgusted, or afraid, or is it that the deviation from the norm that I represent is threatening to them?

But these are all culturally derived attitudes. They have nothing at all to do with my back injury or useless legs. They are more about how people perceive and relate to me than about my condition. They further cloud the issue of a definition of disability.

The ADA definition of disability as a physical impairment would seem to imply that disability is a medical condition. This is certainly a view commonly held by the public at large. And it seems intuitively sound. After all, if an injury or illness put me in this wheelchair, then medical science might have some answers to get me out of it again. You can't blame the public for holding tenaciously onto this view, either. They have been convinced of it by two very powerful media machines: Christopher Reeve and the major telethons.

Reeve and I share a remarkably parallel lifeline. He's exactly, to the week, two years older than I am. His two older children are each two years older than my two children. If I had been aware of this pattern, I would have stayed in bed the last week in May 1997, exactly two years after Reeve suffered the tragic accident that paralyzed him. But like a fool I went out and got hit by a truck exactly two years to the week after he suffered his crippling accident. Go figure.

My first reaction to Reeve's misfortune was the same as everyone else's. I was saddened by the tragedy and inspired by his determination to move forward. He was clearly making an impact in terms of public awareness of spinal cord injury, fundraising, and accelerating the work toward a cure.

But after I was injured and had spent some time adjusting to my new reality, I looked at Reeve's response more critically. I discovered that much of the rest of the disability community was also critical. The reason is that Reeve seems to focus his energy and message exclusively on finding a cure for spinal cord injury. That's the only message we hear from him. The implication is that people with disabilities can only be whole if they can be cured, that life with a disability has no value unless the condition can be reversed. As Reeve testified before Congress regarding the president's health-related budget request for 2000,

> Without your support, spinal cord victims will continue to sit in wheelchairs, draining the resources of insurance companies as well as Medicaid, Medicare, VA hospitals, and nursing homes. With your continued support, it is very possible that within the next three to five years people who are now afflicted with a wide variety of disabilities will be able to overcome them. They will regain their rightful place in society, rejoin the workforce, and at last be relieved of the suffering they and their families have had to endure. (2002, 95)

Speaking as a person with a disability, I don't see myself sitting in my wheelchair draining resources. I'm not waiting for federal funding in order to regain my rightful place in society. I'm a little miffed, to put it mildly, that the powerful beacon of Reeve's message to the American people paints me and others like me in such an unflattering light. My book is dedicated to the premise that there's more to disability than the urge to escape from it. But more people will read Reeve's book than mine. Unless you buy a couple of copies for friends and spread the word.

Following a presentation by Reeve at the 1996 Democratic National Convention, Harriet McBryde Johnson, a delegate from South Carolina who also uses a wheelchair, took the floor. She explained to the gathering, "Christopher Reeve is going through a tremendous transformation. It's impossible for most people to imagine, but it happens thousands of times every year. It doesn't make him a disability spokesman. He's still learning. He wants to be cured, but for us it's more important to live our lives, just the way we are. He doesn't speak for us." But don't tell the

American people, who have a love affair with their former Superman. They have their minds made up.

The second pernicious media machine I mentioned is big business charity, which raises money for medical research to cure disabilities. Now, don't get me wrong. I'm not opposed to charity. I'm a minister, for heaven's sake. Our salaries and ministries and buildings are all supported by voluntary donations. Charities tap into the human impulse to do good. They give us a channel to share with people in need. I direct and encourage charitable giving. The big charities are successful money machines for their causes. They have raised billions of dollars for research and have pushed the progress of medical science. But at what price?

The image portrayed by parading Jerry's Kids across the stage during the annual telethon for muscular dystrophy is that disability is a tragic, pitiful condition. "This child will never be asked to the prom," was a slogan recently shown below the photo of a girl with a disability. Well, why not? Is that the fault of her physical condition, or is it rather the fault of a society that looks on people with neuromuscular disease as less than desirable? Using the pity factor to raise money segregates people with disabilities as the objects of pity. It doesn't empower them to adjust to life as it is. It doesn't empower them to struggle against the limiting perceptions of the dominant culture. It casts them as passive recipients of the spare change that society thinks it can afford. They become beggars, the only profession traditionally open to the disabled. The charity industry creates dependency, and degrades, controls, and isolates the "victims."

Jerry Lewis's Muscular Dystrophy Association telethon brings in about $40 million each year. It has raised more than $1 billion since its inception. But the way in which they portray disabled children is an insult, as Marta Russell explains:

> Jerry Lewis perpetuates outdated images of disabled persons as leading tragic lives, as homebound victims waiting for cures. Fantasizing about what life would be like if he were disabled, Lewis told *Parade* magazine, "I realize my life is half, so I must learn to do things half way. I must have to learn to try to be good at being half a person." What is Lewis's message? There is no life without a cure; disabled people are not capable of working, raising children, or participating in the majority culture in any "whole" sense. Lewis's exhibitions perpetuate the damaging myth that our disabled "half" lives are not worth living. (1998, 85)

The disabling message broadcast by Lewis and other telethons wouldn't be so bad if it weren't so pervasive. Charlton points out that, according to surveys, "more people form attitudes about disabilities from telethons than from any other source" (1998, 35). The four largest of them reach a combined audience of 250 million people. Who's going to bother to get personally acquainted with a disabled person, in all the complexity and ambiguity of their experience, if you can be spoon fed your views on disability from some inspirational telethon?

Contemporary disability activists reject what they call the "medicalization" of disability. They insist that one's medical diagnosis is much less important than how a person with a disability is integrated into or excluded from society. In some cases a disabling condition may respond to a cure. People living with that condition may have the option of returning to a previous state of being. Cures are constantly being discovered for conditions that were once thought to be immutable. Reeve expects his condition to be a temporary impairment, as medical research gets closer and closer to understanding spinal cord injury, and he may well be correct. He may get out of that chair one day. But surely this optimism can't be applied across the board as one attempts to define disability. Disability cannot be reduced to a medical deficiency in search of a cure. That would be an unhealthy attitude for me to adopt, a misunderstanding of my condition, and a tragic image to leave with the American public.

One final question cries out for attention before we finish this chapter. If disability can't be simply reduced to a medical question, then what is the relationship between health and disability? I have a disability, but I'm not sick. Curiously, I've never been healthier than I have during the last five years. I can't remember having lost a day to illness in all that time. I used to get sick constantly. I'd catch every cold or flu bug that was in vogue. I think it was from visiting lots of sick people and shaking lots of hands, especially on Sundays. I still shake hands. Now I just wash my hands afterwards. I sit in the receiving line after church shaking hands, and then before I hit the parlor for cookies I stop by the bathroom to wash my hands. I'm convinced this little detour has saved me countless weeks of illness.

I think I'm healthier as a disabled person than I was before because I take better care of myself. I'm more deliberate about controlling the factors that are under my control—perhaps because so many more factors aren't. I am more aware of healthy eating habits, taking vitamins, regular exercise and rest, and good hygiene. As a member of an at-risk population, I get a flu shot every fall. I've been in the hospital several times for follow-up surgeries, but I haven't been sick.

My self-perception undergoes a radical and uncomfortable transformation every time I'm admitted to the hospital for another of my frequent surgeries. When do I stop being a healthy man with a disability and become a patient? Hospital personnel struggle with the issue, too.

When you check in at the front desk, you are instructed to wait until an escort can take you to your room. Invariably these well-meaning escorts will come up behind me to push my chair, then realize, startled, that there are no push handles. "That's because I push myself," I explain, trying to be nice.

When you enter your hospital room, you find your hospital gown waiting on the bed. I hate those things! Have you ever tried to transfer into a wheelchair wearing a long, flowing garment that opens in the back? It takes two people to pull this trick off. The fabric gathers underneath and, because I need both hands to lift and transfer myself, there's nothing I can do to get untangled or reduce my exposure. I refuse to put my gown on until the last possible moment before they wheel me away for surgery, and I struggle out of it again as soon as I can get my tee shirt over the IV site in my arm.

I have to explain to the nurses about the bags and appliances I come equipped with. Nurses have been instructed how to empty urinary and colostomy bags as medical issues rather than disability lifestyle issues. They come in promptly at the start of each shift. They always seem disappointed, maybe even a little put off, when I inform them that I have already taken care of my leg bag, and the colostomy is not currently in need of attention. "May I see for myself?" they ask, sweetly. "No," I answer just as sweetly. You have to be very careful in not offending them outright, because you are surely going to need them. Ann used to put out bowls of candy in my hospital rooms, just to keep the nurses happy. There will come a time, the next day when I return from surgery and for a few days after that, when I will be more than grateful for their services. But for now, the fact that I have appliances and bags and tubing and use a wheelchair does not make me a patient. I have a disability. I am not sick. At least not yet. Besides, in spite of their training and hygiene precautions, they are never as careful about the cleaning of my equipment as I am. It's not their bladders that run the risk of infection; it's mine. I've done this more often than they have. In terms of disability hygiene, I'm the expert here, not the nurses.

Then, as soon as I can following surgery, I get up to empty my own bags and take care of my own hygiene. I know I'm well when I can put on my own shirt and pants. These little things mean a great deal to me, symbolically. Though I'm in the same hospital room, I've stopped being a patient. You have to make these mental adjustments yourself; no one will make them for you.

There is no essential relationship between disability and health. One can be disabled and healthy, or disabled and sick. Theologian Jürgen Moltmann agrees:

There is no differentiation between the healthy and those with disabilities. For every human life has its limitations, vulnerabilities, and weaknesses. We are born needy, and we die helpless. So in truth there is no such thing as a life without disabilities. It is only the ideals of health of a society of the strong which condemn a part of humanity to being "disabled." (110)

This flies in the face of a common understanding of disability as a medical issue. If the person with a disability were only in need of a cure, then one would be justified in calling her or him sick. The medical model would be appropriate. But if disability can be thought of as simply one of a variety of ways of being human, then there is no connection with medical science at all. Disability is more than a medical condition.

Do you see the pattern developing here? The more you look into the notion of disability, the harder it becomes to hit upon a satisfying definition. You can't pin it down neatly. It's not a mere medical condition or a physical impairment. It doesn't have anything essential to do with ability or lack thereof, or deviation from some predetermined norm. Attitude is involved, as well as cultural variations. There seems to be no straightforward, intrinsic definition of disability. Too many questions arise from every angle.

In another chapter we'll look at how disability activists are beginning to define themselves. They have moved beyond seeing themselves as victims in need of charity or medical attention. Empowered by several decades of struggle and consciousness-raising, they have begun to change the ground rules for the discussion of disability. They are claiming for themselves the language and definitions that have traditionally been applied to them by doctors, charities, and therapists. For them, disability is no longer a medical category, now it's political. The disabled are redefining themselves as a minority group, entitled to the same civil rights guaranteed in the constitution as have been claimed by African Americans, women, homosexuals, and others.

Defining the concept of disability is not a static project, accomplished once and for all. It is an ongoing process, dependent on historical, cultural, and sociological factors. In today's North American culture, the definition of disability has become a civil rights issue. People with disabilities have begun to see themselves not as patients, but as a discrete minority group. Treatment becomes a political struggle for rights of access, rather than medical intervention to return the person with a disability to a more "normal" state.

Is there anything beyond the minority group model for defining disability? Maybe not yet, but I can see an even more radical understanding on the horizon. The minority model certainly goes further toward understanding the experience of disability than notions of disability as a result of sin or an object of pity or a deviation from the norm or a medical condition in need of a cure. But it seems to have its limitations. Positing the existence of a minority group implies that the group's boundaries can be defined. Who's in and who's out should be something all parties could agree on. But it may not be as simple as all that. Real life is messy. People move in and out of this "group." Members of the various subgroups within the disability minority may have very little in common with one another. How severe does a disability need to be in order to qualify for admission into the group? How permanent?

Maybe society needs the presence of a militant minority group at the present time to stake out some territory that hadn't previously existed, ensuring rights for people with disabilities who are not willingly afforded access by society at large. This model creates political and intellectual space for people with disabilities to define themselves for a change. But maybe when that project is finished—not that it ever will be, but let's say that's our goal—we can arrive at a yet more enlightened place that recognizes the infinite variety of human expression and ability. The drawback to the minority group model is that it's still an us-or-them, in-or-out, disabled-or-not model. In the real world there's no black and white. There's no in and out. There are infinite shadings of human ability, appearance, and condition. In the best of all possible worlds, access will be afforded to all of them, and inclusion will be a thing taken for granted.

Here's an example. In the area of education, it is now considered progressive methodology to identify students with learning disabilities, and to provide them with special learning models that might more closely meet their needs. The operating assumption behind this model is that there is a "normal" way to learn and then there is a minority group comprised of some "abnormal" or "special needs" students who need special access built into the system in order for them to compete on equal footing with the mainstream. That's considered a progressive view, but it falls short of comprehending reality. My wife, who is a teacher and Christian educator, tells me that in reality there are up to seven modes of learning. I suspect that even that number is arbitrary, and that the variety of learning modes is much greater. There are seven different ways, she says, that students use to take in information. Some are auditory learners, who can process information imparted in a lecture format. Others are more kinetic in style. They need a hands-on, interactive approach. Some learn better in a group format, others process information better by themselves. Each student falls naturally into his or her own style. Whoever decided that there was just one mainstream style of learning, with only a minority of learning-disabled students exhibiting special needs? Aren't we all special and unique in the way in which we approach and interact with the world? In *my* school, every subject should be taught not just by lecture and memorization, but also with play-dough and pipe cleaners and music and dance and drama and poetry and crayons and playgroups. Mairs suggests that our black-and-white definitions of disability are far too confining. "Binary thinking is merely a habit of mind," she writes, "and despite the comfort of order and familiarity it offers, it doesn't apprehend reality, which is, let's face it, a frightful jumble. Gifts get handed out higgledy-piggledy" (1996, 13).

Who has a disability? Who's "normal"? Where do you draw the line? I learned in college philosophy that when the answers to the questions become silly, you're asking the wrong questions.

When we finally come to an acceptance of the human being as an infinitely variable creature, this book will have become obsolete. With any luck I will have sold several thousand copies first, but that's the risk I take. That's the danger in delving into the notion of disability too deeply. There's an internal contradiction at the heart of the matter. Once disability is adequately understood as a normal condition of human experience, there will be no need for a discussion of disability as a special category of human experience. There will be no such thing as disability. There will be only a marvelous diversity of human beings, each one located at one point or another on an endless continuum of abilities, each ability only one in an expansive bundle of tasks and functions and activities that, taken together, comprise what it means to be human.

Unfortunately, the complexity of this truth is hard to convey to a high school class or middle school assembly in just twenty minutes. And it doesn't lend itself to telethon sound bites.

Chapter 9

Crippled by Culture

*C*ulture is disabling. Let me put that another way. Initially, I assumed that I was handicapped by my inability to walk following the hit-and-run accident that left me in a wheelchair. By that and by the pain and internal problems resulting from the accident. But I was wrong. Physical deviation from the conventional, by itself, does not a disability make. Disability is what your culture says it is.

Culture gives meaning to everything. People are rarely aware of that fact, though, because they live within a culture and see everything from the perspective of that culture. Unless we have seen reality from within a different culture, we believe that our cultural perspective is the only perspective there is. We're cultural fundamentalists. We think we see the truth, but what we're really seeing is only our culture's definition of truth. Culture colors everything. Charlton writes:

> The modern world is composed of thousands of cultures, each in its own ways of thinking about other people, nature, family and community, social phenomena, and so on. Culture is sustained through customs, rituals, mythology, signs and

symbols, and institutions such as religion and the mass media. Each of these informs the beliefs and attitudes that contribute to disability oppression. (1998, 25)

Our understanding of the concept of disability, like our understanding of every other concept, is provided by the culture we live in. It's a socially constructed definition that varies according to the culture that does the defining. The meaning of disability differs from culture to culture. Treatment of those who are disabled also varies widely. Accommodation of people with disabilities follows from the culturally determined understanding of disability.

Allow me to elaborate. Some societies determine a man's value by his productive earning ability. If a physical impairment limits that ability, the man's very personhood is diminished. In some places a woman is valued according to her reproductive potential. If that is limited, she is handicapped. In cultures that place an inordinate value on personal appearance, deviation from the norm will be disabling. In some cultures blindness, hearing impairment, mental illness, developmental difficulties, mobility problems may leave a person stigmatized, stranded and isolated, channeled into demeaning work, or warehoused with no possibility of employment at all. On the other hand, in other cultures these variations in abilities may make no real difference at all. In yet other places these conditions may actually become social assets. Whether a physical or mental disability becomes a handicap to a person's dignity and potential all depends on the cultural setting. Disability, again, is primarily a cultural construct, and only secondarily a physically determined given.

Ann and I have spent a total of six years in Central America and Mexico, mainly among peasant and working class communities. In such contexts persons with disabilities tend to be severely disadvantaged. In developing nations, where even majorities are unemployed or underemployed, where basic human services such as health care and education are in short supply even for nondisabled people, persons with disabilities are on the tail end of the social contract. They are the last ones in line in the distribution of social goods and services.

In fact, in many developing nations there may be no social contract. Public resources are in such short supply that the average citizen is on his or her own. Governments may not see it as their responsibility to take care of their citizens. Opportunities for the disabled, assuming they survive childhood, are limited or nonexistent. They can either beg for a meager living or they're kept at home and cared for by family members. Money for assistive technology, such as wheelchairs, communication devices, computers, and accessible public transportation is scarce. Independent living is rarely a socially desirable value nor a realistic goal for persons with significant disabilities living in underdeveloped countries. The equipment and opportunities I take for granted simply don't exist there. Independence for persons with disabilities is not even on the radar screen.

Charlton points out that:

> So-called economic miracles have done little to cure the symptoms of underdevelopment for people with disabilities. Diseases like polio, eliminated elsewhere, still exist. Industrial accidents are more common in the less industrialized periphery than in the metropolis. Employment is unattainable. Millions of people with disabilities are starving, and many more are hungry. Underdevelopment has produced misery for hundreds of millions of people with disabilities. People with disabilities are the poorest, most isolated group in the poorest, most isolated places. (1998, 43)

He goes on to say that most people in underdeveloped countries who sustain spinal cord injuries usually die within a year or two of their injury, from pressure sores or bladder infections. One hundred million people have disabilities caused by malnutrition. Politics, economics, poverty, powerlessness, medical abandonment, and disability are all tied together in a bewildering web.

We rarely came across persons with disabilities out in public in rural or working class barrios in Mexico or Central America. No buses or businesses or public facilities were accessible, and functional wheelchairs or adaptive technology were not even a distant dream. In cities disabled people might appear riding on homemade carts, darting between traffic or finding a corner on the sidewalk to live out their days. They live off what coins passersby drop in their tin cups. In rural Yucatán, where people sleep in hammocks strung up at night throughout their small adobe houses, the elderly or disabled may spend their days swinging peacefully in a hammock in the front room. Grandma hangs out there while the mother of the house diligently pounds out tortillas, the kids run in and out past her, and neighbors pass in the street calling out greetings. A bottle of water, a plate of tortillas, and maybe a bedpan are all within reach. The television, if there is one, is tuned to her favorite station. When there's a ride available to market in the next pueblo, she may be dumped unceremoniously in the back of a pickup truck along with the pigs and chickens and the rest of the family. People with disabilities ask and receive no quarter. No handicap van drives out to pick them up. No special handicap parking tag ensures them a place by the door. In Cancún, when I needed to get up the two steps into my hotel, I simply caught the eye of the kid who worked behind the counter and was hauled in. It may not be the worst existence, living with a disability in Central America, and there is some evidence that people with disabilities are included as participants in family and community life, but there is not a hint of an independent, empowered existence.

One commentator from Mexico, Fernando Rodriguez, reports:

> By and large, people with disabilities in Mexico are very isolated, both because of their family's attitudes and because of all the access issues. Of course, people with disabilities who have money do not experience these problems in the same way because they can pay for transportation, for help to get into buildings, and so on. In my country, independent living really does not exist. The primary reasons for this are backward attitudes and the lack of economic development. (Charlton 1998, 85)

The situation in Nicaragua is a little different, although the politics and economics are similar. Up to two-thirds of the population is unemployed. We couldn't figure out how families survived. Many people live off the Managua city dump, scavenging things to eat or sell. One day, on a whim, I swung onto the back of a garbage truck going by our home and rode with the garbage men into the landfill. There was an entire community there, pawing through the garbage. Hordes of hopeful vendors clog the street corners at each stoplight, selling everything from lottery tickets to lizards. You'd think, under such extreme circumstances, that the disabled wouldn't stand a chance. Indeed, there are few services or accessible facilities offered, and little accessible transportation is available. But, due to Nicaragua's unique history and culture, the perception of persons with disabilities is radically different than in other Central American countries. Nicaragua has been at war for decades. During the 1970s, increasing numbers of people joined the armed struggle against the corrupt and brutal dictatorship of Anastacio Somoza. His family had been in power for half a century. He owned, privately, over one-third of the productive land in Nicaragua.

The revolution was successful in overthrowing the Somoza dynasty in 1979, and the more socially progressive government of the Sandinistas poured what limited resources they had into social services such as education and health care. The new administration, in fact, was recognized by the World Health Organization and by UNICEF for their efforts on behalf of social outreach. Brigades of teachers almost eliminated illiteracy, and "barefoot doctors" distributed health care for the first time into remote rural regions. But the U.S. government, suspicious of the socialistic policies of the new Nicaraguan leaders and their ties to the Eastern block nations, soon instituted a policy to undermine the Sandinistas. Besides diplomatic and economic pressures, the United States funded and helped direct a resistance army consisting of former National Guard members and others disillusioned with the revolutionary regime. The Contra forces, as they were called, inflicted serious damage on the Nicaraguan economy, security, and people, leaving thousands of citizens disabled. Landmines left over from the Contra War were still a problem in remote areas when we were there in the early 1990s. People with disabilities became a common sight in the city. Rehab programs for the injured proliferated. A prosthesis factory opened near the neighborhood in which we lived. And the war-injured—and by extension other people with a variety of impairments—were treated with respect as heroes of the revolution. I wrote an article for the *Christian Century* about a former National Guard member who had been injured by the Sandinistas, and had eventually returned to work as a Mennonite pastor. On the day I found him, he was working side by side with a former Sandinistan soldier, building a school building for disadvantaged children in his neighborhood. It was something of a miracle of rehabilitation, transformation, forgiveness, and healing.

Honolulu, I found, is an ideal place to study cultural differences in addressing disability. Hawaii is a tossed salad of ethnic groups and nationalities, all living together on tiny islands surrounded by water extending at least 2,100 miles in every direction. Our hosts for the three-month sabbatical were Steve and Ann Ito. Ann has directed Kokua, a program that coordinates services for students with disabilities at the University of Hawaii, for thirty-two years. *Kokua* means, literally, "help," but as consciousness has been raised over the years, the name has been reinterpreted. Now *kokua* is taken to mean "place of growing." It has been in operation since 1966—and Ann has been there from the beginning—when a group of student tutors asked for a university-wide program to deal with special needs students. This program was in place for twenty-four years before the ADA required it, a fact that Ann mentions with some pride. She's currently seeking funding for a three-year, half-million-dollar project to create guidelines for other colleges and universities on accommodating students with disabilities. The project will cover everything from nursing practices and language at university health clinics to training for admissions counselors.

At the University of Hawaii, Ann administers services for nearly six hundred students with everything from learning disabilities to blindness, hearing impairments, and mobility limitations. There is no question for her that students with disabilities should be integrated fully to the extent of their abilities, in every aspect of university and community life. Ann notes that their disabilities often create more work for the effected students. Medical issues or communication needs often add hours of hard work to their weeks. Ann's office provides services to assist them in meeting their goals. Her students come from all over the world, though more heavily from the U.S. mainland and Asia. She notes some distinct differences in the understanding and integration of persons with disabilities between one culture and another.

Modern day Hawaiians, like Central Americans, make no special deal about disability, Ann says. They are less inclined to look for a social, political, or institutional fix, and more likely to take care of persons with special needs within the family. A family will exhaust its own resources caring for a disabled family member, before expecting social or government resources to kick in. They will carry Grandma up and down stairs and get her where she needs to go. A disabled child is brought into family gatherings and mainstreamed in school. Hawaiian is a culture that seems to be blind (no pun intended) to difference. You see it in the wild diversity of cultures on the islands that are not only tolerated but also celebrated. It's the island culture of aloha; everyone is welcome.

I saw the inclusive *ohana*, or "family," in action several times over the course of the summer I was in Honolulu. When I enter athletic competitions on the mainland, I'm something of an anomaly. Race directors are aware in advance that a wheelchair participant has signed up. They ask what they can do to accommodate me. All the other competitors cheer for the wheelchairs as they start. If they pass us on the course or we pass them, there's always a congratulatory shout. We're "inspirations" to the rest of the field. We are unique.

I was not unique in Hawaii. I entered a 5K race for muscular dystrophy and received no special treatment. I didn't get an early start and nobody cheered for the wheelchair entrant. I didn't even get a T-shirt! The course wound through a park and included several speed bumps and even, amazingly, a couple of curbs. I was on my own to negotiate them. Later, I entered a one-mile open ocean swim on the north shore of Oahu, the same beach where international surfing competitions are held. There is very rough water there. The treatment was the same. I was on my own to get across the sand of the beach, and was given no special start. When I finished, I sat on the sand wondering how I was going to get from there to the finish line, which was another twenty yards up the beach. Finally two bystanders picked me up and dragged me.

At first I was frustrated by such nonchalance. But now I have a theory. My theory is that there is so much raw diversity on Oahu, that one more instance of it, in this case in the form of a guy in a wheelchair who enters athletic events, raises no eyebrows. It's not that there are lots of athletes with disabilities—I never saw another one—but there are so many distinct social groups that any form of diversity is just accepted as is. Here there are Samoans, native Hawaiians, *Haoles* (we mainlanders who tend to be whiter, louder, and less sensitive than the rest), Japanese, Indians, Chinese, Vietnamese, Thai, Filipino, Portuguese, British, Australians, and others. The variety of restaurants is tremendous. We were unable to sample them all, and believe me, we tried. A unique Hawaiian form of humor has grown up in response to it all, one we would not get away with on the mainland. We're too sensitive. But in Hawaii there's no attempt at creating a melting pot. My home state of Iowa, in an extreme form of cultural fundamentalism, is considering passing "English only" legislation. Such a thought would never seriously be entertained in Hawaii. It's a wild and healthy tossed salad out there. Cultural relativism and mutual accommodation—toward people with disabilities as well as people from different heritages—are common practices.

Steve and Ann Ito are caring for a disabled relative. Steve's mother lives in her own home, but she's anything but alone. Two grown daughters take turns staying with her, getting her to daycare and tending to her needs. They're relieved on the weekends by Steve and Ann, who think nothing of spending great chunks of time taking care of her. There is no talk of institutionalization. Career decisions and personal plans will take into account the need to have someone with Grandma.

Oh, I forgot to mention—Ann Ito is blind. She gets up at 4:00 every morning, rides the paratransit "Handi-Van" to work at Kokua, and returns home each night after 9:00 PM Clearly her visual impairment is not an issue for her in living a productive, meaningful life. She was instrumental in setting up the paratransit system on Oahu. They now have about 150 accessible vans driving all over the island, offering curb-to-curb service for only $2 per ride with a day's notice. It's an incredible service, well utilized by residents. I even used it to take my wife, Ann, down to the wharf for a sunset cruise on the occasion of our twenty-sixth anniversary. Efficient, yes, but romantic it wasn't. For the record, I do not recommend taking your spouse out for a special evening in a public paratransit truck. It seemed like a good idea at the time. Someday she'll forgive me.

Where Hawaiians have an open attitude toward the disabled, Ann Ito notes that Asian cultures present more restrictions on opportunities and expectations for persons with disabilities. Among many Asian cultures, people with disabilities are objects of shame and scorn. In Japanese culture, where appearance and conformity are important, disability is seen as something shameful, a disgrace to the family. A person with a disability may be closeted at home to keep the secret from the wider community. But this treatment is gender dependent. In a rigidly patriarchal society, a disabled wife is often discarded, especially if she cannot reproduce. A disabled husband, however, is a different story. His wife will dutifully and sacrificially care for him. Gender roles are much more rigid in Japanese culture than in the United States.

Ann Ito points out that the Chinese will often keep the disabled person in the family a secret. According to a study by Jerome Mindes, "In China, it is not uncommon to hear of mentally ill or retarded adults who have lived their entire lives in back rooms, isolated from all but their immediate family." A Beijing University student told a journalist, "We want children to maintain the family line and support their parents in their old age. Disabled children are useless for either purpose so they become a luxury . . . in China." In Asia, infants who are born with disabilities often end up in orphanages after being abandoned by their families. A new law in China actually requires abortion and even sterilization to prevent the birth of children with disabilities. Infanticide of girls and disabled boys is widely practiced throughout Africa and India.

Gender differences in dealing with persons with disabilities are often significant:

> The cruel treatment of women with disabilities is rooted, in many cultures, in the dehumanization of those women based in part on their dual body status—as women and as women with disabilities. Some women I interviewed reported they had been raised by their families to become good housekeepers but never to become sexually active women. Some said they never had full-size mirrors at home which permitted a view of their bodies as they grew up. One woman said as a child she frequently was lectured, "When your brothers marry, you'll live with them and help take care of their children." Moreover, everyday bodily issues such as appearance, body language, facial expressions, and posture are almost universally neglected, making these issues, especially sexuality, extremely problematic. (Charlton 1998, 58)

John Hockenberry, in his travels as a journalist, always keeps an eye on how other people with disabilities fit in. His observations about living with a disability in the Middle East are interesting. Though sharing the same territory, disabled people in Israel and disabled people in Palestine face radically different experiences. "Israeli crips," he writes, "had lots of gadgets. . . . The culture of disability in Israel is distinctly military in nature. Wheelchairs are technology. Israeli crips look at their chairs like they look at advanced jet fighters" (1995, 236). Hockenberry found progressive treatment centers for people with disabilities, and wholly accessible neighborhoods, at least in Tel Aviv.

His experience in Palestine was decidedly different. "If hanging with Israeli crips was like watching a scene from the movie *Top Gun*, visiting spinal-cord-injured Palestinians was like reliving the valley of the lepers scene from *Ben Hur*. . . . Palestinian crips were not big on either pride or swagger. The Palestinian office for the physically disabled dispenses big, clunky, low-tech, mostly used wheelchairs from the basement of someone's old house down a steep flight of stairs" (1995, 237-238).

It was rare to see disabled Palestinians on the streets. The most severely disabled were commonly institutionalized. Medical care differed from one side of the border to the other. Arab families tended to put their limited resources into the search for a miracle cure for their injured loved one. "Their idea of rehabilitation was to pray for their child to walk again some day." Until the prayers were answered, the person with a disability was confined to some institution or cooped up in a back room at home. They were awarded heroic status as martyrs to the cause, but they were not encouraged to get on with their lives.

Education is a luxury out of reach for the disabled in many countries. Ann Ito and her daughters recently traveled to Japan. She was particularly interested in seeing how the curriculum for the blind may have expanded in recent years. Traditionally, she explains, the blind in Japan have had two career options. They could go into massage or they could be beggars. At Tsuba College in Tokyo, a school for people who are blind or deaf, the curriculum options are still severely limited. The deaf have five courses of study available to them. People who are blind have three. The director of the school asked her, "What can a blind student in Hawaii study?" Her shocked answer was, "Why, anything they want, of course!"

According to Charlton, in some African countries no education is available to children with disabilities. In India only three percent of boys with disabilities are educated. Girls with disabilities have almost no opportunity for an education.

In the United States, education for the disabled has undergone many transformations during the past century. Persons with disabilities have traditionally been segregated and institutionalized. Mainstreaming students with disabilities has been in vogue only for the past few decades. Mainstreaming often meant, in practice, that disabled students might have attended the same schools as the "normal" population but were segregated in their own classrooms. Currently, full inclusion is being explored in an increasing number of schools. Full inclusion integrates students with disabilities into classes with their able-bodied classmates. It seems to have a positive impact not only on the students with disabilities, but also on their nondisabled classmates. Even with these advances, people with severe disabilities are four times more likely than the national average to have less than a ninth grade education.

Language can be a powerful force in the formation of attitudes toward people with disabilities. In Zimbabwe, for example, the words for "cripple" and "blind" denote "failure" and "helpless," respectively. In Managua, Nicaragua, I worked for a time with a Mennonite pastor who used a wheelchair. The other pastors I worked with, while affording him a degree of respect, still referred to him as *un invalido*. The word seemed shockingly value-laden. There is a great discussion about language going on. Words like "cripple" and "gimp" are too charged to use today, except within the disability community itself. "Handicapped" doesn't accurately describe my condition; it describes what happens when someone with my condition bumps up against stairs or narrow doorways. We become handicapped when facilities fail to make full accommodations. Cute, politically correct designations for people with disabilities, such as "other-abled" or "challenged" or "special," hardly seem compelling to the disability community. Describing someone as "disabled" puts the emphasis on the disability, not the person. Currently, it seems least offensive to talk of "a person with a disability," which, at least, puts the person first.

In most places around the world, living with a disability places a person in an economic and political disadvantage. Even in the United States, where conditions and attitudes about disability are much more enlightened, people with disabilities find themselves economically and politically challenged. Up to two-thirds of people with serious disabilities are unemployed. Most of those would prefer to work, but find the barriers, both physical and discriminatory, prohibitive. What I took as a given, being able to return to my employment following a disabling injury, is in fact quite rare. I hear horror stories about pastors with disabilities being passed over for placement. If I had been in a job that required standing, I would have had to retool or join the unemployment lines. People with disabilities are four times more likely than the average U.S. citizen to be living below the poverty line.

John Callahan, an irreverent cartoonist who also happens to be a quadriplegic, shares in graphic detail how difficult it was for him to live on disability payments:

> My SSDI entitlement was just over $600 a month. According to Welfare, that was too princely a sum. They required me to hand over $200 a month as a partial reimbursement for the $800 I was allotted for daily and weekend attendants. My rent, for a small one-bedroom, ground-floor apartment, consumed a further $325. The $75 that remained was real whoopee money. All I had to make it cover were

electricity, phone, groceries, clothing, drawing supplies, envelopes, postage, copying, haircuts, dental bills other than emergency ones, and food for my cat. (1990, 175)

Once Callahan's cartoons started to catch on, and he started receiving payment checks in the mail, he was expected to turn over the unexpected windfall to the government. He made $5,000 in his first two years as a professional cartoonist, and felt guilty over every cent of it. His caseworker increased the frequency of her visits, trying to catch him hording stashes of loot. "She poked into every corner of the apartment in search of contraband Cuisinarts, unregistered girlfriends, or illegal aliens serving as butlers and maids. . . . There is no provision in the law for a gradual shift away from welfare to self-support," he concludes. "I want to get ahead. I have the talent, the ability, the desire, and the moxie to do it. I have twice the drive of the average able-bodied person. What I am being told by the welfare system is, no, we won't let you do it."

An archaic welfare system is not the only barrier to the independent functioning of people with disabilities. Attitudes still get in the way. In 1991, Bree Walker Lampley, a television news anchor, got pregnant. Lampley had a mild disability, a condition called ectrodactyly, which caused a partial fusing of the bones in her hands and feet. She could do her job, and had proven herself to be a competent mother with a previous daughter. Her new child had a 50 percent chance of being born with the condition. But a local radio call-in program made her the subject of one of its shows. The announcer invited people to call in with their responses to the possibility of Walker Lampley bringing a "disfigured" child into the world. The comments that day were revealing. "It's a horribly cruel thing to have the baby, knowing it's going to be deformed," said one caller. "I think it's kind of irresponsible," said another. And finally, "I would rather not be alive than have a disease like that."

In the end, Walker Lampley's baby was born healthy, although with ectrodactyly. She sued the radio station, saying, "This is about my children and all children in the future born with an unconventional appearance." The lawsuit was unsuccessful, but the publicity surrounding the case generated a great deal of support for her and for those who see disability as something more than a tragedy to be avoided.

The way people with disabilities face their surroundings varies from culture to culture. Ann Ito finds that her University of Hawaii students who come from the U.S. mainland are much more likely than disabled students from other parts of the world to confront situations of inaccessibility "adversarily." Mainland students are less likely to accept barriers passively, even less likely to negotiate outcomes, and more apt to litigate.

We who are raised in the dominant culture of the United States tend to feel that our environment can be manipulated to accommodate to our needs. Neighborhoods can organize to have a stop sign installed at a busy intersection, for example. We can sign petitions to close down nightclubs. We feel we're entitled to our own personal pursuit of comfort and convenience. We have come to believe that the world should reflect our needs, that society guarantees our right to life, liberty, and the pursuit of happiness. When we don't get our way, we sue. There are more lawyers per capita in the United States than in any other country. We expect to get our way.

North Americans, for good or bad, are brought up demanding rights and remodeling their environments to suit their personal needs. That explains the ADA, the independent living movement, and the growing perception of disability as something more than a personal tragedy or a medical pathology.

To summarize, disability is not a set and determined condition, defined entirely by biology. It is a culturally dependent construct that varies widely from one culture to another. Perceptions about people with disabilities vary greatly from one place to another, and from one time to another. Treatment of people with disabilities is not consistent from one culture to another. Perceptions about gender differences have an impact. Whether a person with a disability is handicapped or not, how they are regarded and treated, what they might hope to accomplish in life, and how easy that might be for them—all this is dependent not on how well their bodies or senses or minds might work in relation to some real or perceived cultural norm, but on how their culture defines them and whether it permits, encourages, discourages, or denies their full inclusion.

It's not biology; it's sociology.

My injury, recovery, and readjustment take on a whole new meaning in this light. Much of what I have accomplished since my injury has been the result of my hard work and perseverance. That's what it has felt like to me, and that's how many other people see it too. I am, you might remember from chapter 4, an inspiration. But my hard work wouldn't have meant diddly in a culture that didn't accommodate me. In almost any other country in the world, the outcome from my accident would almost certainly have been different.

Toward the end of our term in Managua, I was becoming more and more paranoid about the increasing likelihood of having an accident in the city. I rode my bike there, too, you see. In the worst traffic, among the craziest drivers in the hemisphere, I rode a used mountain bike. For the first months, I even did so without a helmet. I would weave in and out among the cars. I would race buses to bus stops. I would roar down mountain roads at terminal velocity, passing all manner of cars and trucks. It was all very energizing. But as our term was drawing to a close, each time I went out I got more and more paranoid about getting injured or killed in traffic. I suspect that Vietnam War vets experienced the same thing as their tours of duty were drawing to a close. Oh, Lord, don't let this be my time. I finally gave up riding in Managua altogether.

Who would have thought that my number would finally come up in the safe confines of an Iowa farming community? It's a good thing fate waited, actually. I would not have survived the ordeal in Managua. I would certainly have died from my injuries on a Managua street or in a Managua hospital. In Grinnell I was minutes from the trauma center that saved my life. If I had, by some miracle, survived such an accident in Managua, I would have had a much more difficult time returning to my life. Here in Grinnell I had a good job I could come home to. Through that job I had medical insurance that covered most of my expenses and buys me the high-end adaptive equipment I need to get on with my life. None of this would have been available in Nicaragua. I'd be in someone's back room now, or on a street corner. It would be hard to perceive myself as anything but a useless invalid under such circumstances.

The town I came home to responds to my needs for barrier-free access. During the first year following my injury, the city installed curb cuts in every single block between my home and my church, permitting me to roll directly to work. The following year ramps were installed from the street up to the sidewalk in front of my church, up the two-step curb in front of my favorite coffee shop and bike store (Jeff tells me he lobbied hard for it), and to access the post office (don't ask why the local affiliate of the federal government waited for twelve years after passage of the ADA to comply. It's done now, and that's what counts). After my family moved to a more accessible home in another section of town, curbs were cut between that home and the downtown. That wouldn't have happened in Managua. I'm even being paid to write a book about my experiences! As they say, where else but in America? I'm fortunate, as a person with a disability, to be here. I'm not responsible for the culture that gives me these opportunities. I'm in a privileged situation. I know it, and I'm both humbled and grateful for it. In spite of the shortcomings in the United States in dealing with persons with disabilities, it is still the culture with the most empowering image of disability available.

Of course, that's just me talking—a person from a culture that values the independence of the individual, and that sees barriers to full, autonomous existence as responsive to political and moral leverage. I'm one who has reaped the benefits of this system. Someone with a disability from, say, China, who is used to living in a back room and has based his or her self-perception on cultural tradition, might find my existence with disability positively terrifying. It's all relative.

What it means to be a human being is infinitely variable. There are as many definitions as there are cultures. Cultures define personhood in a variety of ways. Who you are as a person is less dependent on your abilities and attributes than it is on what culture you happen to hail from. Our perceptions of reality are entirely relative. Therefore, what it means to be a person with a disability is always subject to cultural interpretation. It's the purview of the social sciences, not physical or medical science.

Chapter 10

Rights or Rehab?

It's a pitched battle, a full-scale war, and they're not taking prisoners on either side. I'm talking about the struggle for control of perceptions, understandings, and language surrounding the issue of disability. What's at stake is the civil rights of an entire community and a slice of the American social contract pie. Billions of dollars are up for grabs. It's a life-and-death struggle, literally, at least for those defined as disabled.

She was an outside agitator. She came to Grinnell to attend a workshop, and she brought with her an entirely new way of looking at disability. Well, maybe not new to everybody, but new to me. And apparently new to Grinnell. It certainly took Jeff, the coffee shop guy, by surprise. I was still working things out on my own here. She was a catalyst from the outside world.

She used a power scooter for mobility. I scoff at power scooters. I can roll rings around people in power scooters. I can enter places they can't, and push at twice their speed on the sidewalk. My kids and I point and laugh at them. There's an episode of *Seinfeld* in which George, faking a limp, is given the use of a Rascal by his employer. He offends a group of senior citizens who are also on power scooters, and a two-mile-per-hour race ensues. He finally gets away by picking up his scooter and running off with it. Of course, I know I shouldn't laugh. One day I, too, will be the proud user of a Rascal. But I'll adjust to that day when it comes. For now, power scooters provide comic relief.

This woman was an advocate for disability rights in a larger city in Iowa. I don't know who pays her salary or what her job entails, but she had a different outlook on functioning with a disability than I did. My project had been to adjust, fit in, adapt, and function in a world organized by the able-bodied, while creating as little wake as possible. It's not always possible in a wheelchair to slink through a crowd or navigate doors and hallways and stairs, but that was my goal. And I had been doing pretty well at it, thank you very much. But this woman would have none of it. Her personal goal was nothing less than the modification of the world to meet her needs. She wasn't going to adjust to a hostile world. She was going to fight back!

She saw everything as an offense to people with disabilities. *Everything.* I heard her making comments about the size of the restroom at the college facility that housed the workshop. The doors into the facility were too hard to pull open. She carried a little fish scale to measure pounds of pull on doorknobs. She discovered several doors that required two more pounds to open than allowed under ADA guidelines, and notified the college staff and shop owners of their delinquencies. Me, I had always prided myself on being strong enough to open doors. My goal was to function without needing to seek assistance or call attention to my condition. But, admittedly, life was more challenging for this lady. She had less upper body strength and she drove a Rascal. For me it was an individual problem addressed by my own resources. For her, it was a flaw in the social arrangement in Grinnell. These differences, I'm learning, aren't just personal idiosyncrasies; they represent opposite sides of a struggle for the hearts and minds—not to mention the sidewalks and doorways—of the American people.

Her complaints made me uncomfortable. See, this was my town. Why hadn't I fixed these problems yet, she seemed to be demanding. What was I doing, anyway, just hanging around? Passing? For God's sake, boy, stand up for your rights!

Jeff collared me the day after the workshop. It seems the lady in the scooter had paid him a visit. Of course, she couldn't get up the step into his shop. So she rolled around through the alley and came in the back door to give him a piece of her mind. Apparently she butted her scooter into the line at the coffee bar, interrupted Jeff while he was making an espresso drink for a customer, and made a very loud scene in the middle of a set by a string band that was playing for about fifty people in the shop at the time. Now, Jeff is a cool dude, but it doesn't take much to push his buttons. She wouldn't, he told me, getting hotter by the minute, go next door to talk to the landlord about their repeated attempts to make the building accessible. She wouldn't let him explain about the wooden ramp they'd built for me that was stolen before I had a chance to use it. "The thing that irked me the most," he said, "was that she was screaming at me about my store being inaccessible *while she was in the freaking store*! She had gotten in without help, made it to the counter without help, and eventually left without help—even though I *wanted* to help her *out* in the worst way, like maybe through the front window! Her biggest handicap is her communication style." Jeff's ponytail was quivering by now. He was loaded for bear. "What makes those people so uppity?" he demanded to know.

This presented me with something of a dilemma. Jeff doesn't see me as one of "those people." I'm a good cripple, you see, the quiet kind who accepts things the way they are. I'm not one of those uppity crips constantly complaining about one thing or another, the ones who think they're entitled to special treatment, who constantly point out the problems in a shrill and intrusive voice. "Yeah, you're right," I told him. "Those people are insufferable." What could I do? I needed my daily coffee fix, and there's nowhere else in town to get coffee this good. But I felt a little like Uncle Tom in a wheelchair.

This issue called for some reflection.

I never signed up to be an advocate for the cause of disability rights. I've been on soapboxes before, to be sure, for such things as civil rights in El Salvador and nuclear disarmament. I've withheld portions of my taxes in symbolic protest against funding the military industrial complex. I've protested against the launching of a trident nuclear submarine christened the *Corpus Christi*. It was named for the city in Texas, of course, but to radical seminary students at Yale Divinity School, versed in Latin and biblical theology, the name means "the Body of Christ," and we were darned if we were going to let the military name a ship capable of annihilating 208 cities with multiple nuclear warheads after our Lord without a whimper of protest. I've advocated for environmental protection and for bicycle and pedestrian support. I've organized workshops on human rights. But I never agreed to be a spokesperson for civil rights for the disability community. It seems a little selfish, somehow, now that I'm in a wheelchair. I was never trained for it. Nobody likes an uppity crip.

Then I had to accompany my son on a college visit in the fall of his senior year in high school. We drove to a venerable institution with a beautiful historic campus a couple of hours from Grinnell. I think it was our first such visit, so I had no preconceived notions. I take that back. I did harbor one preconceived notion. I assumed that the campus would be accessible, at least for the parent of a prospective student making a first visit to the admissions department. This was a decade after the ADA, after all.

After two hours on the road, we arrived on campus, found the admissions office and politely inquired about a restroom. They pointed to a sign on the wall down a hallway where I instantly identified three stairs blocking my access. Oh, sorry. Is there another restroom? Yes, on the second floor, but, oh, wait, you couldn't get there, could you? After some hasty consulting behind the counter among the student volunteers and reception staff, they directed me to an adjoining building. I dutifully rolled over there, finding a door to a men's room an inch too narrow for my chair. I came back in a state of some agitation. When the entire admissions staff came up blank to my entreaties for a genuine accessible restroom somewhere on this god-forsaken campus, a vice president was called for and we went on a lovely tour together. Finally, five buildings later—I'm not making this up—and down a steep hill that I'm sure violated ADA guidelines for incline, we pulled up to a student center that thankfully had a bathroom I could get into. By then I would have been glad to empty my leg bag discreetly into someone's coffee cup.

The vice president and I had a little talk at the end of our visit. I'm not a demanding person. It goes against my nature to seek concessions, especially for myself. I'm hesitant about pointing out flaws. But on this particular day I found myself pointing out, as only an uppity crip can, that his college was woefully inadequate in terms of accessibility for persons with mobility impairments. Didn't they have students in wheelchairs? Hadn't anyone ever visited before who was in a chair? It's been ten years since the Americans with Disabilities Act was passed, the federal legislation that requires accommodation, for God's sake. What have you been doing all this time?

I haven't heard back from him. And my son wasn't accepted at that school. He didn't like it, anyway.

I was beginning to learn how important the ADA was, how it had already impacted my life, the public facilities around me, and my expectations of accommodation. I also discovered that my home-state senator, Tom Harkin, was its initial sponsor. He had fought for the legislation because he had an intimate experience with disability. His brother was deaf. Harkin knew what it was like to be denied access simply on the basis of ability.

The ADA didn't change everything overnight, but it did have an impact. It changed the climate of what was morally the right thing to do in this country regarding treatment of persons with disabilities. It acknowledged that about 43 million people in the United States could be defined as having a serious disability. Critics point out that the count was short by tens of millions, since it failed to include people with a whole variety of disabilities such as learning disabilities, certain mental illnesses, and HIV/AIDS. An additional 7 million people, for example, have a severe, crippling form of arthritis. But it was a start. The ADA took a swing at it. In passing the ADA, Congress also recognized that these people had been "subjected to serious and pervasive discrimination." And it provided federal legal recourse for victims of this discrimination to address their situation. Title I defines disability and addresses employment issues. Title II covers access to public entities, including public transportation. Title III engages the private sector, making discrimination against people with disability illegal in business and public accommodations. "If services are provided, services must be made available to persons with disabilities." Title IV covers telecommunications for persons with disabilities.

With the ADA in place, it became illegal to deny employment to any individual who, apart from his or her disability, was otherwise qualified to do the job (given reasonable accommodation by the employer). Persons with disabilities were entitled to equal enjoyment of goods, services, facilities, advantages, and accommodations.

Many disability activists are critical of the bill. They are quick to point out that there was no enforcement mechanism included in the law—enforcement is consumer driven if it is to happen at all—and it has no affirmative action component like other civil rights legislation to redress past wrongs. It has huge loopholes built into it to let businesses off the hook if they can prove that the required accommodations are too expensive. And the courts have not proven as supportive as had been hoped. But it does create a climate that hadn't existed before. I'm grateful for that because it has provided an environment for me to continue to work toward my potential even after a devastating injury. My integration into the community, as difficult as it may have seemed to me, was vastly easier now than it would have been before passage of the bill. I can take many things for granted that people with disabilities just ten or twenty years earlier had to fight for. Though I'm a reluctant advocate, I recognize that I reap the benefits of struggle and sacrifice that others have made on my behalf.

It is worth spending some time exploring the Americans with Disabilities Act—not just what it does and fails to do and how it came to be, but what it implies about the meaning of disability itself. The movement that brought it into being was not just trying to pressure society to build ramps, print elevator buttons in Braille, widen doorways, and enable people with disabilities to enter the workforce. Its goal was nothing short of a complete restructuring of the political landscape in America, a revision of the entire cultural model for understanding disability. Its leaders were trying to affect hearts and minds, to wrest control of the perception of disability from the halls of medical science and place it squarely in the arena of civil rights. People with disabilities were rejecting being treated as medical patients. They were claiming for themselves the right to be treated as members of an oppressed social class. They proposed that, in spite of tremendous differences between themselves in terms of their disabilities, they still shared a common culture as persons with disabilities. The change represented here is huge. This point cannot be overstated. The ADA represents nothing less than a new paradigm for understanding disability, one that had never surfaced and could not have been imagined previously in human history.

In spite of profound differences between people with disabilities, there is a sense in which every person with a disability shares a common experience. Often the differences are what seem most apparent. Think about the variations represented under the rubric "disabled." We're talking about cancer survivors, diabetics, people with head injuries, people who are blind or deaf, people with mobility impairments, learning disabilities, and mental illnesses—and each group is clamoring for programs and funding to address its own needs. Often they are in competition for scarce resources. Sometimes the solutions for one special interest group clash with those for another. In Grinnell, for example, as the city was busy making curb cuts and ramps for me to roll downtown, I learned that people who are blind and who use the same sidewalks may have more difficulty navigating the corners. They tap the curbs to establish their location.

But in terms of society's understanding and treatment of disability, there is common ground. People with disabilities tend to share, for example, the stigma of being disabled in a society that values physical perfection and a narrow definition of beauty. We are seen as deviants, unconventional, abnormal, outsiders. We share difficulties in getting around, in accessing public facilities, in using equipment designed for use by the majority of the population. Even if we *can* get into the coffee shop by the back door, there's something of a second-class feel to having to enter an establishment through the alley. We share rejection by a skeptical society that is reluctant to hire otherwise qualified applicants simply because of their disabilities. Even on a personal level we find we have things in common that distinguish us from nondisabled people. Put a couple of wheelchair users in a room and we have instant rapport. Talk immediately turns to bladder and bowel issues. We share tips about our Quickies and Top Ends, TiSports and Colours. We recognize each other by coded labels that are incomprehensible to outsiders. "I'm an L-1 incomplete, how about you?" "Oh, you lucky bastard. I'm a complete C-4 quad." (Translation: My spinal cord injury is at the level of the first lumbar vertebra, although the injury is incomplete and I have some movement below the waist. My acquaintance is a quadriplegic, injured at the fourth cervical vertebra, with no movement below the neck.) We check each other out surreptitiously in a crowd. The other day I was rolling through a shopping center and a man in a wheelchair, as he rolled past, gave me a high-five hand slap. I didn't know him from Adam, but I recognized his experience, and he knew mine. Other disabled persons, with other kinds of disabilities, may have even more in common to identify them as a distinct culture. The deaf, for example, have their own language. If a deaf person can read lips as well as communicate through sign language, she or he can legitimately claim to be bilingual. Others may need a translator to speak with the hearing culture.

This new understanding of disability as a distinct minority culture could not have arisen until very recently. The ground had to be prepared politically, intellectually, and emotionally. Society had to grow up in its understanding of disability to make it possible. Romel Mackelprang and Richard Salsgiver (1999) identify three distinct historical models for understanding the notion of disability. The first, what they call the "moral model," sees disability as a moral, not just a physical, imperfection. This was the operative model during biblical times. Illness, suffering, and disability were thought of as divine punishment for sins. Disability was an indication of depravity. In spite of advances in medicine and science, vestiges of this model are still present in popular culture. Note the roll of people with disabilities in such movies as *It's a Wonderful Life* or *Unbreakable*. It's no accident that Captain Hook has a prosthetic arm. The evil Dr. Loveless in the television series and now the movie, *The Wild, Wild West,* uses a wheelchair. The Penguin, arch-villain in *Batman Returns*, turned to a life of crime because he was angry at having been abandoned by his parents in the sewer when they found he was born with a disability. Villains are often depicted as disabled, decrepit, wretched, and bitter. A twisted exterior makes it easier to make sense of a twisted soul. The two go hand in hand in popular cultural assumptions.

The Enlightenment brought a change in models to western thinking. In the mid 1700s, there arose the perception that problems were soluble. The environment could be manipulated. Humans could be perfected. With the development of the proper medical knowledge or surgical technique, people's bodies could be infinitely responsive to healing intervention. This assumption has driven the pursuit of scientific knowledge and has resulted in amazing gains in the understanding of the human body. This is the "medical model" of understanding disability. Do you remember the 1970s television series, *The Six Million Dollar Man*? Each episode was prefaced with images of a terrible plane crash and the salvaging of the injured test pilot. "We have the technology to rebuild him," says the tense, competent medical director. "Stronger, faster, and better than before." According to this model, physical perfectibility is the goal, full recovery through healing is the protocol following injury or illness, or, failing that, physical therapy is designed to bring the patient as close as possible to his or her former experience.

A third model, which has only begun to emerge over the last several decades, is the social/minority model. It removes the definition and locus of disability from the individual and places it on social and cultural forces.

> In contrast to the medical and moral models, the social/minority model of disability views persons with disabilities as a minority group within a dominant non-disabled society. It sees the phenomenon of disability as a social construct much like race or gender. The limitations of disability, widely known as handicaps, come about because of society's definition of disability rather than any innate characteristic of disability. Therefore, intervention is not necessarily with the person who has the disability, but with the society that creates and harbors the definition. (Mackelprang 1999, 40)

It's an issue now of diversity or difference, not deviance or deficit. The experience of disability has become a social and political movement, not a cause for shame or a condition in need of treatment.

The emergence of the disabilities-rights movement is brand new in human history. Two factors seem to have contributed to its emergence just now. The first of these was the growth in numbers of people with disabilities in society. There are simply more of us around now than ever before! Before the end of World War II, most people with serious disabilities simply did not survive. There weren't enough of them to start a movement.

> In World War I, only four hundred men survived with wounds that paralyzed them from the waist down, and 90 percent of them died before they reached home. But in World War II, two thousand paraplegic soldiers survived, and over 85 percent of them were still alive in the late 1960s. The development of antibiotic drugs and new medical procedures improved the odds. As recently as the 1950s, death remained likely in the very early stages of a spinal cord injury as a result of respiratory, bladder, and other health complications. Now doctors neutralize those problems, and paraplegics and quadriplegics can live long, healthy lives. (Shapiro 1994, 5)

Medical advances have greatly expanded the ranks of the disabled. If you think you're seeing more people in wheelchairs, more people who are blind or visually impaired, and more mainstreamed adults with learning or mental disabilities than you did even ten or twenty years ago, it's not just an aberration. There are more of them around, and they are more visible. They are less likely to be hidden at home or at an institution. Having a disability is becoming "normal."

A second factor behind the sea change in self-perception of people with disabilities is the civil rights movement of the 1960s and 1970s. People with disabilities began noticing the change in self-perception of other minority groups. Oppressed groups began reclaiming with pride what had been seen as a stigma, and demanding equal rights. We've seen black power ("Black and beautiful, baby!"), gay pride ("I'm Straight but not Narrow"), and feminism ("A Woman's place is in the House . . . and the Senate"). Now there's a self-identification among the disability community. A retired lady in Grinnell pushes a wheelchair with a bumper sticker on the back that reads, "0 to 10 in 60 Seconds." A mentally retarded girl wears a T-shirt that reads, "I have Ups Syndrome." Marilyn Hamilton, who invented and built the Quickie line of wheelchairs, used to say, "If you can't stand up, stand out!" I have a T-shirt that reads, "It's not what you push. It's what pushes you."

Marca Bristo, president of Access Living of Chicago and chair of the National Counsel on Disability, was paralyzed in a swimming accident as a young woman. She describes how this new, more militant attitude about disability took root in her own experience:

> I found personal power through others who had crossed that bridge before me, others with disabilities who taught me the power of accepting who I was and using my newly changed self to change the world around me.
>
> People taught me that the world looked at us wrong, and that we had a responsibility to help the world see through our eyes. A young girl came to my office in Chicago one day and said, "Before I met you and before I came to Access Living, I thought my wheelchair was too wide for the bathroom doors. Now I know the bathroom doors are too narrow for my wheelchair."
>
> It is that paradigm shift, that change in worldview, that gave the disability-rights community its power. (1999, 66)

This is a brand new way to look at disability. All of a sudden it's not a liability to have a disability. It's a Cause, with a capital C. When Franklin Delano Roosevelt was president, disability was a shameful thing. He had no choice, if he were to remain in political office, but to hide from the public the fact that he had been crippled by polio and used a wheelchair for mobility. He assumed—and rightly so—that the public would have seen his disability as a sign of weakness. Even today, as a memorial is being established for FDR, there is controversy over displaying him as he really was, in a wheelchair, or as he presented himself to the public.

The deaf and the blind were the first to begin to see themselves as distinct minority groups, and to use their identity and power to claim social benefits. A school for the blind was begun in Baltimore in 1812, and Thomas Hopkins Gallaudet founded a school for the deaf in Washington, D.C., in 1817. By the end of the nineteenth century, deaf and blind people were already setting up advocacy groups that proved effective in securing special rights and financial assistance.

You have to be very careful about offering help to newly empowered people with disabilities. They tend to be on the militant side. Kevin Robinson, in an article in *New Mobility* magazine titled "The Last Time I Saw Jeff," writes a tongue-in-cheek account of a blind friend's process of political empowerment. Jeff had become militant about his blindness and warned his friends that offers of help would not be tolerated. One day, a church deacon brought Jeff to church for a social function. On disembarking from the car there was some confusion and more than a little danger on a narrow road:

> "Jeff," he said, "there's a steep drop-off right outside your door. If you'll give me a second to get the kids out I can give you a hand."
>
> It didn't sit well. With a look of disgust, Jeff opened his door, flipped open his long red-and-white cane and stepped from the car. He promptly disappeared from sight.
>
> "I rushed around fast as I could," the deacon told me, "but all I could do was watch him roll, head over heels, with that cane flailing round and round, red-white, red-white, red-white, all the way down the hill."
>
> We watched Jeff's progress for several moments in silence. "Whatcha gonna do now?" I finally asked as Jeff disappeared under the eaves of the distant forest.
>
> "Well," said the deacon, "since Jeff hasn't asked me for any help yet, I reckon I'll get myself a hot dog." (2000, 43)

The Independent Living Movement, a distinctly North American initiative, was started by Ed Roberts in Berkeley, California, in the 1960s. It encouraged persons with disabilities to move out of hospitals, nursing homes, and rehab centers and to live independent lives. Roberts, who died in 1995, was a pioneer in the development of the new paradigm for understanding disability. At a time when African Americans were breaking the color barrier by enrolling in traditionally white schools and universities, Roberts was quietly initiating his own assault on the disability barrier at the University of Southern California at Berkeley. A quadriplegic, he attended an inaccessible college, living in the infirmary because dorms were inaccessible. He was once told by a state vocational rehab program that he was too severely disabled to be employed; he went on to become head of that very agency.

The philosophy of the model Roberts developed revolves around three principles: Those who best know the needs of the disabled are the disabled themselves; these needs can best be met by comprehensive programs that provide a variety of services; and the end goal is as full an integration as possible into the community. All kinds of services were initiated at his Centers for Independent Living to make integration possible: from accessible transportation and housing to employment, education, and networking. In order to be integrated fully and productively into society, all that was needed by persons with disabilities was accommodation. These centers were the missionary outposts of a new way of understanding persons with disabilities and their role in society. Centers for Independent Living are today being established in Europe and Japan.

It was a political battle with economic implications, as people with disabilities began to see themselves as a discrete minority group, and to recognize the discrimination with which they had been treated. As always in politics, it becomes a politics of scarcity. The disability community was clamoring for a piece of the pie, claiming scarce resources that would otherwise have been claimed by other groups. This new movement was going to cost something, and funds would have to come from somewhere. The first law that made it illegal to discriminate on the basis of disability was passed by Congress in 1973. Its wording was copied straight out of the Civil Rights Act of 1964. Then politicians began to see the financial risks involved, and they got cold feet about its implementation. It wasn't signed into law until four years later, after three hundred disabled activists took over the regional offices of Health, Education, and Welfare (HEW) in San Francisco and occupied it for twenty-eight days. This was a watershed moment in the struggle for empowerment of people with disabilities. What had been the individual's cross to bear—a pathological medical condition—now became a minority group issue, a movement, a community defined by oppression and a claim to long-denied rights. Through cooperation, the group discovered it could impact the political landscape of America.

In 1988, deaf students and alumni at Gallaudet University staged a rebellion that declared deaf pride alive and well. Gallaudet was in the process of hiring a new president for the 124-year-old institution. None of the six previous presidents had been deaf. Students felt that it was high time to have a deaf president. But out of a slate of three candidates, the trustees chose the one hearing candidate. She didn't even know American Sign Language. It was a recipe for disaster. The student body was incensed. They closed down the campus and, skillfully using the national media attention focused on their struggle, forced the university to hire its first deaf president.

The disabilities-rights movement had come of age. Two years later, the Americans with Disabilities Act was passed. The scope of the legislation was significant.

> While hardly a panacea, the ADA proposes to ensure the right of Americans with disabilities to move from the margins of society into the mainstream. It promises them equal access to the public sites where their fellow citizens conduct their everyday lives; subways and snack bars, offices and auditoriums, jury boxes and gymnasiums. . . . When he signed the ADA into law, President George H. W. Bush proclaimed, "Let the shameful wall of exclusion finally come tumbling down." (Longmore and Umansky 2001, 1)

It had been a hard-fought political and economic struggle. Although the language of the ADA was modeled after the Civil Rights Act of 1964, which prohibited racial segregation and oppression, the ADA looked to be vastly more expensive. The Civil Rights Act cost nothing to implement. In some cases, it actually saved money, as separate facilities were integrated. Retrofitting society to meet ADA guidelines was going to be costly. Government buildings and public accommodations would have to be remodeled. As new buildings were constructed they would have to be accessible to persons with varieties of disabilities.

The only way such an expansive bill could have been made palatable to conservative politicians and business interests was to weaken it by giving business an out: no one was required to do anything that was considered an undue expense. It was hoped that common sense would rule and that no business would have to incur undue hardship in providing accommodation. There was no enforcement agency. There were no punitive damages allowed, and caps were set on damages that could be collected. In some ways, the bill as finally passed was a pretty watered-down version of a civil rights document. "Give me my due rights," people with disabilities were demanding. "But only if it's not too inconvenient." Would the NAACP have accepted language like that as part of racial segregation legislation, I wonder? "Equal rights now—if it's okay with you all."

Still, the ADA was immensely significant. In one document, it affects two watershed concerns for people with disabilities. First of all, it legally establishes a political framework for the inclusion of people with disabilities in society. The challenges disabled people face in getting from place to place, in finding significant employment, in being allowed to engage as full participants in society, are all addressed in this legislation. It makes discrimination against people with disabilities illegal. It's not just me on my own against the coffee shop step and the college restrooms and the curbs and all the rest. Now I have the weight of the federal government on my side when I press my issues of access. That alone is a huge accomplishment. Speaking as one person who benefits from the ADA, I especially want to express my appreciation for the handy parking places.

But the other thing accomplished by the ADA was even bigger, to my way of thinking. It formalizes this radically new understanding of the concept of disability. It goes beyond the medical model that individualizes the problems of persons with disabilities. With the ADA, people with disabilities are seen in relation to society at large, and society assumes certain responsibilities for their full inclusion. Whatever shortcomings the bill contains, at least it recognizes disability as a legitimate minority group concept. It stakes out and protects certain rights that group is entitled to. This is a transformation in the perception of people with disabilities.

The ADA raises questions for physical rehabilitation and social accommodation. For example, given this new paradigm for understanding disability politically and socially, should physical therapists concentrate on teaching patients in wheelchairs how to jump curbs, or should they put their efforts into training them in political advocacy? Who is "liable" for a handicap? Where does the responsibility for access lie? My dive back into life since my injury has been a personal struggle to overcome the obstacles in my way. Should I have been more proactive in demanding that the social environment be remodeled to suit my needs? Could the confrontational lady in the Rascal have been right?

Since the passage of the Americans with Disabilities Act, some interesting developments have taken place. Its impact has been significant in some areas, but negligible in others. It has made almost no difference in terms of employment. It is still the case that two-thirds of working-age Americans with disabilities are unemployed. The law hasn't been used as much to get people with disabilities into the workforce, as it has to keep workers who are hurt on the job employed. The law has little power to change the employment landscape. A 1999 American Bar Association study of more than one thousand employment lawsuits found that plaintiffs lost their cases over 90 percent of the time.

In terms of modifying the physical landscape, however, the bill has been more effective. Even though most institutions and businesses have been reluctant to initiate new accommodations on their own, people with disabilities have successfully pressured and sued to improve access in hotels, movie theaters, stadiums, schools, department stores, banks, and other facilities. It is becoming more "fashionable" to see ramps and universal signs of access. It amazes me that some new structures are still thrown up every day with no thought of accessibility. I've heard that new homes built with universally accessible designs would cost no more than 5 percent more than the expense of a traditional home. But if you wait until you need to remodel an existing home, you'll pay a lot more than that.

Even with these modest gains, however, there has been a growing backlash to the ADA legislation. As I'm writing this manuscript there is a legal battle taking shape between the airlines and persons who are larger than "average." The *Honolulu Advertiser* reported on June 20, 2002, that the airlines were cracking down on oversized fliers taking up two seats while paying for only one. "We sell seats on airplanes," explained a Southwest Airlines official. "If a customer uses two seats, they should pay for two seats."

The article revealed that airline seats are typically seventeen and a half inches wide. Now wait a minute. Have you ever been on a long flight, with the armrests digging into your sides, your neighbors tripping over you to get to the restroom, and the kid behind you banging on your seat the whole way? There's nothing "normal" about the space the average person is given on an airline. The seats are none too wide for "normal" sized people who try to squeeze in and spend several hours on a long flight. My current wheelchair cushion width is seventeen inches. Airline seats give me just an extra quarter inch on each side. And I'm not a big guy. I weigh 160 pounds dripping wet.

Miriam Berg, president of the Council on Size and Weight Discrimination, entered the discussion and reframed it from an argument about individual deviance into terms of the social/minority model. She responded, "If a person takes up more than one seat, that's not the problem of the person, that's the problem of the seat." Physical accommodations need to recognize a wide diversity of size and ability among the population. That's the message of this new paradigm. It's not deviance, it's diversity.

A recently introduced bill would require attorneys filing ADA suits to warn businesses ninety days in advance, in order to encourage compliance. A recent *Wall Street Journal* headline complained, "Under the ADA, We May All Be Disabled." The article reported that more and more people were claiming special treatment under the ADA. Indeed, in one affluent high school, fully one-third of the student body is officially regarded as disabled, entitling these students to expensive tutoring, computer equipment, and special services. Disability activists warn that the "ADA is shrinking." They are reluctant to go back to congress seeking to strengthen any of its provisions, for fear that this new political climate may roll back some of what is already in place. They lament that the civil rights leadership in the country seems oblivious to the inclusion of disability rights as an agenda item.

What do I think about the issue? I'm still not sure. It's a process, coming to understand disability as a civil rights issue. I couldn't have entertained this model when I first rolled out of rehab. It simply wouldn't have occurred to me. There was work I had to do, and I had to do it on my own, in adjusting to life as a person newly disabled. That's what they had trained me for. I'm coming to understand disability as a civil rights issue, but I'm not completely in that camp yet. I'm not sure you can roll the whole understanding of disability into a minority model. I don't want to transform every relationship in my small town into one of confrontation. I don't want to offend Jeff or jeopardize my access to gourmet coffee. I don't want to put the burden of my injury on everyone around me. My Calvinistic work ethic kicks in here; I don't want to make other people responsible for problems that I need to work out for myself.

Yet my condition is not purely a symptom of personal weakness that I need to overcome. Stairs where there could just as easily have been ramps, narrow doors that could just as easily have been cut wider, and attitudes that stigmatize people in wheelchairs and with other disabilities have no place in a town that prides itself in being hospitable. If my condition is a symptom of human diversity, then my hometown should make allowances for people of all ability levels to participate as fully as possible. And if nobody else is going to fight that battle, then I may have to. Who better than me to notice these deficiencies and recruit allies to help work to correct them? I can look at it as something I can give back to the place that reared and nurtured and cut some ramps for me.

Because battles have already been waged, you don't have to become political to live with a disability. But you can if you want to. And maybe you should. Only here in the United States, and only now at the start of the twenty-first century, do we who live with disabilities have the opportunity to make such a choice. Whether you take up that mantle or not, people with disabilities today benefit from the efforts of those who have preceded them. The rights and ramps and perceptions we take for granted now are the fruits of hard-fought battles. We're not completely defined by society's rigid definition of disability. Disabilities-rights activists have staked out a new territory for us. Like Neil Armstrong planting an American flag on the moon, Ed Roberts and others have staked a claim on behalf of people with disabilities in the social and political dialogue of the day. We can choose to take up that flag if we wish. If not, at least the territory is open to us.

That opportunity is another of the many gifts that have been made apparent to me.

Chapter 11

Rolling Reflections

Think of this final chapter as an album of postcards from my sojourn in the land of disability. Or snapshots from a family vacation. Only this vacation is not one I'm coming back from. These reflections revolve around the wheelchair, the symbol of my new limitations, but at the same time the guarantor of mobility, speed, and independence. Consider this my spin on things.

A minister and two of his parishioners were out in a small boat fishing, when they realized that they'd left their extra bait on the dock. "Not to worry," said one of the church members. "I'll go get it." And with that, he stepped over the transom of the boat and walked across the top of the water to the dock. He retrieved the tub of bait and returned to the boat the same way. Because the other parishioner didn't say anything about this strange occurrence, the minister didn't either.

Soon, the three men grew hungry. The other parishioner said, "Be right back," and he stepped out of the boat and walked across the water in the same way as his companion. He went to the bait shop, got a bag of pretzels, and returned over the water to the boat. By now, the minister was full of wonder, but he didn't say anything.

Soon, after all those pretzels, the men got thirsty. This time, the minister popped up. "I'll go for beer," he said. And he stepped over the side of the boat and sank like a rock.

His two parishioners turned to each other, and one said to the other, "Maybe we should have told him where the tree stumps were."

This chapter is a continuation of my attempts to indicate where, in the foreign culture of the experience of disability, the stumps are.

Scott Draper ordered my first wheelchair shortly before I was released into the world. Scott was the rehabilitation engineer at the physical therapy department in which I found myself. He showed me a catalogue. "Here's what you should get. What do you think?"

What was I to say? "Great," I told Scott. "It looks fine to me." One of his jobs was to match my injury level, physical abilities, and personality to the machine he constructed for me out of the catalogue. It's an exacting science, I've since learned. Thankfully, long gone are the days when you call up the drug store and order an Everest and Jennings or Invacare wheelchair over the phone. It's no longer one-size-fits-all. That has made for some tremendous advances in mobility for the disabled masses. But it has also lowered the gauntlet when it comes to finding a chair that fits.

The chair he ordered for me was made by Quickie Corporation. It was nothing like the heavy folding chairs with the leather slings you see in hospitals. For one thing, it had a rigid frame that didn't fold up. "Rigid chairs are better for performance," Scott assured me. "Performance?" I wondered if we were talking about trained bear shows. Juggling acts maybe, or magic or balloon animals? No, he corrected, they simply roll better, more efficiently with less push. Less wiggle in the frame.

Now I understood the principle. It was like a bike frame. You want the most rigid bicycle frame possible to ensure that the energy you put into the pedals gets transferred with the least amount of waste directly into forward momentum. Wheelchairs are the same way. Chairs with rigid frames don't wobble. They track straight and return your investment of energy with forward motion. The also weigh half as much as a hospital frame—twenty-five pounds compared to fifty pounds. They're often made of aluminum alloy, the same material as good bike frames. Mine came with a low-slung back, armrests, and antitip bars in the back. Scott told me that most active wheelchair users jettison the add-ons quickly. They strip their chairs down to next to nothing. It didn't take me long to lower the back of my seat even more, to strip off the armrests, and to remove the antitip bars. I flipped over backwards only a few times before I learned where my center of gravity was and how to maintain a vertical posture. Insurance paid for everything but the designer colors listed in the brochure. I chose a neon purple color for the chair, even though I had to pay an extra hundred bucks out-of-pocket for my extravagance.

I had no idea of the significance of what I was now riding, or what it would eventually come to mean to me. The Quickie brand wheelchair was a relatively new arrival on the market. Its development was intimately related to the rise of the new, more assertive identity for persons with disabilities that was explored in the previous chapter. Marilyn Hamilton, an avid Californian sports enthusiast, was responsible. One summer day in 1978 she was injured in a hang glider accident and became paraplegic. She was impatient with physical therapy and refused to accept the clunky hospital wheelchair they tried to put her in. She talked her hang gliding friends into building her an ultra-light wheelchair out of the same aluminum tubing the gliders were made from. The result was a wheelchair that was incredibly light and strong. "Hamilton had reinvented the wheelchair. She took a piece of medical equipment and made it fun and sporty. She took the universal symbol of sickness and turned it into a symbol of disability self-pride." At that moment in my recovery, Hamilton's motto "If you can't stand up, stand out" sounded pretty good to me (I've since toned it down a notch or two). Her chair was such an improvement that she started her own wheelchair company, selling chairs as fast as she could crank them out. Wheelchair users had doubled from 1960 to 1980, so there was a growing market for her product.

The new chairs catered to a new and growing group of people with disabilities who were defining themselves in new ways. They were no longer medical patients; they were a social minority group, clamoring for their rights, independence, and curb cuts. The new chair that Hamilton produced was sleek. It looked more like a racing bike than a traditional wheelchair. The tubing under the rider almost disappeared from sight. It was sporty and maneuverable. And it came in designer colors, to satisfy the growing consumer demand for novelty. Even the name of the new company, "Quickie," was a sign of its placement in the market. One advertisement slogan quipped, "You need a Quickie." They were selling wheelchairs with sexual double entendre!

Twenty years later, Quickie was still turning out cutting-edge chairs. God bless Scott, my rehab engineer, for recognizing the possibilities when he found me my first one. My chair rolled well. It had a low-slung back in black nylon. It was a remarkable fit, for having been a wild guess on the part of the technician. It was fast. Oh, not at first. The wheelchair is only as fast as the engine. I rolled around a one-mile measured trail on the edge of town to see how it would feel and how long it would take me. Yes, I was back to my old competitive habits, putting a stopwatch to every activity. Twenty-eight minutes was what I recorded that first circuit, just over two miles per hour. And I was beat. But I went back to the track several times a week, until I got my times down to seven or seven and a half minutes per mile. Now I was rolling. That was the pace I used to jog! Before long I entered a local 5K race in that chair and was immensely satisfied to have beaten some of the able-bodied field.

I started taking walks with my family on the sidewalks around our house. A couple of blocks seemed long enough at first. It took full concentration, I was finding, to drive the chair. A crack in the sidewalk, a stick on the road, a pothole or just an uneven surface could send me flying off the front of my chair if I wasn't careful. Short wheelbase, you know. I have to pop little wheelies over every little imperfection. Even now it takes careful attention when I'm wheeling. In fact, it takes even more attention now, because the new chair I have boasts even smaller front caster wheels and a shorter wheelbase.

I took longer and longer strolls in the chair. It was fun and not too taxing to roll to my office and back. I found I could roll longer distances—and faster—than was comfortable for pedestrians on foot. Ann and my kids are constantly whining at me to slow down. Left to my own now, I probably stroll comfortably at six or seven miles per hour, compared to about four miles per hour for a fast walker. On a long straight stretch, if the sidewalk is not slanted to one side or the other, my arms become the pistons that my legs had been on my bicycle. Lean and push. Pop back up, breathe deep. Lean and push. The rhythm becomes a mantra, and I'm carried along with the wind in my face.

The chair becomes a decided advantage on long shopping trips to the mall. My companions are dragging, looking for a place to sit down. But I carry my own personal chair with me. I could roll through malls for hours. And sometimes, with my daughter, I do. She's the only one in the family now who still has the stamina to out-shop me. The mall was my first solo excursion. I can't remember what errand took me there, but it was an experience that tested my new identity as disabled. I caught people's attention. No one looks you in the eye for long in the mall unless they're trying to catch your attention. I watched people's eyes. First, they glanced at me as they would at anyone they happen to come upon, then they looked away, again normally. But then it would register. Here's a person moving differently. Instead of bobbing along, step-by-step, this one is rolling smoothly. He's shorter. Oh, it's a man in a wheelchair. As the realization would dawn on them, that would be the last I would see of their eyes. Yes, it's a man in a wheelchair. Quick. Look away. Don't let him catch you staring, for God's sake!

Except for the children. They were fascinated. Their eyes locked onto my wheels, my hands and arms pushing them, my legs. They would whisper to their mom or dad, "That man's in a wheelchair. Look." And the parents would always hush them. "Shhh. Don't point."

Sometimes I do wheelies and other wheelchair tricks to impress kids. Their eyes open wide and smiles spread across their whole face. But usually they get dragged away by parents who are concerned that they will embarrass me. Or themselves.

On those first excursions into the community I was self-conscious and shy. I hurried in, made my purchase, and fled to the safety of my car. What were they thinking about me? What did I look like to other people now? In the past I had had a specific image of my body and self. I was confident in my walk, in my style of clothing, in my physique, in my hair. It wasn't a big thing, but I knew who I was. Now, in a wheelchair, what would be noticed about me? They were seeing only the wheelchair. It didn't matter what else I might have had to offer; the wheelchair was the first impression.

My chair has become much more to me than a piece of adaptive equipment. It is an extension of my flesh. It is my legs. It represents mobility. It supplements my physical abilities. It is always at my side when I'm sitting on the couch or in bed. When my kids get in it and roll off, I become a little nervous. My current church moderator, who is also the youth group leader, likes to roll around in it. He's teaching himself wheelies, though he still has a lot to learn. When I check my chair at the ramp leading to commercial airlines, I'm always anxious about getting it back when we land. I don't like it removed from me. I need it to access connecting flights. "No," I tell the ticket agent. "An airport wheelchair to get to my next flight is not acceptable." This chair is my prosthesis, an extension of who I am. A substitute is not adequate, even for short distances. Would you be willing to be given someone else's shoes to walk around in? Someone else's glasses to read with? Someone else's toothbrush? You get the point.

The chair served me for four years, but even as high-tech and carefully measured as it was, I was learning it had its drawbacks. The chair was too wide, for one thing. There were countless bathroom doors that seemed to be just one inch too narrow for this chair. Part of the blame was mine. In the impact five years ago, my pelvis was shattered and has healed with a gap between the two halves. It's called an "open book fracture." It cuts a strange image on an X-ray. I sit pretty wide now. But there was a gap of about an inch between my hips and the edge of the cushion, another little gap between the cushion and the inside of the wheels, yet another between the inside of the wheels and the outside of the push rims.

Those inches and fractions add up. My chair was wider than any chair I ever ran across in use by active wheelers. It was something of an embarrassment, not to mention of limited usefulness. In comparison to pushing a narrower chair, with wheel width about the same as my shoulder width, this Quickie chair put a great deal more strain on my shoulders than necessary. Shoulder strain is a huge issue for wheelchair users. Shoulders aren't designed to take the regular stress that we put on them. When your arms take over the work of mobility from your legs, they do double duty. Bob Kaloupek, a man in Grinnell who has been using a wheelchair for fifty years (Ann and I visited him soon after my release from the hospital, and he's been a useful role model and mentor), shakes his head when I roll by pushing my racing wheelchair or cranking my handcycle. "Your shoulders will wear out," he warns. So anything that adds shoulder strain needs to be examined. Little things count. The chair also turned out to be a little too low for the length of my legs from ankle to knee, which resulted in me sitting too hard on my butt bones. And it was longer than it needed to be, limiting the maneuverability of the whole thing.

Scott had warned me that a first wheelchair for a newly-injured person might not be satisfactory for very long. He was right. As my skills improved and my body adjusted to its new position, I decided I needed something sportier.

I began to notice other wheelchair users. We look each other over, sizing each other up. How smoothly do they roll? How long do you suppose they've been injured? What level of injury? How do you suppose they see me? What kind of chair are they in? What brand of tires? Are they strong and independent or do they seem weak and dependent? We don't ask each other these questions out loud. That would be rude, a violation of the unspoken rules of etiquette. But, at least in the place I'm at now, I'm busy sizing up the "competition." I'm better at being disabled than that person, aren't I? I rolled by a guy in the shopping center a few days ago. He was a few years older than I, grizzled and worn, but still pushing his own chair, in a respectable piece of equipment, wearing gloves, and obviously independent. When he passed I nodded my head in his direction. We *knew* each other, though we were strangers.

I began noticing the equipment used by other active and athletic wheelers, some of which seemed even more exciting than my Quickie. Quickie as a company had gotten big. It was bought out by an even bigger medical supply company. Its cutting-edge reputation was losing ground to smaller, more daredevil entrepreneurial companies, with even more in-your-face advertising campaigns. Wheelchairs with names such as "barracuda," "boing," "champion," "reactor," "rebel," "X-treme," "impact," "hammer," "heat," and "nitro" were being introduced. The wheelchair catalogue sounds like a lineup of professional wrestlers! One company offered a full-color catalogue featuring tattooed, muscular men with scantily-clad women draped over their chairs. Ann caught me with one of their ads. "What are you looking at?" she demanded, suspiciously. Guiltily, I quickly shuffled the pages. "Nothing, honey. I'm just reading the articles. I mean, just shopping for a wheelchair."

A new brand of wheelchair appeared, the TiSport, manufactured from airplane-grade titanium. That's what they were beginning to make high-end bikes from. Titanium weighs next to nothing. Its strength-to-weight ratio is astounding, superior to almost every other metal. The chair had borrowed even more than my Quickie from bicycle technology. Performance bikes had been around for a century, seeking out ever lighter, more streamlined and functional designs. No sense for the wheelchair industry to reinvent the wheel, so to speak. The TiSport appeared on the Internet and in catalogues, receiving the highest levels of customer satisfaction. Wheelchair athletes I knew were raving about it. Mary Thompson, my Grinnell wheelchair racer friend, got one. Maybe it was time to shop for a replacement for my trusty steed.

Shopping for a wheelchair, though, is an exercise in futility. You can't find a selection of wheelchairs in any store. No place has a back room full of varieties of brands and sizes and styles. You might be lucky enough to find a disability-related expo; there are several of these product exhibitions scheduled around the country each year. The closest one to me is in Chicago, five hours away. But even if you find a product line you like, they won't have a chair on hand that fits you. Every body is different. Every chair is custom designed. You have to buy them from a medical rehab center, or through your insurance company, or directly from a catalogue or off the Internet. Is there any other product you can think of that you are expected to buy, sight unseen, at the recommendation of some professional? Especially a product whose fit and specifications are so exacting and important. Every body measurement must be taken into account to assure the best biomechanical fit. There's science involved. Too small on certain measurements and you run a greater risk of pressure sores. Too big and you stress the shoulders more. Even then preferences in such measurements as center of gravity and seat "dump" or "squeeze" enter into play. You need to be centered directly over the wheels so you can get the longest push around and down on the wheel, rather than simply chopping at it as it comes up. It's quite a puzzle. You wouldn't buy a pair of pants that you couldn't try on first. You'd never buy a car that you couldn't test drive. But you're expected to buy a wheelchair, in which you'll spend almost all of your waking hours, with absolutely no opportunity to take the product for a test spin. I was frustrated.

But, as so often seems to happen in this new life of mine, perseverance provided a solution. A happy coincidence opened the way for me to try out one of these new chairs. Stuck in St. Mary's Hospital, part of Mayo Medical Clinic in Rochester, Minnesota, for several weeks following one of many bladder surgeries, I toured the rehab department and found a sample model of the TiSport titanium chair. With the help of Anderson's Medical Supply Company across the street from the hospital (they haven't paid me a dime for this endorsement, by the way), I tried the chair they had in stock, made what adjustments were possible, took additional measurements and made more than a few guesses about where I might like such things as center of gravity and lumbar support height and angle, filled out an order form, took a deep breath, and turned it over to Scott, my own rehab technician, to maneuver through insurance and try to order me a chair. That's another whole obstacle course. I leave those negotiations to the professionals. It took months, but in the end a chair was delivered. And it was perfect. It may seem silly to see a man so positively giddy over a wheelchair, of all things, but when you spend as much time in a piece of equipment as I do, little things mean a lot.

A year after I got my new chair, I spent a long weekend in Spokane as an invited participant at Bloomsday Road Race. Bloomsday is the largest individually timed foot race in the United States. Fifty thousand runners take part every year. The one-millionth participant in the race was identified the year I took part. That's a lot of runners! They pull out all the stops for wheelchair competitors. They paid my airfare to come out from Iowa, put me up in the official race headquarters hotel for the weekend, and wined and dined me for days. And I'm no elite racer! I learned more about functioning in a wheelchair that weekend by rubbing wheels with professional and world-class athletes than I had figured out on my own in Grinnell during the previous four years. We learn from each other where the stumps are, because we have a lot in common. We're all reinventing our lives. Some have gotten better at it than others.

The race itself was a disaster. It rained, it snowed, it was hilly, I did poorly. But my point here is that, in my new TiSport, I was envied and courted by more accomplished wheelers, just as I had examined and compared the equipment of others. My racing equipment was a piece of junk, compared with that of the other racers, but my everyday chair was in high regard. Must have been the right one.

Do I have a right to such expensive equipment—especially in light of the fact that most people with disabilities in America and around the world would find this equipment far out of their reach? When insurance pays, it drives up rates for everyone. When Medicare pays, it costs tax dollars. I have been criticized for seeking out the best equipment. One acquaintance complained, "His toys are better than mine." But understand, anything less than the absolute best piece of adaptive equipment only serves to increase my disability. I will continue to claw for the best available, and to support that struggle for anyone else as well.

You may have trouble understanding a wheeler's devotion to his or her chair. But the right chair makes it possible to do things and be someone you can't be in the wrong chair. In the wrong chair, I'd be disabled all over again. This new chair is the right chair. Somehow they have shaved the weight down to around fifteen pounds. Strangers who handle my chair always comment on its weight, or lack thereof. Tossing the frame across my lap into my car is a breeze. The new chair will extend the life of my shoulders for years. One effortless push and it will roll for yards. We recently remodeled our new house, laying down a hard surface flooring from the garage at one end of the long ranch house to the bedroom at the other. With one mighty shove I can roll all the way from the garage to the side of my bed.

Life is good.

The walls take something of a beating on these high-speed passes, though, because wheelchair users don't push the wheels for every maneuver. For short trips, say, across the kitchen, you shove off a table or counter top and catch yourself on the fridge or stove. Pray the stove isn't on when you grab it. It's like a weightless ballet. Hockenberry's experience with pushing off and catching himself on available surfaces is what he claimed qualified him as a candidate for the first journalist in space. You probably aren't aware that NASA was intending, before the disastrous explosion of the space shuttle *Challenger*, to send a civilian journalist into space. Hockenberry says that it was coming down to a face-off between him and Walter Cronkite. NASA ended up scrapping that project. But the truth remains: piloting a wheelchair in the kitchen is like floating in a weightless environment.

Rolling down a hallway provides similar shortcuts. Instead of always pushing the wheels for momentum and steering, it's much easier, when negotiating a corner, to grab a piece of the door frame molding on the way by and swing around, using it as a fulcrum. I've gotten to be such an expert at that move at church that I can swing into my office from the hallway at full speed. It drives the secretary crazy. On the rare occasions when I happen to miss catching the door frame, I go crashing into the wall at the end of the hall. It's starting to leave marks. On the wall as well as my face.

My wheelchair is more than a medical device. In Hawaii, my kids dragged me to the beach at Waikiki several times a week. With some effort I was able to push the wheelchair over the sand to the edge of the surf, and then ease myself into the water. It involves popping a wheelie the whole way and shoving with all my strength to gain a few inches at a time. It's awkward and slow, but it works. And, of course, I want to do this on my own. What I hadn't realized was that salt water and sand were working their way into the delicate ball bearings of the front casters. My oversight became apparent one day when they seized up and simply would not move.

Now, for a wheelchair user, this is more than a mechanical problem. It's not like having your car break down and calling the garage for a fix and a replacement. It's not just an inconvenience when a wheelchair breaks down. It's a whole new disability. With a chair that doesn't work, I can't even get up from the bed. I become a true invalid, in every sense of the word. I spent an entire morning and half a can of WD40 spray, along with an ice pick, a screwdriver, a pair of pliers, and a big hammer, trying to loosen up the caster. It works now, but my confidence is somewhat shaken. Yet another reminder of the contingency of living with a disability.

It's been interesting to note that my attachment to my chair as a prosthetic device has extended to my car as well. Three years ago I bought a new car. One of the members of my weekly Bible study looks at me like the church is paying me too much. Maybe so, but hear me out. I researched this car, a Suburu Forester. It's as small as I could go, with the requisite room to pull my wheelchair frame over my lap in the driver's seat and optional room in the back for someone to place my chair if I'm hauling passengers. The chair fits back there with no need to dismantle it. Hand controls are installed, of course. It has a relatively high clearance and all-wheel drive to plow through snow. Remember, if I get stuck in a snowdrift, there's no getting out and walking for help. The car is trouble-free. It adds an element of confidence to my daily living. When I'm driving it around town, on business or errands, I do so with the sense that the car, like my chair, is just another mobility aid. It's yet another prosthesis.

Every social encounter in a wheelchair becomes an exercise in uncertainty. I've found I must be the patient teacher. Years ago, when I rode that weekend bike ride with Deb, the blind woman, she confided in me after the weekend was over that she had spent the whole two days subtly educating me. And that I was a slow learner. I'm glad she waited till it was over to tell me.

Sometimes I do need help maneuvering in public, and have to find ways to ask for it. In a crowded restaurant one night, the only accessible route to the bathroom was blocked by a row of people sitting at a long table, every one of their chairs pushed back into the aisle. By the looks of the table, littered with several empty pitchers of beer, they were having a good time. No one paid the slightest attention to a man in a wheelchair waiting patiently for them to notice him so that he could get to the bathroom. They made it necessary for me to tap each one on the shoulder and ask for passage. Each of eight rowdy men. I had to interrupt the dinner conversation eight times to get by. And here's the kicker: when I come out of the bathroom not more than two minutes later, the chairs were back in the aisle and I was forced to repeat the process all over again. Times like this make me wish I carried a cattle prod. "Wheelchair coming through. Zap!"

Crowds have a hard time parting for a man in a wheelchair. I'm two feet too short to be noticed, for one thing. Eye contact tends to be quite horizontal in a crowd. People aren't looking up or down, they're looking at each other's faces. You roll around on the floor beneath the radar screens of most standing people. My face isn't on the same plane. My view is much more mundane. I'm looking at belt buckles and buttocks.

Wheelchairs take up lots more room as they attempt to cut through a group of people. I cut a wide swath. There's no question of slinking in between Joe and the buffet table. I have to clear out the crowd in order to get through. "Hello, people, I'm down here. I'd like to get through, please. Might I have just a few more inches of room? Hey, I'm talking to you. Move it or lose it!"

To help a person in a wheelchair or not to help. That is the question. People usually try to give assistance to people with disabilities. Unfortunately, they don't always know how to do that, and they don't always ask how it might best be accomplished. I'm the expert here. Just ask me. If a nondisabled stranger and I approach an inward-swinging door at the same time, they will invariably push the door open for me. At that point they find themselves in the awkward position of standing there blocking my path of entry. And I'm much wider than they had thought I was. Now they're faced with the dilemma of standing back and holding the door open as wide as they can, creating a little tunnel for me to roll through, or squeezing back against the door and hoping I can avoid rolling over their toes. The only way for me to avoid the certain embarrassment that I know is coming, is for me to scoot ahead and plow the door open, holding it in place for them. That causes its own confusion, too—having a crippled guy hold the door open for you must be embarrassing—but at least we both get through the door without serious injury to either of us.

Once, before I knew better, I let two grown men attempt to dismantle my chair and put in the back hatch of my car. It was dark at the time and I was tired. How could I have known how badly it would turn out? I thought I was in good hands—one of my helpers was a competent carpenter, good with his hands, and the other was an engineer. Between my verbal instructions and their well-intentioned but misguided fumblings in the dark, it took them twenty minutes to accomplish the task I could have completed in two. Now that I always insist on managing my own chair disassembly and reassembly, people who witness my routine are amazed at how streamlined it has become. "My, how quickly you do that." Jeff sometimes watches me from across the street at the coffee shop when I park in front of my church. He says it looks like a ballet. I would guess that a person *would* get pretty accomplished at something she or he does ten times a day for five years. What amazes me is the fact that many people in my social circles have no idea how I get in and out of my car, how I drive, how I dress, and how I manage to get around. They know I do it, but the mechanics have, for all this time, been a mystery to them.

Most refreshing was a young man who was staffing the counter at a video rental shop in Grinnell. I had a video to return, and parked just outside the large plate glass window facing the desk where the young man was stationed. He watched me intently as I opened my door and began to swing pieces of chair over my lap and onto the parking lot. I wouldn't have minded if he had come outside then and offered to take the video from me, but he just stood and watched. As I transferred into my chair and headed toward the door, he jumped there ahead of me, met me outside, and took the video. "That's pretty neat," he said. "Can you show me how you do that? Is it hard? How long have you been doing this? What happened to you? I've never seen a wheelchair like this. Is it pretty uncommon?" This young man, by suspending any preconceived notions he might have had, in one chance encounter deepened his understanding of what it was like to live with a disability. How refreshing it was for me to be able to explain my new life to someone genuinely interested!

Wheelchairs are messy machines. In spite of recent advances in materials and biomechanics, their means of propulsion is still very primitive. Think of it. We can put a man on the moon and talk instantaneously with people all around the world, but we still propel a wheelchair by pushing on the wheels! How fast or far could you go on a bike if you drove it like that? Engineers are working on improving chairs with gears and cranks, but then it becomes a handcycle and not nearly as maneuverable in cramped spaces. Power chairs are also on the cutting edge of technology. There's a new chair, the IBOT 3000, that can stand its user up on two wheels and can actually ascend and descend stairs. It does it all with gyroscopes and computers. You can pick it up for the cost of a modest house. Some of the power chairs I saw in the hospital being set up for use by quads cost $10,000 to $15,000.

Weather is a huge factor in deciding whether to go out for the day or not. I have had days on end when I was unable—or simply refused—to venture out of the house. Snow, if it's slippery, removes the friction you need for your wheels. And if the snow is piled up more than an inch or two deep the wheelchair becomes a large and unmoving lawn ornament. I once rolled down my ramp in a snowstorm. That part was easy enough. But when I had rolled to just beyond the end of the ramp and my forward momentum stopped, I was as stalled as if I were a stone. My wheels were turning, but I wasn't going anywhere. I had to wait for someone in my family to look out the window and notice my plight.

Whatever you roll over while pushing a wheelchair—say in the men's room at a truck stop or under the trees in the park where the pigeons are nesting and the neighbors just walked their dog (a big dog, let's say)—follows you home. It's on your wheels. When you push your wheels, it gets on your hands. On entering your home, you can't wipe your wheels as you would wipe your feet. You can't take off your wheels like you take your shoes off. Dog poop and pigeon poop and lord knows what from the public restroom comes inside with you and tracks across your beige carpet which is rapidly become more of a brownish color, especially in the traffic pattern created by the rolling of your wheels.

I have worked out a couple of solutions to this problem. I have a couple of old towels I leave by the back door. Holding them against the tires as I roll a couple of complete revolutions of the wheels cleans things up fairly well and only tracks into the kitchen as far as two turns of the wheels. That's fifty-two inches, if you're counting. On really snowy days I have a spare set of wheels equipped with knobby snow tires that I can pop on in place of my regular indoor tires. Of course, I'm then stuck with the knobbies for the rest of the day until I return home. As I roll into church, businesses, the hospital, or anywhere else in town, I track prodigious amounts of snow and guck into otherwise clean and neat establishments all over town.

Another trick that wheelchair users learn pretty quickly is to use gloves while pushing in questionable terrain. Hockenberry recommends handball gloves. I tried them after reading his book, but found them too fragile. They usually come only in white, too, and I wanted a more manly color. I thought I'd stumbled on a good alternative when I tried football-receiver gloves. They're sticky and designed to help players catch the ball. Using them in a wheelchair, they grip the push rims like they're glued on. Unfortunately, they're useless in slowing forward momentum. They have two speeds: go and stop. They're too sticky.

I finally hit upon black baseball batting gloves. They run twenty bucks a pair, last a long time, and look good. They're only on sale during the spring season, so I buy my year's supply of three or four pairs every spring.

Selecting wheelchair-appropriate clothing has been an issue of self-discovery. The best thing to wear in a wheelchair, besides nothing at all, is pajamas and hospital pants. That, in fact, is what I did wear for some weeks after leaving the hospital, until I decided it was time to get dressed. Then I had to find clothing that fits in a seated position and is easy enough to pull on and doesn't get ruined by dirty wheels. I gave up sport coats and suits right away, except for funerals and weddings. And then I find that I sometimes get only one wearing between trips to the cleaners. Imagine your $200 suit coat rubbing on your wheels at a rainy graveside service. Sunday church doesn't even rate a suit anymore. It's hard to stay dry in a wheelchair during a rainstorm. My lap becomes a puddle and my cushion absorbs whatever rolls off my jacket. A purely utilitarian approach might be to wear a poncho, but the image of a cripple rolling in a poncho was more than I could bear. Wheelers can't use umbrellas. Our hands are occupied. My daughter invented a holding system for attaching umbrellas to a wheelchair. She called it the "Dryrider." She took it to the state level of competition in the InventIowa contest, and won a $50 savings bond with it. I actually used it for a while, but the longer you're in a wheelchair the more you learn to streamline your life, and I soon tired of the extra equipment.

One Sunday we visited the mall after church. On this particular Sunday I had pulled out all the stops in the clothing department. Man, I looked hot, if I do say so myself. I must have been depressed about something, so I had gotten really dressed up. I wore gray tweed slacks. Black polished shoes with dress socks. A white tailored dress shirt. Conservative dress tie, not the hand-painted hula dancer tie I normally prefer. And to top it all off, the new black suspenders Ann had given me. I felt like a lawyer, or the CEO of some Fortune 500 company. In that outfit, rolling around with the Sunday afternoon crowd at the mall, Ann noticed a difference in people's reactions. Normally people part for me, glance once, notice a person in a wheelchair, and walk on. Today, Ann found, people were craning their necks for a second look. There was a very real attention factor going on. Why?

We came to the conclusion that a well-dressed man in a wheelchair is an anomaly, a violation of expectations, something curious. Like a pig with wings or a frog singing opera. You just don't expect a crippled guy to be professional, well dressed, and successful looking. It presented a perceptual dissonance. It was the best thing I could have done to broaden people's understandings of disability. It was a great ego boost, too.

I didn't subscribe for long to Marilyn Hamilton's philosophy of living with disability. I've seen too many people in wheelchairs adopt a show-persona, with long hair or freaky clothes or an attitude. I'd adapt her saying to this: "If you can't stand up, at least show up." Make it an issue of perseverance, not outlandishness. My goal is to approximate my former self as closely as possible. I prefer jeans and a T-shirt. Because jeans are harder for me to wear now, given my plumbing configuration and seated stature, khaki Dockers often have to substitute. I want to be seen as a "normal" guy who uses a wheelchair to get around. I know it's a vanity, but what can I do?

I live in a wheelchair now. I will continue to do so for the rest of my life, until I breathe my last breath, or until my kids let the air out of my tires, whichever comes first. The fact that I live in a wheelchair is neither good nor bad, in and of itself. It just is. It is a neutral description of myself, much like saying that my eyes are blue and my hair is blonde.

It's a different life than the one I lived before. It's far from easy, and not without its moments of sadness, anger, pain, grief, inconvenience, and embarrassment. But, like moving to a foreign country and learning to fit in, it's a life I find I can get used to. It's not a tragedy. I'm not here to provide an object of pity or inspiration. This new life is defined by more than what it is missing. I'm not waiting for doctors to come up with a cure for who I am now. I'm also not content to sit at home waiting for the world to accommodate me. I have some fantastic gifts to offer still, and the world had better figure out ways to include me—even on wheels—or it will be that much poorer for its oversight.

You may join me here some day. Get your own chair if you do. Mine is in use. You may get here suddenly through some traumatic accident or illness. You may arrive more slowly, through a degenerative disease that gives you time to reflect on your losses. Or you may get here naturally, as you age and decline. The one constant is that you won't come here willingly. No one in their right mind would give up abilities they once had. My advice is not to be afraid. Disability happens. Keep your wits about you and get the lay of the land before you panic.

Maybe, come to think of it, this adjustment process is less like knowing where the stumps are than it is not being afraid of getting wet. When I was five, my parents started taking me to swimming lessons. It took two years of lessons before I would put my head under water. Every time the instructor told us to put our heads under, I would get out of the water, screaming, and run all the way home. After two years of this, I found I really wanted to learn to put my head in the water, so I practiced all winter in the bathtub. When the next summer rolled around, I passed my first swimming lesson. I put my face in the water. The watery environment wasn't what I had feared. It was peaceful and quiet, a relaxing place to float. Over the years it has provided me exercise, competition, solace, and self-esteem. During my summer in Hawaii, I spent nearly an hour one day snorkeling, following a sea turtle. This huge creature floated like a bird under the waves. It seemed utterly unperturbed by my presence just above it, close enough to touch. There's a whole world down there, full of color, excitement, and life. What would I have missed if I had been unable to overcome my fears when I was five and learning to swim?

Life with a disability can be a magical world. Or at least better than the alternative. Don't be afraid to embrace it. Get your face wet. Don't let yourself be defined by social stereotypes governing people with disabilities. Look around for the sea turtles. Swim with them for a while and learn how they live.

As long as you're alive, the adventures keep coming like unsolicited gifts. How rude it would be to leave them wrapped and unopened.

Bibliography

Bishop, Marilyn E. *Religion and Disability: Essays in Scripture, Theology, and Ethics.* Kansas City: Sheed & Ward, 1995.

Block, Jennie Weiss. *Copious Hosting: A Theology of Access for People with Disabilities.* New York: Continuum, 2002.

Bristo, Marca. "Power to Change the World." *Paraplegia News,* October 1999.

Buechner, Frederick. *Wishful Thinking: A Theological ABC.* New York: Harper & Row, 1973.

Callahan, John. *Don't Worry, He Won't Get Far on Foot.* New York: Random House, 1990.

Charlton, James I. *Nothing About Us Without Us: Disability Oppression and Empowerment.* Berkeley, CA: University of California Press, 1998.

Corbet, Barry. "The Conquest of the Ordinary." *New Mobility,* March 2000.

Crase, Cliff. "Reasons & Remarks: Disability Cool." *Paraplegia News,* July 1999.

Crossan, John Dominic. *Jesus: A Revolutionary Biography.* San Francisco: HarperSanFrancisco, 1994.

Dobbs, Jean. "The Berkeley Scene: The Ed Roberts Campus & the Power of Nine." *New Mobility,* May 2000.

Eiesland, Nancy L. *The Disabled God: Toward a Liberatory Theology of Disability.* Nashville: Abingdon Press, 1994.

Eiesland, Nancy L. and Don E. Saliers, eds. *Human Disability and the Service of God: Reassessing Religious Practice.* Nashville: Abingdon Press, 1998.

Forbes, James, interviewed by Bill Moyers. *Washington Week Special Report,* PBS, September 12, 2001.

Fox, Michael J. *Lucky Man: A Memoir.* New York: Hyperion, 2002.

Fries, Kenny, ed. *Staring Back: The Disability Experience from the Inside Out.* New York: Penguin Putnam, 1997.

Govig, Stewart D. *Strong at the Broken Places: Persons with Disabilities and the Church.* Louisville: Westminster/John Knox Press, 1989.

Hahn, Harlan. "Can Disability Be Beautiful?" in *Perspectives on Disability.* 2nd ed. Palo Alto, CA: Health Markets Research, 1993.

Hockenberry, John. *Moving Violations: War Zones, Wheelchairs, and Declarations of Independence.* New York: Hyperion, 1995.

Ingstad, Benedicte and Susan Reynolds Whyte. "Disability and Culture: An Overview." in *Disability and Culture.* Benedicte Ingstad and Susan Reynolds Whyte, eds. Berkeley: University of California Press, 1995.

Johnson, Mary. "The ADA at 10: A Retrospective View." *New Mobility,* June 2000.

Karp, Gary. *Life on Wheels: For the Active Wheelchair User.* Beijing: O'Reilly, 1999.

Kelsey, Morton T. *Healing and Christianity in Ancient Thought and Modern Times.* New York: Harper & Row, 1973.

Killmer, Richard L. "Forgiveness." Louisville: The Presbyterian Peacemaking Program.

Kushner, Harold S. *When Bad Things Happen to Good People.* New York: Harper Collins, 1981.

Lane, Nancy J. "A Theology of Anger When Living with a Disability," in *The Psychological and Social Impact of Disability*, Robert P. Marinelli and Arthur F. Delloito, eds. New York: Springer Publishing Company, 1999.

Leavet, Ronnie Linda, ed. *Cross-Cultural Rehabilitation: An International Perspective.* New York: W. B. Saunders, 1999.

Linton, Simi. *Claiming Disability: Knowledge and Identity.* New York: New York University Press, 1998.

Longmore, Paul K. and Lauri Umansky, eds. *The New Disability History: American Perspectives.* New York: New York University Press, 2001.

Mackelprang, Romel and Richard Salsgiver. *Disability: A Diversity Model Approach in Human Service Perspective.* Pacific Grove, Calif.: Brooks/Cole, 1999.

Mairs, Nancy. *Carnal Acts: Essays.* New York: HarperCollins, 1990.

———. *Waist-High in the World: A Life among the Nondisabled.* Boston: Beacon Press, 1996.

McBryde Johnson, Harriet. "Conventional Wisdom, Part One." *New Mobility*, September 2000.

———. "Conventional Wisdom, Part Two." *New Mobility*, October 2000.

Nagler, Mark, ed. *Perspectives on Disability: Texts and Readings on Disability.* Palo Alto, CA: Health Markets Research, 1990.

National Organization on Disability. "The State of the Union, 2002: What's the Picture for Americans with Disabilities?" *Paraplegia News*, April 2002.

Palmer, Sara, Ph.D., Kay Harris Kriegsman, Ph.D., and Jeffrey Palmer M.D. *Spinal Cord Injury: A Guide for Living.* Baltimore: Johns Hopkins University Press, 2000.

Price, June. "My Spin: The Olympics of Life." *New Mobility*, October 2000.

Price, Reynolds. *A Whole New Life.* New York: Scribner, 1994.

Reeve, Christopher. *Still Me.* New York: Random House, 1998.

———.*Nothing is Impossible: Reflections on a New Life.* New York: Random House, 2002.

Robinson, Kevin. "The Last Time I Saw Jeff." *New Mobility,* January 2000.

Russell, Marta. *Beyond Ramps.* Monroe, Maine: Common Courtesy Press, 1998.

Shapiro, Joseph P. *No Pity: People with Disabilities Forging a New Civil Rights Movement.* New York: Random House, 1994.

Sheldon, William D. "Is the ADA Shrinking?" *New Mobility*, June 2000.

Webb-Mitchell, Brett. *Dancing with Disabilities: Opening the Church to All God's Children.* Cleveland, Ohio: United Church Press, 1996.

Wink, Walter. "Holy and Without Blemish Before God: Disability and Normalcy." *Auburn Views*, 1, no. 1 (Spring, 1993).

OTHER RESOURCES FROM AUGSBURG

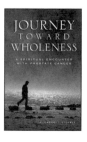

Journey toward Wholeness by R. Carroll Stegall
244 pages, 0-8066-4595-4

The story of Stegall's experience with prostate cancer. Stegall brings his gifts as a storyteller and his perspective as a person o faith to a work that informs and helps enable cancer-sufferers (especially men) and their families to better articulate their fea anxieties, and hopes as they stuggle through the experience.

And We Fly Away by Ray Ashford
80 pages, 0-8066-4570-9

The moving story of the punishing, yet extraordinarily graceful, final years and death of the author's wife. Ashford's own emergence from sorrow is marked by the conviction that death is not the end, but a marvelous beginning.

God's Tender Words for Life's Tough Moments by Margaret Houk
96 pages, 0-8066-4551-2

God wants to help us through our trying times, great or small. The divine words of strength, love, help, and mercy gathered and arranged in *God's Tender Words for Life's Tough Moments* wi move the reader's heart, just as they have moved human hearts for centuries.

In a Dark Wood by Linda Jones and Sophie Stanes
240 pages, 0-8006-3624-4

Features a diverse group of voices describing unlikely and often moving journeys toward or away from faith—Protestants, Catholics, and Jews; laypeople and religious professionals; activists, poets, politicians, and ordinary people. In addition, dozens of readings, poems, and prayers reflect on belief and doubt, on the loss of faith and its rediscovery.

Available wherever books are sold.